Operation Condor

OPERATION CONDOR

ROMMEL'S SPY

John Eppler

Translated by S. Seago

MACDONALD AND JANE'S · LONDON

Dedicated to my wife Denise

Macdonald and Jane's Publishers, Limited
8, Shepherdess Walk
London N1 7LW

ISBN 356 08419 1

Printed in Great Britain by
REDWOOD BURN LIMITED
Trowbridge & Esher

Contents

Family Matters

The house stood facing the Nile. In the long wall fronting on the street there was a large opening. It was a wide high gateway in which hung an ancient, heavy, elaborately carved cedar-wood door screening the interior from the gaze of the curious.

The house was bare and exposed to the merciless sun. Only at dusk, when the sun sank into the western desert, did the house throw a deep shadow across the entire width of the street and into the palm grove along the water's edge.

The dust of Egypt had no time to settle on the house; every year a fresh coat of whitewash was applied. But despite this outward cleanliness, there was nothing fashionable or frivolous but rather something severe and puritanical about its fastidiousness. The only exception was the gate, covered in oriental ornamentation, rich in ancient carvings.

Day and night, nodding in the heat, a huge Nubian sat in front of the gate, his black skin gleaming in the sunlight. On his head sat an immaculately clean turban; his snow-white cloak fell down to the ground round about him in regular folds.

Behind the gate lay a dark alley that opened into a wide sunlit patio, aflame with roses. Narrow mosaic footpaths led to a round pool. The court was surrounded by an arcade, which, shady and cool, gave shelter from the scorching heat. Along the wall stood long divans heaped with cushions, on which the men of the family reposed, smoking their hubble-bubbles and chatting.

Besides the great gateway and a narrow opening at the southern end of the patio there were two other doors in the courtyard. One, leading to the harem, was guarded by a fat dark-skinned eunuch of indeterminate age. The other door was not guarded by anyone. It led to the salamlik, where the men dwelt.

The entire façade consisted of a series of loggias three storeys high, screened by wooden shutters decorated with intricate lattice work. Behind these shutters sat the wives of the clan—white-bosomed Egyptian women eating vast quantities of sweetmeats and casting bored glances over the Nile. Below the river front of the house, rowboats were fastened to a long wooden jetty in the river.

Every morning and night a blind old Ulema holding a gnarled stick in front of him walked along the eastern colonnade, and about halfway along sat down on a stool whose legs were inset with sayings from the Koran picked out in filigree. Only then did he begin to recite a chapter from the Koran in a nasal sing-song. When he had finished, without saying another word, he would leave the patio and pass through a little door made in the big gate and disappear into the palm grove.

Every morning at precisely the same time small boys carrying long-necked copper jugs and small coffee cups hurried across the rose-spattered courtyard and disappeared behind the little wooden door leading to the immense kitchen and servants' quarters of the house. They were serving coffee to the fat women in the harem.

Under the arcade sat the men, who sipped their coffee amid loud salaams and much Arab chatter. A pitch-black Berber carrying a copper brazier slowly walked round the four sides of the covered way, trailing the scent of sandalwood and smoke and singing an Arabic song under his breath.

This was the house in which I grew up. It was here that the breath of adventure first brushed my cheek, and I knew that as long as I lived it would never let me go.

Each year, after the month of Ramadan, the great family gathered from far and wide in this house for a festival celebrating the end of weeks of fasting. They included relations from Arabia—the Mother Country—sweeping in like travelling knights of old, on horses and on camels impatient to deposit their outlandish riders at their destination. With them came massive, heavily armed bodyguards riding fleet-footed meharis.

The visitors wore black cloaks thrown over white kaftans; inside their bandoliers were stuck the razor-sharp daggers of the Janissary. Their faces were thin, passionate and wild, hardened and furrowed by the hot sand of the desert; their proud, thin-bridged noses and black eyes smouldering fire showed them to be true Bedouins. Their beards were cut after the fashion of each particular tribe, and their hair was held fast under a white head-cloth girt with a black cord intertwined with gold.

In late August 1930, when I was sixteen and had returned from visiting the spas of Europe with my parents, the Nile overflowed its banks, spreading a vast sheet of water over the land. For all that it stood on the bank of the giant river, our house had been built to resist the worst floods. As the turbulent yellow masses of water flowed sluggishly towards the Mediterranean and flooded the entire countryside in the process, the whitewashed house stood visible from miles away, alone like an island, adjoined only by the swamped palm grove. The trunks of the palm trees stood deep in water, and, after the river had returned to its bed, the year's high-water mark could be seen on the trunks of the trees. Anyone who has lived long enough on its shores is familiar with the annual flooding of the Nile and can never forget the giant river.

Standing on one of the balconies looking across the Nile to the West, one could make out the outlines of three pyramids on the horizon, where the marshy waterlogged delta was lost in the Libyan desert. In the morning, before the wall of humidity descended on the countryside, from the roof garden looking south-west one could see the greatest graveyard in the world—Sakkara, the dwellings of the dead. Its underground chambers and galleries are enormous charnel houses, each the size of an immense villa. In these lofty dark places sixty-four huge bullocks were interred in enormous sarcophagi in sixty-four gigantic chambers.

Thousands of workers must have had their shoulders torn raw by the ropes with which they dragged the granite blocks to the site for the chambers of the bullocks; hundreds must have collapsed; hundreds of others must have been moved in to take their place; and all this for a fat beast—sacred Apis—which spent its life ruminating until death. Not much has altered since then. The ancient masters have been replaced by others, the bulls are no longer holy and are no longer placed in funeral chambers, but the fellaheen still stand waist deep in water—until the flat-worms that infest the water kill them. Carved into a stone set in one of the pyramids is an ancient Theban proverb: 'Nothing new under the Egyptian sun.'

Since my homecoming I had been living, like the other male members of the family, in one of the self-contained apartments giving on to the patio. No woman was allowed to set foot here, and an almost oppressive silence reigned. It was an outward sign that I had become a man—I was entitled to my own quarters! Hardly a sound penetrated the rooms, which were cool in summer and pleasant in winter. The harsh sunlight filtered through the half-closed shutters, which gave out on to the flower-filled inner garden.

By the orders of the head of the family, a dark-skinned Bisharin, brought from one of the family farms in the Sudan, lay outside at the door and was prepared to vouch for my safety with his life.

My rooms were on the top floor and there was a way up to the roof, where the gardener had created a garden with hundreds of potted plants. As a shelter against the relentless sun and frequent sandstorms, a structure similar to a Bedouin tent had been erected. Under this, of an evening, one could enjoy the breeze that regularly sprang up after sundown, bringing to the whole of the river country a breath of refreshing cool sea air. In this part of the world, life—at least for the happy wealthy few who did not need to work—did not begin until evening.

There is something reassuring, something protective, about large families; especially their sense of belonging is profound. It was wonderful to live in this house, because on the one hand you felt completely free and on the other you knew that you were safe from all outside threats.

This year, as the great festival of Beiram, following the fasting of Ramadan, was coming to a close and the family began to disperse, the men in the family decided, as was the custom, to take me for a while to the land of their origin, Arabia. The order came from the head of the clan and there was no gainsaying it. The command from above was 'no compromise'; it was no excuse that I, a stranger in the midst of the family, had entered it through the marriage of my mother—a circumstance beyond my control. I counted as a member of the family, and, like all the others, had to follow the laws of the clan.

When I was only a young lad they had seen to it, because of the dictates of religion, that I should be circumcised. To make this solemn occasion particularly memorable, an enormous banquet was laid on; but I stood there frightened to death as the surgeon-barber, armed with a sharpened razor and accompanied by a sheikh intoning from the Koran, rid me of my foreskin. My poor mother, appalled by such goings-on, and ignorant of such a practice in her European homeland, crept to her own quarters in tears; but the men in the family, amid much banter, salvoes of rifle shots and general hubbub, took me into their midst. Despite the tears running down my cheeks, they assured me that I was, as of that moment, a true Moslem for all time, and especially an invincible Bedouin. Like other lads in the country, from this hour on I attended the Moslem school and there learnt by heart the Surahs of the Holy Koran. In Europe, where I was frequently sent for periods of schooling, my friends were astonished to hear me quoting the Surahs. They understood not a word, and for them it was something wild and exotic. But some, knowing nothing of religion, called me a heathen. The Orient was then very far from Europe, since one could not get there in a few hours' flying time.

So it was arranged that I was to join the tribe that camped in the Oasis of Ajun-Musa in the Sinai Desert. I would wander the length and breadth of the Arabian peninsula and live as a Bedouin among Bedouins. Soon after I was put into a well-upholstered railway carriage and made a comfortable journey to Suez. It was the last prosaic trip I was to have for a considerable time. From then on I travelled without benefit of cushions.

Outside the railway station, in the shade of a plane tree, sat two Bedouins, awaiting my arrival. They were swathed from head to foot in cloth, except for a small slit to look through. Europeans are no use at waiting. They are always in a hurry. These two men of the desert, however, were sitting motionless in the shade, like the camels lying on the ground next to them, chewing their cuds and gazing into the void.

The Arabs rose and, after many deep bows, and with every imaginable good wish for blessings from Allah, they stuck their muskets into leather holsters hanging from their saddles, and we mounted the camels. With myself between the other two, we set off southward over the sand towards our tribal encampment.

In the cool pre-dawn twilight Ishmael Abdel Kader, my uncle, strode out of his tent to the riding camels, which lay in a circle to one side of the camp. Further off the pack camels squatted, ruminating, kept in place by the household servants, invariably called 'little brothers'. It was on these camels that the women and children would ride.

Other servants took down the tents, which were packed and loaded on to the beasts. A Bedouin rolled up the carpet on which Ishmael had spent the night and carried it to his master's pack animal.

As was fitting for the head of the clan, Abdel Kader gave the lead. He gripped the boss of his saddle, drove his knees into the flanks of the animal and called out: 'Insh' Allah!' The man holding the reins let go, and the well-trained mehari bounded to its feet without a sound.

Abdel Kader rose up in coordination with the beast's movement and swung his leg over the back of the animal. Settled in the saddle, with a magnificent gesture he gathered his djellaba around with one sweep of his arm. Proud, self-assured, defiant, he alone was responsible for the welfare of a thousand Bedouins, their wives and their children, their goats, sheep, camels and horses.

The animals moved along at a steady pace; we had to press our thighs against the saddles to control the onward surge of our mounts. Then came the command from Ishmael, penetrating and imperious: 'Yellah!'

In nasal tones the head drover chanted his couplet, giving rhythm and tempo to the ride, and we went forth across the endless sands. Behind us the women and children followed at a steady unhurrying pace.

The sun emerged from behind the red-hued mountains. The desert ahead stretched before us, still under a pall of grey and blues. In the distance, on the rim of the wadi, more black hills were silhouetted against the sky, and over the surface of the featureless plain the warming air began to shimmer.

The caravan threaded its way through a countryside filled with harsh and withered stunted thorny scrub, on which the camels fed at night. Slowly, step by step, this gave way to small dunes of sand.

The sun became as hard as glass and began to burn our faces. The gleaming sands dazzled our eyes, and our eyelids began to droop. Soon the merciless rays of the sun would turn us to stone in this land without shadow, without trees, without gardens. It was another two days to the next oasis—and in between, nothing but sand, rocks, desert and burning sun! The monotony of the scenery was accompanied by the steady chanting of the men as we proceeded at a steady pace, neither walk nor trot. The repetitive humming was meant as a diversion on the long march, but what was meant to keep others alert only made me sleepy.

I rode side by side with Ishmael Abdel Kader, who, from the beginning of the journey, had made not the least concession to me. Only after I had seen to my camel and set up my tent was I, like every other man in the caravan, given permission to drink. He refused to let me have a slave. I was to be toughened and to be made to take pride in this journey, in this ordeal of initiation which had been approved for me only after long arguments with his brother.

Ishmael Abdel Kader belonged to the older generation, to those who reject everything new and regard it with distrust. As an Arab he was a descendant of Ishmael, the rejected son of Abraham and his Egyptian slave Hagar. As the prophecy said, he was a wild ass, one who calls the desert his home, laughs at towns and never takes orders from any master. He was an Arab, wandering through the desert, forever seeking water and fresh pastures for his animals. He was a wild lawless man, acknowledging no rules other than those dictated by tradition, free of any yoke, his own master.

He had a low opinion of Europe, which he had recently visited, because he was convinced that the schools did not equip a man to live as a man should. A free Bedouin had no need of schools like those. A free Bedouin who wanted to learn to read and write went to the Koran school, and there he learned the meaning of being a pious Moslem, obeying meticulously every last law of Islam, that religion of the Prophet which alone is made for the desert.

It is a religion that asks only that one should distinguish truth from untruth, which leaves no room for doubt, which needs no intermediary between Allah and Man, which has no nonsense about it, which will tolerate no images, either of Allah or of saints, which has no priests in flowing vestments, only the faithful to pray five times a day to Allah while they prostrate themselves in the direction of Mecca. The faithful need no altars, because the place to pray to Allah is everywhere—all over the world. The true believer can be at one with Him in any oasis and on every square inch of earth. The mosque is not the house of Allah, only a place where the faithful gather to pray together. Allah needs no house, no ceremony, no baptism. You come, you pray, you go. How different from those infidels!

Of his attitude towards Europeans he made only one exception—my mother, the wife of his brother. To every other Moslem she was an unbeliever—but not to him. His affection for my mother was the only aberration in this most conservative of Bedouin chiefs.

Soon after I was born, just before the World War I, my mother's favourite uncle died, leaving her to inherit his modest hotel in Alexandria. My parents duly moved there, and while my father carried on his travels as an investment adviser for European and English mining and oil companies, my mother ran the hotel. It was not a grand hotel, but an above-average discreet bourgeois establishment. It was there that Salah Gaafar kept a suite apart from his family home for his private use. Naturally he got to know my parents very well, and was careful to see that during her husband's lengthy absences my mother was neither bored nor bothered by any of the other tenants. After my father's sudden death Salah Gaafar married my mother and adopted me.

At first Ishmael Abdel Kader Gaafar did not want to approve of this marriage of his favourite relative to a widow and infidel, but soon her good looks and good sense charmed him as much as they had my step-father. She alone had the right to talk to him and not to stay in the harem like the other women of the clan. She was allowed to go as she would but could not enter the salamlik, which is reserved for the men.

Whenever he went to Cairo to visit the members of his family, he would shower my mother with presents—the choicest gifts you could find at the Khan el Khalili. He seemed to know every merchant in this, the greatest of all bazaars, which stretched out like a spider's web from the great Midan el Ataba el Khadra in the middle of the town to the narrowest alleyways of the Bab el Nasr. In this labyrinth of merchandise two men could not walk abreast. Here the precious treasures of the Orient were to be found and here all the merchants knew that Ishmael Abdel Kader would buy them for his German relative.

These treasures were for the woman from the land of the infidels, living right there in the middle of an Arab family—a family shut off, set in ancient ways, where tradition and religion were jealously guarded. This woman was cherished in a family proud of its origins, proud of having been among the first to have risen to eminence in Arabia; a family that had helped to spread Islam all over the world and settled eventually on the Nile.

Yet Ishmael Abder Kader came nowhere near being able to understand that with me, even inexperienced in the ways of the world as I was, he would have no success. He could not believe that the stubbornness of his character, the unerring instinct that had protected him in a thousand ways in the broiling hell of Sinai, and his intuition, which otherwise never failed him, would not do the trick this time—would not prevent my defection from the culture and civilization of Arabia. It did not occur to him that the family of which he was so proud was bound to fall apart; and that its disintegration had already begun with my adolescence and that of my stepbrothers and cousins. He refused to accept that we did not give a damn for wandering in the desert on horseback or camel, for conducting tribal feuds, for eating rock-hard dates under the merciless Arabian sun, or for drinking camel's milk. We had become soft, he would have said, and spoilt by riches. For me, this ride to Mecca in January 1931—the year 1349 of the Hijra—was a ride into the past, into adventure but nothing else.

Ishmael Abder Kader was fifty years old and at the height of his powers. He was upright and as thin as a rake, his face lean and sun-tanned. He was the personification of the true Bedouin. His vast wealth had not led him into a dissolute life, as it had his brothers in town.

He had four wives, as the Prophet allowed. That is what his ancestors had done and he did not want to change one iota of it. Ishmael was an Arab and proud to be the head of a clan. It was his place in life to fight and to lead his people in an orderly fashion through the deserts. A thousand years they had wandered thus, and they could not imagine that it would be otherwise in another thousand years' time, for this was the will of Allah. It was no use protesting against Kismet.

When you leave the sea of sand, it is just like arriving in port after an ocean voyage. Hour after hour you scan the empty land hoping to catch the merest glimpse of your destination. At last, on the far horizon, you see a tiny dot that with every step gradually grows larger in the boundless distance.

An oasis!

The palms are grey with desert dust. Their fan-shaped branches are hanging limp and tired and their trunks are furrowed like the faces of old fishermen.

Darkness was falling as we approached the water wells, riding over the sands and filing through the palm groves. The sun setting behind the Barkan cast black silhouettes along the ground. The road was bordered with meagre scrub; there was not a blade of grass and, instead of green meadows, nothing but drifts of sand and old palm trees powdered by the hot breezes.

'How terrible the sun can be!' said Ahmed, who was riding by my side.

Every individual characteristic had disappeared from the landscape, and only the last sharp thin mauve streak of the horizon remained of the day, with a few blood-red clouds looming in the gathering dark. From ahead we could hear the nasal tones of the drover, the rhythm of whose calls was accelerating as we approached the middle of the oasis. Water, like a magnet, draws everything to itself in this wilderness. We rode into the grey island briskly but calmly despite our thirst, which would now be quenched for a good long while.

The Taste for Adventure

We were on the road that led to the Holy City of Islam—Mecca—the point towards which millions of Moslems throughout the world offer their prayers five times a day. Ishmael Abdel Kader, with me riding by his side, was about to cross the boundaries beyond which, in accordance with Moslem tradition, no infidel or demon is allowed to walk or ride. Only the faithful were permitted to live within that circle.

I could sense the fervour of my fellow travellers, the excitement which filled them at the thought that we were approaching our goal. Ahmed, in whose company I spent most of my time during the ride, told me one morning soon after breaking camp: 'Only three more days, Hussein, before we put on the Ihram.' That is the pilgrims' garment, made of two seamless pieces of woollen cloth, one wrapped around the legs, the other worn over the torso and one shoulder. I knew—and I could have told Ahmed as much, even if I had been stoned for saying it—that our pilgrimage to the Kaaba, with its black stone, was no more than the extension of the ancient tradition of the idolatrous dwellers of Arabia before the days of Mohammed. A convenient gathering at the Holy Stone, in the middle of the desert, later developed into an annual fair.

By the very act of setting foot upon that sacred ground I was about to fulfil one of the five duties placed upon the faithful by Allah—the Hadj to Mecca. The moment I left that place of pilgrimage I became a Hadji. The principal duties towards Allah are faith and submission to His holy will. That is the real meaning of the word Islam. Anyone who submits himself *is* a Moslem; and that is just what I, who knew the European world, whose mother was Christian by birth (a religion she taught me behind the back of her Arab family), could not do.

I continually felt the need to dissemble and the result was an attitude of estrangement, which made me feel insecure. I was having to struggle with pangs of conscience.

But for all of us this journey we were making together, this pilgrimage, had a deeply moving significance. For many, it was the culmination of their entire lives. They—and this included myself—could barely wait for the moment when we would set foot in the Haram, with its four domes, its immense colonnades and its vast courtyard, in the middle of which stood the chamber containing the Kaaba stone, the vast cube hung with black silk given regularly either by the city of Cairo or the city of Damascus. After that we would drink the holy water of the well of Zamzam and walk seven times round the Kaaba.

Only a selected few have ever entered the empty and darkened chamber, for the Prophet said: 'Allah wants to dwell alone in a darkened chamber.' Then we would kiss the black stone let into the wall. It was originally white, and turned black only because it absorbed the sins of the pilgrims through contact with their mouths.

In Arabia the story goes that on the day this stone was set into the eastern corner of the wall of the Kaaba the tribes of Hedja were quarrelling among themselves. Each wanted to carry the stone to its appointed place. The Prophet ordered the stone to be laid upon a carpet, told the head of each tribe to get hold of a corner and then set the stone with his own hand into the place where it is to this day.

Like thousands of other pilgrims or Hadjis we would then run to the nearby hills of Safa and Marwa, and continue our pilgrimage barefoot to Mount Arafat. On the way back we would sacrifice sheep and camels in the Mina and stone the devil by throwing pebbles against a stele that stands there, symbolizing evil incarnate. We would do everything precisely in accordance with the Sunna 2/192, and would then visit the tomb of the Prophet King at Medina, because a pilgrimage without that visit is not a true pilgrimage.

They are stubborn and hot-blooded, these Bedouins, like wild asses, but they can be as pious as lambs. They believe profoundly in the Prophetic revelations that Allah had given them the deserts and steppes of Arabia as a place to dwell and bade them spend their lives seeking green pastures for their beasts; they believe they have no master to serve and that therefore they are free men. That is what makes them so attractive, despite the fact that they are also lawless, and never will they do what they do not want to do.

A Bedouin never bothers about the feelings of others. He will seek his goal quite ruthlessly. He does his own thing. The desert, the heat, the sun and the wind with which he has to live are also merciless, and they have made him into what he is. Throughout his life a Bedouin will nurse a sense of superiority. This applies to the Bedouin specifically, not to Arabs in general.

To us Europeans their religion appears a miracle. In seven hundred years Islam had spread throughout Asia Minor, then along the coast and some way into the interior of Africa, to half of Sicily and Spain, and through vast areas of the Far East, knocking at last on the doors of China. It produced a culture that is among the most splendid on this earth. It is a religion out of the desert and for the desert—simple and hard. It knows only truth and untruth. In Paradise it knows only joy and happiness: in Hell only terror and agony. There is nothing in between, just like the desert. Hot by day, cold at night. Light and shade. There are no half-tones; everything is clear and easy to understand. It knows no priest and no initiation; no one has any privileges; all are equal. It is a religion for men!

For some people a particular environment is necessary to trigger off their latent mental or physical potential. This ride on the back of my camel through the merciless wilderness of the Arabian Peninsula was the most beautiful gift of my life. It stripped away all pretence; it swept away all the doubt I had brought along with me from the modern world, so captivated was I by everything around me. Whatever religious doubts I had, I felt that I belonged to my companions on the journey. We lived together, rode side by side under the searing sun, lay together, exhausted, after punishing sandstorms, and spent the nights together, dog tired after the day's march we had put behind us, over sand and boulder-strewn desert, under the silent star-studded night sky.

It was at Hadda that we left the desert, Abdel Kader, Ahmed and I. The others had gone on to Kummaah, east of Mecca, with the animals. Beneath the hill on which we stood lay Jiddah, a town on the Red Sea coast, broiling in the shimmering heat.

My journey was over.

We rode the remaining few kilometres down into the town. The sun stood stark and white hot in the sky. We had left Wadi Fatima behind us and within the ruined ancient walls of Jiddah the coral-built houses of five and six storeys were coming into view. There was not a tree, not a shrub to be seen, only sand and beaten earth in the ravine-like streets. On the façades of the houses, stuck like swallow's nests, were innumerable balconies, all screened up to the height of a man. In a country where there was virtually no wood thousands of artistically decorated moucharabies, made of precious imported Indian teak, hung on the outside walls. Both the wood and the artists, Abdel Kader explained in answer to my astonished enquiries, for many years came from the Malay Archipelago—hence the Indonesian style of the balconies and façades.

Abdel Kader rode ahead of us in the narrow spaces left between the rows of squatting vendors with their wares spread out before them. It did not occur to him to dismount from his camel; he just steered the beast, with the air of a man who knew where he was going, through the chattering multitude.

A fanatical falconer, he was looking for a hunting bird. Several of these dismal birds of prey could be seen sitting about on their perches in front of his tent, with their attendant, who spent all his time feeding them, grooming them and training them. After an endless palaver, Abdel Kader eventually settled on the bird of his choice, a fine falcon. The vendor placed the hood upon the falcon's head and fastened its tethers to the pommel of Abdel Kader's saddle, whereupon the bird sank its talons into the wooden part of the saddle and began to rock himself in step with the gait of the mehari, as if he had sat there from the beginning of time.

The air was unbearably hot, the sea was like liquid lead, and there was not a breath of wind. The barren square by the jetty was deserted.

Two hours later we boarded the dhow, a fine long boat, which I had engaged when we had first entered the town. The skipper had ordered a comfortable place to be made ready for me in the stern near the rudder. My quarters were furnished with a wide straw palliasse, covered in a thick comfortable rug, and cushions everywhere. The whole place was upholstered with cushions. It was a first-class berth, in which I was to cross the Red Sea to Egypt as far as Quseir. After brief farewells, Abdel Kader and Ahmed rode off across the square towards the desert. Soon they had become little more than two small black shapes.

The sun, a dark red disc, sank into the sea and night came out of the desert. A light breeze from the south-east soon began to gather strength.

The makouda, the head man in the crew, grasped the rudder in his huge hands, the r'eis shouted his commands across the deck in a hoarse voice, the triangular sail billowed in the following breeze and the bows of the dhow began to slice through the waves. We began to make more headway and Jiddah disappeared into the night. Only the outlines of the buildings could be picked out by the light of the rising moon. Once more I was on my way to modern houses, with all the usual comforts, elegant women and rich pashas; where one kills time in nightclubs and on golf courses; where in other words, one lives a 'civilised' life.

Chapter 1

Wild Oats

Between Lake Albert and Lake Kyoga, the Imperial Airways flying boat banked and turned south-east. In less than an hour, we would be in Port Bell. Beneath us a herd of buffalo plodded through the rain-soaked plain. The pilot turned the machine until its nose pointed towards Lake Victoria before us. He began his descent. For me, the flight would soon be over.

'Where to, stranger?' asked a voice near me as I stepped out of the arrival hut on to the wooden jetty that led to the Lake shore. The voice was that of a red-bearded fellow, leaning negligently against the wooden paling. There were great round sweat stains caked with salt under the armpits of his old faded unwashed shirt. The rest of him did not look as if it had just got out of a bath, either.

'What do you mean—where to, stranger? I don't like being addressed by people I don't know, Mister.'

'Whisky-Wolf', he remarked dryly and without altering his negligent posture. 'And the stress is on Whisky—please! The Wolf bit is only a kind of appendage.'

I crossed the jetty and called to a boy loitering nearby to carry my luggage. Suddenly there was Redbeard walking by my side; I had not heard him coming up to me. He spoke English with an accent, and he smelt strongly of booze. It will not do me any good, I thought, to be seen with this character. A bit too cocky for my taste, what's more. I'll make a point of getting rid of him as quickly as I can. Not for another six months, when I was leaving the goldfields of Lupa, did I manage to do that, however. But in the course of time he showed himself to be an amiable enough cove who, after we had got to know one another properly, provided me with a lot of laughs.

'To make myself perfectly clear, Mister, I am going into Kampala. And so, this is where you get off.' No sooner had I said it than there he was sitting next to me in the clapped-out Dodge I had hired for my journey to the hotel. The black driver took no notice. He must have thought the bearded character and I were together.

Since my companion did not appear to me to be travelling through Africa with a bulging wallet, I dismissed the driver at the hotel and walked into the entrance hall, leaving him standing in the doorway. Should he insist on coming in, that was his affair; I would not know him. He seemed to have worked things out for himself already; he started crossing the street in leisurely fashion, waving goodbye from the opposite side in the way one leaves an old friend one has brought to the station to catch his train.

After a hot bath I felt ravenous, and wanted something to eat in the hotel restaurant. Although I have never been very fond of English cooking, a really good steak, which was something they did know how to prepare, would do me good. I crossed the entrance lobby on my way to the restaurant, and there, in a deep armchair, slouched Red-beard, in his frayed trousers and his unwashed shirt. He sat there as if he had been a guest in the place for years. His clothes, which would have been out of place in any other setting, were nevertheless not particularly noticeable because the place was full of Europeans in weird get-ups. This was after all the gateway to the wilderness, which began immediately beyond the last hut in town.

'Now, where were we?' he asked in his funny English, walking by my side into the dining room.

'We weren't anywhere, Mister. We said goodbye outside the hotel. If you are booked into a room as well, I can't stop you coming into the dining room with me; but I most particularly want to eat in peace by myself.'

This speech did not seem to make the slightest impression. Without a word, he strode by my side up to a table and was seated as I was pulling back my chair. Calling the boy with his middle and forefinger, he ordered whisky at the top of his voice, demanding that two glasses of the stuff appear on the table instantly. The boy obliged.

'Welcome to Kampala', he said, gulping the Scotch down in one.

I said in German: 'No one can stand on one leg for long. Let's have another.' I said it because I wanted to see the look on his face, to see how he would take it.

'It's that damned Saxon dialect of mine. It's always gives me away. But what the hell!'

It did not matter a damn to him that I had addressed him in his native tongue. He took it as a matter of course. I thought: The cheek of the bastard!

'As far as the room is concerned, which needless to say I do not have, being skint at the moment, I accept it gladly as a signing-on present. My toothbrush is in my pocket; and, as you can see, I don't need a razor. I have grown this ginger beard because in the bush razor blades are a bit of a job to get.'

It is difficult to convey the cool with which he shot me this line—no trace of any inhibitions, something he had evidently never heard of.

'Look, Mister, do I really look like the chairman of the local benevolent society? You gave me that bit about the invitation as if you had a letter of introduction in your pocket. I'll be glad to pay for the drink you have ordered magnificently, and I don't mind throwing in dinner, but that's as far as it goes.'

'Relax, stranger. You'll get used to it. It's better to prospect for gold with an experienced old bird than to rush into the unknown like a greenhorn. A great deal more expensive, and more dangerous. You're still wet behind the ears. You can't be more than eighteen, can you? And I don't need to tell you that you've run away from home.'

He was right about the running away. Cairo and Alexandria, once I had returned a Hadji two years ago, no longer held my interest. It was not enough to play high jinks with some equally bored cousins in the streets, cafés, nightclubs and bordellos. I longed for something to excite and test me as the desert had. When Imperial Airways announced the inauguration of the London to Cape service, I was determined to fly it and find real adventure—on my own. So, with the almost unwilling connivance of my stepfather and the cooperation of his family, I raised enough money to try my hand at gold prospecting in the Lupa. I think that they hoped I would exhaust my lust for adventure and that I would return a bit bruised and settle down to becoming a judge like my grandfather.

'What's the big joke?' I asked.

'No joke; only it's better when partners know where they stand.' He had a relaxed charm about him, unfortunately not matched by his appearance. A cool customer should at least afford a well-pressed suit. It must have been my youth that had given him such self-assurance.

'And what do you suppose our positions are?'

'Don't make it hard for me, stranger; you got the idea ages ago of what I am getting at. You want to get to the Lupa—so do I. You have folding money—and I haven't a penny. You know nothing about panning gold and I know all there is to know about it because I am an old prospector. You know, I am one of those who can prospect for gold and booze, and do both things well. In 1900 I panned for gold on the Yukon. I've staked claims in the Golden Heart of Alaska—and on Bonanza Creek on the Klondike, I became part and parcel of the landscape. Ask any real prospector who Whisky-Wolf is—he'll tell you.'

He slapped his hand on the table and availed himself of a fourth Scotch. I still had my reservations and said, 'Oh, I'm sure they'll greet you with open arms on the Lupa, when we turn up. I suppose every prospector worth his name will be there. And when old Whisky-Wolf comes waltzing in, every bar in the place will run out of whisky. And if I know my Africa, there will be difficulties in restocking. What I want to know is what you want with a chap like me, who would be nothing but a hindrance to you? You could manage the 300 km across Lake Victoria as far as Mwanza without cash; there is always one more place going begging on a sailing boat. From there it's another good 800 km to the Lupa across savannah and bush and mountain country. But then what's that to a hard-bitten gold digger who's criss-crossed Alaska?'

'It's nothing. All you have to do is to be careful at the water-holes—lions tend to be creeping about. And they have no respect for gold prospectors. Otherwise the whole thing's child play—for Whisky-Wolf. One good thing, it's not as cold as in Alaska.'

I stood up. The boat across Lake Victoria left early and I wanted to get some sleep. At the reception desk I got Redbeard a room key. 'Breakfast at seven!' I told him.

In my room I fell to thinking; this might be a sensible way to get to the Lupa. The fact of the matter was that I *was* a greenhorn, and he was bound to understand about panning for gold. After all it would be better for me to learn the business in his company. That way I would avoid the mistakes I would be bound to make if I went on my own. When I came downstairs in the morning, he was ready for me in the lobby. Big, broad-shouldered, narrow-hipped, he stood there, damned well preserved for his age. As he came towards me, he moved like an animal—alert, supple, powerful.

'Hello, stranger', he said as if we had shared the same bedroom.

'The boat leaves in an hour, Digger, but I won't leave without some breakfast; there won't be anything decent to eat on board.'

'I've had mine already. Scotch and condensed milk. You must try some. Fantastic!'

'Makes me sick just to think of it. You and your bloody whisky. And now, condensed milk of all things. I bet you cook with the bloody stuff!'

After breakfast I saw that the driver had pulled up outside the hotel entrance. We got in and he drove like a lunatic as he took off to the Lake shore.

'Give these Charlies a car to play with and they're like children. Knock down anything that stands in the way.'

At Karacho the black driver pulled up at the landing stage. The paddle steamer that lay there was not exactly brand new. She was heavily laden and low in the water. Her sides and all metal parts were rusty; a fresh coat of paint would have done her no harm.

The skipper, an Englishman, looked all right. The African who stood at the wheel was grey at the temples.

'Mwanza, sar?' he asked grinning.

'Yes, and this gentleman too.'

'Ndio, Bwana.'

He must have thought 'this gentleman' a very *funny* gentleman. Surely he had never seen one quite like him, with trousers as frayed as that. He left the wheel and came across the deck to set us up a couple of deckchairs in a shady spot. That was all Whisky-Wolf had been waiting for. He hailed a boy and ordered a Scotch, 'without soda, mind'.

Unless I stopped him, my friend would polish off a barrel of the stuff. In Swahili I made it clear to the boy that whisky was to be provided only if I ordered it. Whisky-Wolf did not understand a word, but for the rest of the voyage did not address a single word to me.

The islands off our route lay purple in the mist. A light breeze was coming off the plain as the steamer pointed south. The skipper took the wheel himself. The paddles churned up a mighty spray, and slowly the clapped-out old tub chugged down the fairway, into open water. We arrived on the other side of the lake in the dead of night and stayed on board until sunrise. From the eastern shore, almost 200 km away, blew a keen cold wind. I pulled the blankets about my ears. Africa is a cold land—with occasional hot sunshine!

When morning came, we left the paddle steamer and sat at a round and very wobbly table on the main street of Mwanza having breakfast. It was from here that I wanted to start my trek, provided I could find a vehicle in passable condition. Should I be unlucky, I would have to take the train to Tabora and pay the browned-off digger his fare, because he was penniless.

Before I left home, I had chatted up various available uncles and aunts and organized a collection, making them promise not to whisper a word about it to my mother. They kept their promise to the letter, at least until I caught the plane. The collection did not exactly make me into a millionaire, but added to my allowance. I have to admit that it came to quite a tidy sum. What would I find once I got to the Lupa? In the meantime I would have to go easy on the money.

Whisky-Wolf naturally had other ideas. During breakfast he compiled a list for provisions as long as your arm, enough to supply a regiment of gold prospectors. The emphasis was naturally on whisky. It would have taken a whole truck for his blasted Scotch alone. I began to make substantial cuts in the list. He left the table disdainfully and was not to be seen again for the rest of the day.

It was only 9 o'clock but the heat of the sun was already unbearable. I walked around the Indian shops, trying to find a suitable motor car. At the bottom of the street there was a garage. In front of it sat a bearded Sikh in the shadow of his workshop, flicking at fat flies with a whisk. It is hopeless to look for the make of one's choice on the edge of the wilderness, but I was no greenhorn when it came to cross-country vehicles, having crossed the desert both in Egypt and in the Sudan, several times. I was particularly keen to find a Model T or Model A Ford. It did not have to be in perfect condition but it would have to shift 750 kg without giving any trouble. I was prepared to make a few minor modifications to make it suitable for cross-country work. The Indian heard me out and nodded understandingly.

He must have been one of those chaps who had come to the country right after the British had arrived—ever since which he had been hating everyone who came his way, I thought. He was making a great show of thinking very hard, as if he could find me a Rolls-Royce at least. His idea was to palm me off with something that would cost a bomb and run as badly as possible; after a hundred miles I would find myself stuck in the savannah with my sozzled digger. This Indian probably hoped that we would then serve as supper for a pair of nice big hyenas and disappear without a trace.

'Have you anything against a Chevrolet? Must it absolutely be a Ford?' He stood up and made as if to go into the workshop. He wanted to show me this Chevvy.

'Mr David Jordan has a Ford.' It was the voice of an African from beneath a car that stood in the middle of the workshop, its front end jacked up. Slowly a head appeared from under the car, followed by an old pair of greasy overalls from which all the buttons were missing. The African stood up, towering a good two feet over us, his grin flashing snow-white teeth.

'Bwana Major Jordan's Ford excellent Ford. We are always fixing it when he come from safari.' No one can switch straight from one sales pitch to another as quickly as a really cunning Indian. 'Come back this afternoon, I will have the Major's Ford here for you. You can have a test drive', said the Sikh.

What a ticking off that African will get, I thought, returning up the street to my hotel. The Sikh was dead set on flogging me the clapped-out Chevrolet and now his own mechanic has spoilt his game for him.

Talk about a cross-country vehicle! When I went back for the Ford in the afternoon, I realized that that Englishman must have been a safari fiend. The car was really fitted out to cope with the roughest terrain. He had even built his own condenser to recycle the cooling water when it overheated, and had looped it into the cooling system.

Whisky-Wolf was not at the hotel. The African sitting on a ramshackle chair in front of it, staring vacantly in front of him, naturally had no idea where he was. It's not often that a boozer can be found in a church, and since not every corner in Mwanza had a church, I started my search at the first of the better sort of dives that I could find. As always when one is looking for something or someone, the object of the search is in the last place to be investigated. And this was no exception. I found him, bawling and blind drunk, sitting on a bar stool in the company of two Scotch-soaked British Tommies. 'Your drinking friends are going to come down with the DTs. Come on, Blotto, let's go!'

I took hold of the gold prospector, draped his arm over my right shoulder, and dropped him into the car outside. We had not covered a hundred yards when he began to snore. I had to decide whether to take him along or whether to ditch him in this hole. In the end I delayed the decision until morning to see how well he slept it off and if he were in shape. I began strongly to regret my gold fever.

We set out at the crack of dawn, hoping to get somewhere near Tabora by nightfall. The idea was to cover at least 250 km. When I had taken over the Ford, the Indian had said: 'Two days to Tabora? You must be joking, sir. You will surely be there before sundown tomorrow evening. In any case you will have a most comfortable night with my good friend Bahadur, who runs the best hotel in Tabora. All you will have to do is to put your foot down hard on the accelerator. This Ford, which I have personally most carefully prepared for you, will cover the ground like a bird. There is nothing that can catch up with it! Be sure to give my friend my best regards, sir. He will look after you as if you were a Prince.'

Being familiar with Oriental optimism in all its shapes and forms, I decided I would be lucky to cover 250 km on the first day. An hour later, only 30 km further on, I knew that I would not even manage that. After two hours I was beginning to wonder whether it might be possible to fit my backbone with shock absorbers. Of course none of this bothered my companion, who was snoring away loudly. His head was lolling over the backrest, and from his breath came the strong whiff of a distillery. Gold prospectors obviously do not share in the tedious discomforts of travel to the African bush. They are above such trifles.

Before us lay the endless plain, full of grazing herds, which took no notice of us at all. Three drowsy lions aroused by the noise of the motor veered off to the right only a yard or so from the car without even turning their heads to look at us. They loped off with an easy gait, heavy-footed but very elegant, towards a clump of thorn trees that offered them shade. The heat was growing unbearable. They were keen to find some refuge.

'Have you gone out of your head, you idiot? Stop this crate at once. We're not at the zoo. I don't feel like ending up as dinner for one of those chaps!'

Redbeard had awakened just as the three lions crossed our track. Now he was paralysed with fright.

'You're going on as if I hadn't seen them. Offer them a whisky. I am sure they'd like it', he said.

'You can stop playing games now, Digger. We're probably going to spend the night in the open. That'll give you a chance to study lions thoroughly. At the moment they are dead lazy and quite harmless.'

Slowly Whisky-Wolf sat up next to me in the car. He scanned the surrounding landscape anxiously. The three big cats were stretched lazily under the thorn trees.

His fear gone, the true Digger came to the fore again. 'On the Klondike', he bragged, 'there were bears. Commonplace, they were. And what bears! Compared with them, these three lions are nothing but overgrown pussy cats. And let me tell you, stranger, bears are a damn sight more dangerous!'

'Just wait, you great bladder of booze, just wait till nightfall; you'll creep under the car and shit yourself.'

It was noon; the sun stood overhead. Before us a township came into view in the shimmering air. It must be Shinyanga. The Sikh had told me that there was an Indian duka at the place, run, naturally, by one of his many friends. There I was to top up with petrol, of which one could never have enough in the bush. They stuck together, these African Asians, like sulphur and brimstone. Hardly had my passenger clapped eyes on the first huts than he began to show signs of anxiety.

'Why not stop in this Nigger town? Better a stinking kraal than sleeping out in the open.'

'We'll get ourselves a jerry can of petrol and go straight on. You don't think I want this trip to last a fortnight, do you?'

Beyond the township the way became slightly hilly. It was still hot, but the sun was beginning to go down as we went rolling through a rocky hollow. It could hardly be called driving. I would have to look about for higher ground to set up camp, to get a view of the terrain. At the end of shallow vale a game track led off to the right, crossing our path. If was only a stone's throw away from a patch of reeds, and behind the reeds there must have been a watering hole—a most unsuitable place for an overnight stop. The water-hole would be crawling with lions the moment game started to come down to drink.

A little further on there was a hill with some trees; that would be the place. 'Stop snoring, Digger—make yourself useful. Get out the tarpaulin so we can fasten it to the car and set up the tent.'

He had not even noticed that I had pulled up. He climbed out of the Ford with a stupid expression on his face, not very happy to have to spend the night here, but he did begin to busy himself. I called to him to look out for some dry twigs to make a fire while I looked about to see if I could find some meat on the hoof. I was not very keen on meat out of a tin.

Nothing stirred as far as the eye could see. I was about to stow the Springfield away in the car again when I saw a bull rhino, pricking up his ears and scenting the air, a little to the east of me. He was not aware of my presence, since I was downwind of him. What a fantastic shot, I thought! So we won't eat bully beef, you can't miss this one. There won't be another like this in a hurry. I raised my rifle, and immediately lowered it again.

It occurred to me that if you really must prove your blasted manhood in this way, then you had better find something that can defend itself. Any fool can bang away with a gun. The rhino stood for a good while in the setting sun. Suddenly, he loped down the slope and went crashing into the bush.

We ate bully beef.

My plan was to tackle an even longer stage the next day, if I could do so without flogging the car to death. We broke camp very early. The sun was just showing over the horizon. Along the road ahead of us was an unforgettable Asian itinerant merchant, walking alone, loaded up to the ears, who looked neither right or left as I overtook him. Even if he had asked for a lift, I could not have found room for him. The car was too full.

We covered the rest of the distance to Lupa in four days. Whisky-Wolf spent the remaining nights under the chassis. He had not touched a drop of whisky since we had set out. Slowly he began to look more or less normal. The only time he ran away had been when I had skinned and gutted a zebra. He could not stand the sight of dead animals, but he had no objections to consuming enormous chunks of meat.

A goodly number of amazing types had found their way to the Lupa before us. We were by no means the first! It seems that gold exercises a magnetic attraction on some beings. The most peculiar figures were running around all over the place. Most of the assembled characters were possibly a little older than me, but they were mostly young men who had run away from home. Among them were some black sheep who had drifted here with a fat remittance and best wishes from their families, provided they never showed their faces at home again.

There was of course a bar, or rather a shack that did service as one, presided over by a fat German blonde somewhat past her best. Drinks, which flowed liberally, were paid for in gold nuggets. She was unwilling to accept money and took it only from newcomers.

I have read somewhere that there is a certain smell about hunger. Moreover the writer said that he had caught a whiff of that smell from black men in Africa—it was acrid, dry and penetrating. Throughout my youth, and now here in Central Africa, I had this smell in my nostrils, but where I smelt it, among blacks, there was no hunger. It is the smell of Negroes. But let us not be conceited or proud. We are of course bound to imagine that white men do not smell. To a black, however, we smell just as unpleasant, and our smell is just as penetrating. Many black men have told me so.

We were all hungry for gold, and we must have stank of it. Sitting around a bar and swapping stories was no way to get rich. The next six months or so were spent mostly in the field. Whisky-Wolf and I, usually just the two of us but occasionally with some of the other hopefuls, would bound into the loaded car and drive into the Lupa confident that we would find that strike that would make us rich. Then come nightfall, or after camping for a couple of days, we would return with some small sacks filled with gold nuggets, or with very little, or most often with none. Invariably we would all meet at the bar to boast or commiserate. Whichever it was, it was done to drink. The nuggets we used to pay for our drinks were valued in an interesting way. Rose, the barmaid, had a balance made of two small Eno's salts cans, one of which was filled with sand; the other, when weighted with small pieces of gold, was worth the price of a drink.

Rose, who was not without her appeal to some of the older men, dispensed the drink, fetched the playing cards and chatted us up in the hot smoke-filled shed, night after night, until we were all too tired or too drunk or too broke to go on. She did not seem 'past it' but she was either the most discreet woman in the world or cared only for the gold she wrung from us. Not a man there, drunk or sober, could boast that he had ever kissed her, let alone gone to bed with her. This was amazing because Fritz, her husband, although a strong and virile man, was so fat that copulation seemed an impossibility. As the weeks went by this sexual puzzle occupied more and more of René's thoughts. 'How does he do it? How can he? How can *they*?'

Then one evening after we had all returned from the field where Whisky-Wolf and I had really done very well, it happened. We got into a poker game that went on so long that René and I wiped out Fritz. Rose refused to lend him more money, and rather than listen to his begging for a stake, she left the bar to be looked after by someone else. René proposed continuing on credit, and Fritz fell in with the idea. When he had lost the next three hands, René shuffled the deck of cards together and leaned across the table with his face almost touching Fat Fritz's.

'Fritz', he said, 'you fat sloppy fool, you'll never win and Rose'll never give you the money you've just lost. How do you expect to pay us? Do you think we'll just forget about it? We won't but I have a proposition. We'll let you off the hook if you tell us one thing. How do you and Rose fuck?'

Fritz's eyes at first were as big as billiard balls, but then slowly a drunken grin began to form. A glaze of pleasure suffused his sweating face as he leaned back in his chair and said, 'She's on top', and roared with laughter. So did we.

'You really are a lazy bastard, aren't you.'

The René I have just mentioned was the man who for style and daring stood head and shoulders above the rest. His name was Fedor Magnus Christoph René von Rehbinder. He was an Estonian count and came from Revel (now called Tallin). He was also a baron of some place or other in Sweden, and kept the name of the barony in reserve, up his sleeve. Even in his faded khaki he cut an impressive figure.

When he had had a lot to drink before going to bed, which was more often than not, he would recount how he was actually also Prince Koutzebou, which had happened to him somehow as a result of a marriage in his family and had something to do with Romania. Each time he told me this I called him a liar. Whisky-Wolf, by this time not exactly sober either, would interject: 'Shut up. Drunks and children tell the truth.'

René had been a Czarist Guards Officer, and we stayed good friends until his death a few years ago. He did not exaggerate too much. After all, we all exaggerate a little!

René had been a Czarist Guards Officer, though there was no need for him to mention it. He had swallowed a most indigestible ramrod and was still as upright in his bearing as ever. Captured by the Germans during World War I, he had had a nice rest in a prisoner-of-war camp. René hardly ever mentioned those times. If one asked him questions about it, he immediately fell silent. Somewhere along the line there must have been a marriage into a German aristocratic family, but he hardly ever spoke of this.

His best story was one he always told with a great deal of verve. According to this, he was present when the Russian Prince Yousopov, supposedly a distant relation of his, had killed Rasputin. He would recount this tale in such minute detail that it was as if he were writing a thriller.

Poisoned cakes, of which the monk swallowed dozens without turning a hair, without as much as giving a belch, played a part in the story. The Prince, the Count, the Grand Duke Dimitri and other friends had sat opposite Rasputin waiting for the great hulk of a fellow to keel over. But nothing of the sort happened. On the contrary, he kept asking for more. They tried bullets, but had no success. There was no killing that bear. The Count thereupon fetched an axe and the Prince a potato sack. The Prince hit him over the head with the axe, and together they and their friends bundled the monk into the sack and carried him through the garden of the palace, where this sinister drama had been played out, to the frozen River Neva, cut a hole in the ice and pushed him under. Next morning he was found at a weir. His head was sticking out of the sack. He was dead at last.

After the war Russia became a distinctly unhealthy spot for aristocrats. René left Germany, stopped off in Cairo and quickly married an American heiress. The object of his attentions was connected with chewing gum back in the States, and since Americans are very fond of chewing the stuff, she was unbelievably rich. René Rehbinder was a fine looking man. Counts can be fine looking and he looked better than most. But it was his title the rich lady from America was after. René's forefathers had had something to do with the Teutonic Knights. They had marched into the Baltic area long ago and his great-great-grandfather, or an even more remote ancestor, had settled in Russia. But, he confided in us, his looks interested her not at all. So he, with due ceremony, gave her his name. Now she was both rich and the possessor of an ancient title. As soon as the law allowed, the Count and the chewing-gum Countess went straight to an attorney. He received a lot of money and she went back to the chewing-gum factory, taking the ancient title along with her.

René went to Abyssinia, bought himself some racehorses and raced them in Addis Ababa. Although that city in those days was little known to Europeans, a great deal went on there, including horse racing.

Because his horses frequently won, he made the acquaintance of the Regent, Ras Tafari, and the Empress Judith. As an attractive looking and well-bred man—that is, as far as women were concerned—and a Count to boot, he had entrée to the Court. Ras Tafari was the brilliant son of Prince (Ras) Makonnen and a grandnephew of the late Emperor Menelik II. Deposing the Emperor Lij Masu during the war, he became regent for the young Empress Judith. Twelve years later, in 1928, he was crowned King of Ethiopia. In 1930 Judith's timely and mysterious death left the title and power of Emperor available, and as Haile Selassie he grabbed it. René, Count Rehbinder, took a trip to the Lupa.

In fact René was really the only worthwhile man among the lot of us. The rest were either tyro adventurers who might grow out of it, as any young person grows out of certain phases, or wastrels, idlers or eccentrics. Yet almost none of them were without a redeeming feature. Not one was as a good a storyteller as René, yet some were excellent mechanics, and others quick on their feet, with excellent reflexes, which proved useful in brawls. Another was a hopelessly lazy romantic with a heart of gold, full of kindly advice that he totally ignored for himself. And with all his drinking and filthy habits Whisky-Wolf was marvellous, not to say brilliant, at following up a source of gold once he had spotted it. Following his methods, and learning quickly despite the frequency with which we returned with too little or no gold at all, I began myself to spot the signs that could lead to a good couple of days' panning. Whisky-Wolf could certainly have made out better if his greed for gold had not been drowned by his greed for whisky. Much luck as we had, with increasing frequency it all went on drink and renewed equipment. Not having his lust for drink I was able to transfer a good deal of my gold into drafts on Barclay's Bank. As the weeks went on into months, and when René's often-told tales were beginning to pall, I went off by myself for occasional forays into the bush, if not only to escape the company, then perhaps to find myself.

One night, wanting a nightcap on my return from a short lion-hunting trip, I went into the shed that served as a bar. René had just launched into one of his Addis Ababa stories for the umpteenth time. He was telling them yet again of the accession of the Negus when I came in the door.

Whisky-Wolf stood on the table round which they all sat—Al the Slaker, who each day drank away every last grain of any gold he found; Long Feet Samuel, who had absconded from the New York Police; Bill the Sundowner, who hated work of any kind; a couple of aristocrats from Europe somewhat down on their luck; and Lord Lovelace, with his shorts made of dinner-jacket trousers cut off at the knee. They were a choice bunch of characters, each one of whom could have filled a long adventure film with his life story. They were singing dirty songs in English, and only René's speech was still unslurred. 'I have been waiting for you', he said to me, as I stepped up to the table.

'Why?'

'Because I want to get away from here. Will you come with me?'

'OK, I'll come.' I had realized for some days now that I had had enough of this place. I had seen and experienced everything I had wanted to, and accomplished everything I had come for. It was enough.

'One should leave when saying goodbye is still just a little painful', the Count said. I drained my glass.

The next morning the Ford was made ready and we made the journey to Dar-es-Salaam over the sandy tracks that do service as roads in Africa. We shot our own meat as we went along and bought our victuals and our spirits in the Indian dukas. At Dar-es-Salaam we would again live the life of everyday mortals.

Chapter 2

Invitation to Adventure

As the sun was rising, I went down to the beach and swam out into the Mediterranean. Ilona, the lovely Hungarian I had picked up in the bar the night before, lay in my bed. She had said nothing as I made for the door. We had had a late night.

I had arrived in Beirut the previous afternoon from Alexandria, and had booked in at the Hotel Saint George. I was to meet a stranger at 8.30 that evening, 15 May 1937—a stranger who had come all the way from Istanbul just to make my acquaintance. The meeting had been arranged by the German Embassy in Cairo, which was acting on orders from the Abwehr headquarters in Berlin to collect names and addresses of all people with German blood living abroad. I was a particularly interesting contact for the Abwehr because in Egypt I was a known member of an important Arab family and very few people knew that I was half German. The Attaché at the German Embassy in Cairo had added to the suspense of the prearranged meeting in Beirut by telling me that when the stranger, whose name was Haller, contacted me, he would give me a torn-off half of page 145 of Juliette Adams's book *L'Angleterre en Egypte*. The sign of recognition would be that the two halves would match. I had put my half of the page in the pocket of my dinner jacket, which was then packed at the very bottom of my suitcase.

At 8.20 that evening, while I was getting dressed, the reception desk rang through to announce that someone was waiting to meet me. It was ten minutes before the appointed time. Then there was a knock on my door. Before I had time to reply, it opened and there he stood, framed in the doorway. He was fair and unusually tall, with rather watery blue eyes. A soldier in mufti—a real German.

I thought as he stood before me, How could anyone send a man looking like that to keep a secret rendezvous in the East? I would attract more attention just crossing the street with him than if I walked stark naked into one of the best shops in town.

Smiling, he pulled his half of the page from his pocket, said 'Haller', and handed me the sheet. I did not even need to fit the two parts together, since I had memorized the last words on the upper half and the first words on the lower. The upper ended with the words 'in old Egypt' and the lower half, his scrap of the paper, began 'to consecrate my youth, my strength, my life'. They fitted.

Until we reached the bar, we had made only small talk—the weather, the sea, the town and other things of no particular consequence. The barman gave us each a tot of his best whisky. I took Haller by the arm and led him to a small round table standing a little to one side in a part of the room that lay in shadow. Then he said: 'You know that we don't think it's of any importance for you to do your two years' military service with the army proper. It is for this reason that the Attaché in Cairo arranged this meeting. We have other things in mind for you.'

'I would like to make it clear once and for all, dear Herr Haller, that it's no use making plans for me, because I will never go along with people arranging my life. I am open to propositions, which I shall accept or decline, but I would not advise anyone giving me orders.'

'Since you are German and born in 1914, you must serve your two years with the forces. That is a decree of the Führer's which you must obey, like anybody else. But we are reasonable people, we are prepared to talk—especially in the case of Germans living abroad, like yourself. In cases like yours, there are always—possibilities.'

'I hold two passports, one German, one Egyptian. It is the Egyptian one I have with me. The other one is at home.'

I was beginning to feel very hungry. I had earlier reserved a table in the hotel restaurant, assuming that the man I was to meet wished to spend the evening talking, although I had had no idea what it was he wished to discuss so urgently.

'Have you any objection to a good Oriental dinner during which we could have our chat? It's always pleasanter that way.'

I got up and led him from the bar to the big restaurant, which occupied the whole width of the hotel. After we had sat down at our table, I handed him my Egyptian passport. He took it and leafed through it slowly with a solemn face. Then he said: 'Do you always travel with this passport? It seems extraordinarily full of stamps and visas.'

'I have had numerous holidays visiting relatives in the east and when my father takes his annual tours of the spas of Europe my mother and I go with him. So it's not surprising that it is a rather full passport. When I am in Germany from time to time, I have found it useful to have my German passport with me. Otherwise it is more convenient to use this one. That way people do not question you nor stare at you quizzically. Actually I have noticed this only recently—things have changed so radically in Germany.'

He seemed annoyed by my remark, and his mouth had a pinched look about it. Slowly he took a sip of wine and then said, 'No need to be offensive, my dear chap!'

'Take it whichever way you will. It was an observation, that's all. An impression I gained during my recent travels—no judgement.'

It was quite obvious that he wanted something special from me. He would not have travelled all this way, nor the Germans have paid my return fare from Cairo to Beirut just because I had pretty blue eyes!

'I need hardly tell you that we are fully informed about you, down to the tiniest detail. We know precisely with whom we are dealing. That is what I am here for, and that is why I wish to talk to you.' He picked up his glass, emptied it at one gulp, and licked his lips delicately: 'Really a first class wine, my dear friend—first class!'

'It's a Château la Tour Bellegarde, 1931, Herr Haller', I said, and I thought, He eats and drinks like a connoisseur. If only he looked less agressively Aryan! He helped himself to some more of the grilled quail on his plate, as well as to some more cooked olives, chewed deliberately and slowly and, with a raised eyebrow, said: 'Let's get down to business.'

There was something rather insolent about his manner. I said to myself, He won't get anywhere with you, Johnny; you don't like supercilious bastards. I rather think he's going to waste his time. Or, if he wants to get anywhere with you, darling Haller had better change his tune.

He must have known that he could not simply say, Report to So-and-So and he will give you such and such orders.

'As you say, let's get down to business.'

He took another drink of the Bordeaux, carefully placed his glass on the table, pulled up the left sleeve of his jacket slightly, glanced at his wristwatch and said: 'My colleague Rohde will be here in a quarter of an hour. Until then I should like to discuss our proposition with you in somewhat more detail.'

'This Rohde, would he be your chief?'

'In a certain sense—yes, I suppose he is. He is, as it were, responsible for the Middle East; but he is a very pleasant man to work for. Should you accept our proposition, you will have a lot to do with him. You will find he is very easy to get on with.'

I remembered what the Attaché in Cairo—a man with the most impeccable manners—had told me during a round of golf at the Guezira Sporting Club on one occasion. He had said that Germany enjoyed special advantages in the Middle East, because so many of her people there had a talent for languages and, what was more important, good contacts. I was reminded of the Attaché's remark because I was beginning to see what Haller was getting at. As for manners, he could have done worse than to take a lesson from the young Attaché.

The mood of the evening rapidly changed after Rohde arrived, and I began to take rather more interest in the German proposition. This gentleman was the very opposite of the stilted Haller. He was of medium height, with a look of the outdoor man about him; and he was dark and well-dressed, with faultless manners. He sat down, relaxed and began to chat easily of this and that as if we were old acquaintances. At first it was just small talk but then Rohde began to direct the conversation. Haller leaned back in his chair and did not say another word for the rest of the evening. Not a single word. The underling had done his duty. Now that your Lord and Master has turned up, I thought, you might as well run along home. Should we come to an arrangement, I must avoid having to play a role like yours. That kind of dumb obedience was not for me.

'It would be a waste of time', said Rohde, 'to make a little speech about the Fatherland, a sense of duty and service to the people. I really can't expect you to feel such things. The gap between you and the new Germany is too great. You live in a different world. So I shall go straight to our proposition.'

'I have already told Herr Haller that I would consider your proposition, and I agree with you that any philosophising would be a waste of time. If you have anything interesting, and particularly anything that smacks of an adventure, to propose, I am eager to hear about it.'

I knew well enough what these gentlemen had up their sleeves.

'Like any other army, we need exact information about military conditions in other countries', he continued. 'It is my job to provide this for the Middle East. As Military Attaché in Greece and Turkey, my own freedom of movement is limited; I would draw too much attention to myself. I therefore need trusted men, who are at home in the Levant. The most suitable are men like you, who, while having bonds of kinship with Germany, are resident here—in other words, are fully integrated in the Middle East. You, of course, fit these requirements, which is why we have got in touch with you and why I am suggesting that we collaborate. Should you agree, we can discuss details.

'Before we turn to the social part of this evening I should warn you, if you agree to work with us, that secret service work is no picnic; it is dangerous and requires courage. Should anything ever go wrong, you can never say that you know me, and of course I would never admit to knowing you. You would be on your own, without any hope of assistance. I am telling you this so that you can give it your mature consideration, and because I would like relations between us to be open and above board. Should we fail to come to an arrangement, forget all about this conversation—it never happened.'

Well, at least he had made himself perfectly clear. The frankness of the man was attractive, and I could quite see myself working with him without regretting it. I could safely say that, in any circumstances, I would not blame Rohde for anything.

'You realise I am not doing this out of patriotism', I said, 'although a certain feeling of belonging does play a part. My youth, as you rightly say, was different from that of a young man who grew up exclusively in Germany. I am more Egyptian than German and luckily for you for all practical purposes we are nothing but a British colony; otherwise my interests would be confined exclusively to this country.'

'Egypt is no colony', interrupted Rohde. 'Technically, it became an independent state in 1922. I grant you the British had certain privileges, which according to last week's agreement in Montreux they are going to relinquish. But the main decisions are supposed to be taken in the future by the King and his Government.'

'Yes, that's precisely how the British see it, and particularly how they would like it to look now, despite last week's decision—after all, in 1929 they agreed to all this. That's why soon after the war they made our independence conditional on four special laws: to guarantee the lines of communication of the British Empire; to protect Egypt against any foreign attack, and against direct or indirect foreign intervention; to protect foreign interests and all minorities, which means

British ones in particular; and to give them suzerainty of the Sudan. Otherwise, Herr Rohde, we are quite independent!'

At that time, in 1937, the British ruled Egypt by playing the King and the Wafd off against one another. There were three forces ranged against each other in the country: the British; the King, who was anti-British; and Nahas Pasha's Wafd Party, which disapproved of the King and to which my father belonged. It was not for nothing that some young people who objected to the British occupation had joined the Ichwan el Muslimin, led by Hassan el Banna, and were cautiously heartened by the reaffirmation of the 1922 treaty, and the convention by which Britain gave up its extra-territorial claims. This Moslem Brotherhood consisted mostly of students and intellectuals; but more important was the adherence of the sons of the pashas and beys—in other words, those who long ceased to have faith in the so-called independence, or in the supposedly hereditary rights of our fathers. And then there was another movement. It was the successor to the Old National Party, a passionate enemy of Britain, and consisted of young people with whom I was very friendly. There was also Ahmed Hussein, leader of the Greenshirts, the Misr Èl Fatat or Young Egypt Party. He published a book, *Im'ami*, as his testament of faith. It was his *Mein Kampf*, because his hero was Adolf Hitler. I found the whole thing a bit overdone, but otherwise he was a fine fellow.

'All I want to say, Herr Rohde, is that you are on the wrong track when you say that Egypt is independent. I am afraid that for a long time, despite the Montreux convention, we will remain Lancashire's cotton plantation, as we say—those of us, that is, who don't believe in this new agreement. These considerations will certainly affect my decision whether or not to accept your proposition. Important as adventure is to me—you might say it's in my blood—it is not the decisive factor. And one thing more. If, and I mean if, I should decide tomorrow to accept your proposition, you must understand that I don't do it for the money. I don't need to take risks such as these just for what's in it for me.'

'Very well, let's get on with this tomorrow morning, my dear chap. Think about it, and I shall too.' Then Rohde stood up and said: 'There is bound to be a good nightclub here, surely? We'll go there and talk about other things. Let's enjoy ourselves.'

As we entered the club, a girl was doing some sort of a dance on the floor. While I was watching the soft and airy movements of her slender hands in the white spotlight, the head waiter came up to us. He led us to a table right at the front, next to the dance floor. He had divined instinctively that here was a case where money was no object.

Rohde was staying at the Hotel Metropole, which everyone in the Middle East knew was under German management. He should have known better! Even though I was not yet a member of any intelligence service, I would have expected a man in his position to avoid so obvious a German connection. Such loyalty was appropriate only at home.

The French secret service would not be asleep. I decided therefore not to agree to meet at the Metropole but let him come to the Saint George; let him, moreover, come without Herr Haller who, as far as I was concerned, had been around too long.

The next morning, after a swim in the Mediterranean, I sat on the terrace, having rung Rohde to tell him what I had decided. He accepted without a word, although we had already made an appointment to meet at his place. Possibly he had realized why I wanted to avoid the Metropole, and agreed to come to my room instead. There I accepted the German's proposal, and we made an appointment to meet again on 20 July 1937 in Athens, where we could cross the t's and dot the i's.

It was then I realized that I had forever dashed any hopes that my family had had that my lust for adventure had been sated. I knew I would never become the lawyer or judge they dreamed I would be.

Chapter 3

Hidden Trumps

The *Khedive Ismael* was a passenger ship that plied between Piraeus, Famagusta, Beirut and Alexandria. It was fitted out handsomely and was in those days the pleasantest boat in the area, second only to the luxury liners that called at Alexandria as part of their cruises on the Seven Seas. I had often sailed on her. The cabins and state rooms were most elegantly decorated and furnished, proof of a highly sophisticated taste. To travel aboard her was never dull. The entertainment was select and the passengers agreeable.

Having left Beirut in the early hours of the morning, I spent the time at sea under one of the awnings that had been rigged up on the fore and after decks. It was getting hotter. The hot Sherkiya from Sinai, slightly cooler than it feels in the desert, was strong enough to make a howling sound as it blew through the awnings.

Act One had gone without a hitch in Beirut. In a month's time when I was due to meet Rohde in Athens, we would see!

By the time the ship tied up, Alexandria would be filled by the annual family exodus from Cairo to escape the heat, and I would be able to stay in that colourful city, with its romantic squares and quarters and holiday atmosphere. There was the Grande Corniche, a kilometre long, with its innumerable cafés along the sea, Glyminopoulos, Camp Caesar (where I was born), Cleopatra, San Stefano, Sidi Bishr and many other places. Alexandria is still almost in Europe; Greek and Italian predominate, and Arabic sounds just a bit alien. It is a city of crafty Oriental money-makers, a place where a man who does not care for this way of life is considered mad. Such a man would be regarded with caution and even embarrassment. But most incomprehensible of all in Alexandria were those people who were already rich and did not wish to get even richer, those playboys who haunted the town in summer time and populated the casinos and cabarets.

The Gaafars owned a house and some land at the seaside, near Montazah. The fine sandy beach began right at our walls, and from childhood days I remember the wonderful view of the Mediterranean from the balconies and terraces of our house. In the great park, along one of the walls, stood palms and some agave trees; and in one corner there were pomegranate trees. At the right time of year bougainvillea bloomed against another wall in the garden. As children, we found this park a little eerie after dark.

A favourite Egyptian proverb proclaims, 'Egypt, Mother of the World' (Misr Umm' ed dunniya'), and Egypt is indeed the most beautiful country in the world—for those who are rich! In those days, nearly a century after the Khedive Mohammed Ali, all the land still belonged to the landowner class, whose great wealth contrasted with the poverty of town and countryside. The presence of the British meant that the landowners could go on accumulating ever greater wealth. The political alliance between England and the pashas, with the Royal Family and its lackeys, kept the fellaheen in their place. About the only gain they had achieved was that compulsory labour had been abolished in 1893, except where the Khedive himself had ordered it. The slave had become a free man, but his pocket and belly were empty. The pasha and the bey dominated Egyptian life. The land belonged to them, and England watched vigilantly to make sure that it stayed that way. The wealthy families were all related, and intermarried and lived as a caste of lords in Cairo and Alexandria, making trips to Europe to enjoy the pleasures of life and play the nabob. The fellah was exploited by these families, and if he seemed apathetic, it was because hunger, servitude, injustice and ignorance make for apathy.

Lying in my deckchair aboard the *Khedive Ismael*, the wide blue sea spread out before me, with everything that a young man could wish for already mine, I was still not entirely content. I had become suddenly aware that my visit to Beirut and my meeting with Rohde could give me opportunities to promote the new ideas that were burgeoning in Egypt. Some progressive people had realized that there must be radical remedies. The desire for change had gripped the young intellectual élite, including some sons of the feudal landowners.

One of my innumerable cousins, Nabil, a professor at the Azhar University, that renowned bastion of Islamic theology, had for some years belonged to the Ichwan el Muslimin and was one of the 'Adjutants' of Hassan el Banna, the Führer of the Moslem Brotherhood. The aim of this organization was to rid the valley of the Nile of foreign rule and to obtain justice for the Egyptian people. The Brotherhood combined in its philosophy the oldest and best Islamic traditions. Its long-term aims were Pan-Arab and Pan-Islamic. It also had a secret and very efficient intelligence service.

The King, the British and the Pashas were all against the Brotherhood in theory. But in fact they also financed it, because of the political situation at that time, when each of these factions was trying to gain an advantage over the other.

At the customs I got a porter to take my luggage home in a taxi. My immediate destination was Saad Zaghloul Square, where Nabil frequented one of the cafés when he was in Alex. It was the meeting place of the Brotherhood. There were two questions I wanted him to answer. Could a line to the German Secret Service be useful to the Brotherhood, and if so, how would such a partnership affect the Brotherhood? Secondly, could I, as a member—even if only an insignificant one—have an interview with Hassan el Banna?

Nabil sat flicking his ivory-handled fly whisk, a nargileh before him, out of which there came, with every pull he took, the soft gurgling of bubbles. He looked very composed, his immaculate teeth sparkling white as snow as he smiled when I came towards him. The mandatory greetings and questions about my trip having been gone through, Nabil asked me straight out what was on my mind.

'What I have come to see you about is something we can't discuss at home. They'd think we were mad.'

'Then we must ring and tell them we won't be home for dinner. You are in luck, you know. Hassan el Banna is in town and I have an appointment with him tonight. Before we left Cairo, I once mentioned to Hassan that we were cousins and that you had ties with Germany—even if only family ones. You shall talk to him. You have come at the right moment.'

As we made our way through the Midan Orabi, to the Mosque of el-Khaid Ibrahim, I was preoccupied with mixed feelings of confidence and doubt. Surely it was impossible to arrive at one's goal so easily. There must be a catch somewhere.

Nabil, as a fanatical member of the Brotherhood, had an influential position in Hassan el Banna's circle of founders, much to the chagrin of his family, who rejected and even resisted the Brotherhood. It was not surprising that Nabil had stepped out of line; after talking to him, I thought I might have done the same in his place. For his father, whom he regarded as a kind of brothel creeper and who lived the life of the wealthy Levantine, he had nothing but contempt. Towards seven in the evening my uncle would leave his palace, where the whole clan lived, and would not be seen there again until dawn. He would spend the night in the society of the belly-dancers and Arab singers who haunted the countless night-spots and Oriental theatres of Cairo. There was no dancer freshly arrived from Europe on whom he was not the first to lavish his money. The owners of the night-spots saw to that and he was a big spender.

He cared nothing for his wife and children; for him they did not exist. Always dressed in the latest fashion, wearing his fez at a rakish angle over his left ear, a 'King Fuad' moustache under his nose, he was the epitome of dashing Egyptian manhood. Very slender, covered in gold and jewellery, my uncle was one of the best known of the smart set, about whom stories circulated in every café.

I had decided to seek out Nabil immediately after my arrival in Alexandria and have a good talk with him, as there was little more than a month left before I was due to meet Rohde in Athens.

The weather was ideal, the sea calm. Night had fallen, and the light from the Ras el-Tin lighthouse swept over the calm water. We sailed through the narrow fairway and into the great glittering harbour basin of Alexandria.

'In the name of Allah, the all-compassionate and the all-merciful', whispered Nabil as we went through the gate of the mosque, took off our shoes and entered the outer hall. All Moslems quote from the Koran as they enter a mosque—Allah is the absolute, He is the only God, the Almighty, the just. Man's duty to Allah is faith and complete submission to His will. That is the meaning of the word Islam. He who submits is a Moslem. Allah is a living reality to an extent the ordinary European Christian simply cannot comprehend.

Hassan el Banna was facing a group of men, both young and old, who sat in semi-circle around him and listened to his dissertation, delivered in rounded poetical cadences. He had the power of oratory as only Orientals can have, with an affect on the hearer that is little short of hypnotic. I had imagined him taller. His deep-set eyes burnt with a fire that seemed to consume all those who were present. I disliked this and felt uneasy—fanatics are dangerous. I decided, before I made up my mind about him, to speak to him and get to know him. His snow-white eh'ma was wrapped untidily about his head. On top one could make out a red spot where the top of his tarboosh was showing. A straggly black beard framed his cheeks, upper lip and chin. His face was like one of those in old Turkish miniatures. As he saw us enter the hall, he stood up and came towards us. Then he led me to a corner of the hall, where we sat on the floor. 'Marhaba', he said. 'Welcome. I am glad to make your acquaintance. Your cousin has told me a great deal about you.'

I went straight to the point and asked him the question I had intended to put to Nabil. He looked at me for a long time, his eyes narrowed to a slit, without answering. Then he spoke very slowly. 'You are not the first to ask me this question. Some weeks ago, in Cairo, an Italian came to see me. Now that Mussolini is the self-appointed 'Protector of Islam', he is trying to establish his influence over the nationalist elements in Egypt in order to play them off against Britain.'

I interrupted him: 'At the moment, I am not trying to do anything, Hassan bey, nothing at all. No one has sent me.' I did not want him to think that I had been sent by someone, since I was after all still a free agent and had not yet made up my mind whether I would work for Rohde or not. It was too soon to speak on behalf of someone I had spoken with only twice before.

'Good', he said. 'We are first and foremost an Arab and a religious movement. Nabil will have told you that I am no friend of the Europeans. Nevertheless I have taken from them several ideas that suited my purpose, which doesn't mean that I agree with them in all things. I am opposed to their influence—otherwise the British could stay in this country for ever. Whatever happens, there can be no compromise about the predominance of Islam in Egyptian life, as long as I have anything to say about it. That is precisely what the Europeans don't want, and the Germans are no exception.'

I thought, Now there's the rub. But then he went on.

'Nevertheless it's important, in order to reach our goal, to explore every avenue. Should you have a contact—or shall we say, should you find one—I have nothing against it. That is on condition that our interests are protected and that I myself have no contact in this matter with anyone but you—except of course Nabil, which goes without saying. He has my implicit trust.'

We discussed all sorts of things then until, impelled by hunger, we went to one of the Arab restaurants on the Grande Corniche.

A few days later I was sitting in the Casino San Stefano, having a cup of coffee and looking out to sea. I had to be alone to think in peace about the events of recent weeks. I had to make plans. I had to make a decision soon. Either I would work for Rohde and his organization, or I would come back here, to the same old round. But I wanted no more of that; I had lived long enough in a gilded cage.

What was it that Swabian peasant had called down to me from the bridge when I had fallen into the frozen stream up to my neck in the ice? 'When the donkey does too well, he runs on to the ice!'

The old man had not lifted a finger to fish me out. 'Now you just figure out how to get out of there', and, staying put on the bridge, he gave me a long hard look as I crawled, sopping wet, out of the river. 'If you were my boy', he said, 'I would tan your hide for you.'

Perhaps it would be best to keep my fingers out of this one. The fire could easily become too hot. This connection with the Germans might be useful—or dangerous. At any rate, I reasoned, I must not make up my mind in Athens until I have established a really firm position for myself in Egypt. That would be my trump card. I could put forward concrete terms only if I had something to offer. On the other hand, it had been the Germans who had approached me, and they must have had a good reason. In fact, Rohde had said so quite openly and without beating about the bush. Still, my contacts with the Moslem Brotherhood were not enough. I needed something more.

It was then that I thought about Ahmed Hussein, the Führer of the Greenshirts. Ever since the signing of the Anglo-Egyptian Treaty the previous year Hussein's followers had taken an extremely hostile attitude towards the British. They regarded the treaty as a rotten compromise, merely affirming the same British intentions made in 1929 and still not granting Egypt the right to govern itself and the Sudan. I had not seen him since last August when, on the eve of his journey to attend the Nuremberg Party Rally, he had asked me for advice about his trip. I did not find him very likeable. Still, even if he was not one of my favourite people, I felt I should call on him. Then there was Ahmed Radwan, who had particularly good connections in nationalist circles. These consisted mostly of young officers putting their heads together; these, too, could be very useful. To be in a strong bargaining position I had to hurry and make my contacts.

Later that afternoon my old school friend Kahil and I were engaged in our usual game of chess at the Café Ibrahimija. He told me that if I wanted to I could meet Ahmed Hussein in Tanta. Kahil, who was one of the founder members of the Greenshirts, offered to accompany me there the next day.

'I'll fetch you tomorrow morning. We'll be there in a few hours and could be back late in the afternoon.'

The distance to Tanta on the Delta road and Damanhour was about 120 km. The journey took at least two hours in a normal car because one continually met donkeys and camels in no hurry to get off the road. I had just run in my new Lancia and was tearing through the villages along the irrigation canals near Tanta, making liberal use of the horn. I wanted to be there by noon. But the journey took more than two hours and we arrived after twelve. Tanta is half-way to Cairo in the south-eastern part of the Delta, and boasts a much venerated holy man, Sheik Said el-Badawi, who lies buried in a splendid mosque named after him.

The Sheik lies well-protected behind immense bronze railings at which the faithful offer up their prayers and then kiss the bronze bars. His memorial is covered with an immense black velvet cloth. Every year in April and August there are great festivals in memory of Badawi. Members of my family who live near Tanta on a farm made a pilgrimage to the mosque every Mouled, because they believed that this would protect them from all illness. Nevertheless, should one of them fall ill, it was no fault of Badawi's but because the Afridis were so evil that even he fought against them in vain. Next Mouled they would make the pilgrimage all over again quite unperturbed.

We were out of luck—Ahmed Hussein too was at the holy man's grave. He was praying as we entered the mosque, to which his friends had sent us, so we were bound to do likewise and to join the prayers at the Doh'r. Reciting the Sunnas, I thought to myself, I would rather have a decent meal than spend the time in prayer.

When prayers were over and Ahmed Hussein and I had talked, he agreed that, should my plans come to fruition, I could count on his help. His journey to Nuremberg had yielded him precious little apart from one contact—someone he described as an old gentleman who had lived a few years in Egypt and was now working in some organization or other where he played some unspecified role. Ahmed Hussein had also collected some invitations and consumed a great deal of alcohol, which had not agreed with him at all.

All that remained now to complete my list of contacts was to meet a few of the young officers belonging to other nationalist organizations. One of them, Hussein Zulfikar Sabri, whom I already knew slightly, was in Cairo, so my next move had to be a quick flight there.

Naturally, when I mentioned my plans to anyone, I spoke only in terms comprehensible to someone in the nationalist movement. Nor could I speak in more exact detail, since everything was still in the kite-flying stage. Nothing specific had been arranged, and I could easily make myself look ridiculous should nothing come of the whole business with the Germans.

At Almaza Airport I was astonished to see Group Captain Tom Forrester, an old acquaintance, walking towards me across the forecourt. I instinctively stepped back a few paces from the waiting taxi. I *would* meet that Englishman here, of all places!

'Glad to see you, Hussein. We must have another round of golf some time—we haven't had a game for ages!' His tone was sarcastic. He had taken me by surprise. But my distrust was almost immediately allayed. Nervousness was the last thing on earth I could afford.

Forrester was most affable and on that hot windless clear day it was a pleasure to accept his invitation to go to the Turf Club for a drink. I dismissed the taxi and we drove through the wonderful city of Cairo.

'How are you getting on with your flying time?' he asked me. 'Has Milton let you take a kite up yet—I mean solo?'

'Yes, the last time he let me take up a Moth for a short spin, just over the airfield. All by myself. I suppose he wasn't really meant to, but I shall be taking my test soon, and as old Milton says, I am bound to pass. So he took a chance on it.'

'The de Havilland Moth will fly by itself, you know, Hussein. It's absolutely foolproof. That's why he trusted you with the old kite. It's probably the safest plane in existence at the moment and Milton is a first-class instructor. I wish we had one as good as that in the RAF. He is a really good pilot.'

Then we had lunch together at the Guezira Sporting Club. Since Tom Forrester was a most entertaining chap, and good fun, we lolled round the swimming pool after lunch and larked around with the pretty girls swimming there. After all, I did not have to be at the Egyptian Army Officers' Club in Zamalek before the afternoon to meet

Hussein for a game of squash—and to find out from him what was going on among the young officers in the Egyptian army.

Thanks to the Anglo-Egyptian Treaty, even men from the middle classes now had a chance to become officers, a possibility hitherto only open to the rich. The first group of 'new' officers who had recently obtained their commissions became disenchanted when they discovered that the army was riddled with corruption. Being idealists, they could not understand how such a thing was possible. They were anti-British but not pro-German, and were not really interested in what was happening in Germany or Italy. There were few contacts with intelligence organizations in either of these countries, and such as there might be were most likely with the Italians. There was a sizeable Italian colony in Egypt and it was conceivable that contacts had been established there. The number of German nationals in Egypt was insignificant. About the true situation in Germany the average young Egyptian officer knew as much as I—which was nothing. Only what was in the papers. A few considered Hitler as a great leader, but really this was just a form of hero worship for someone who had revitalized the German army.

Most of the officers sympathized with the Brotherhood, and some were active in it. They formed themselves into loosely knit groups, but without any formal organization. There was as yet no move to get anything going—they were still groping in the dark.

Many years later, Anwar el-Sadat looked back on all this from the commanding heights he had reached, forgetting in the process that Hussein Zulfikar had been the leader of a cell before he had been. Although unsuccessful in an attempt to fly General Azziz el-Masri Pasha out and over to the Afrika-Korps, Hussein Zulfikar had been the first not only to organize a cell but also to be active in the nationalist movement, at great risk to himself. Often it is the first who later becomes the last.

At that time there was no really clear purpose behind the thinking of the young Egyptians. The intellectuals spoke with hatred of British rule and of the minions who were prepared to carry out the demands of British politics because in the process they became grossly rich, as only a corrupt Oriental can. The British may have been installed in the country as conquerors, but they were surrounded by hatred.

The revolution of 1919, almost completely ignored in Europe, had long been forgotten. Saad Zaghloul, its leader, had become a folk hero and there were statues of him all over the country. But it had done no real good. Mustafa Nahas Pasha, Zaghloul's successor and head of the Wafd Party, was a very different kettle of fish from his predecessor, and it was he who made an accommodation with Britain.

Concurrently there was also an insignificant liberal faction in Egypt, which may have been under German influence, because a number of those who belonged to it had studied in post-war Germany. But its influence was negligible. Although almost imperceptible at first, a process of ferment was beginning among the young officers; but unfortunately they lacked a charismatic figure who could have galvanized them into action. There was, of course, General Azziz el-Masri, a man who was the idol of the young officers but who seemed to lack faith in them. The outlook for change was by no means favourable.

Masri was the only man who fulfilled Zulfikar's requirements of idealism combined with an eagerness to do something—to build up a cell and to extend it. He was of mixed Circassian and Arabic origin, and a hardened enemy of Enver Pasha in the days of the Ottoman Empire (Enver Pasha himself being a proponent of Turkish rule). Later Masri had become Commander-in-Chief of the Sherifian troops of Abdullah, the Emir of Mecca, and had fought on the side of the Ottomans against the Italians in Tripolitania. Fighting with Lawrence for Arab independence, he had led a battalion of volunteers from Mesopotamia and Syria. He was a gallant and splendid champion of the Arab cause.

There was a cool wind coming from the Nile as Zulfikar and I crossed the bridge and passed by the Kasr el-Nil barracks, in front of which Tommies sat drinking their beer. At the Midan Soliman Pasha we sat down in one of the cafés in the square.

I have a lasting affection for Arab coffee houses, with their tumultuous noise, the calls of the proprietors (who shout every order at the tops of their voices), the chattering customers, the yells of the vendors of ground-nuts and cakes, the perspiring Berbers who serve the coffee, and the nargileh smokers who, lost to the world, oblivious to all the sounds and smells of the Orient, enjoy their hashish. When we had found ourselves a table amid all the hubub, I asked Zulfikar straight out, if I should put the questions to him one day, whether he would be willing to do some work with me which was not without risk; and whether, should he agree to do it, he would stick to it.

Without hesitation, he agreed immediately.

I now knew that I could meet Rohde in Athens with a couple of bargaining points in my favour.

Chapter 4

A Bargain Sealed

Just at this time something happened that might have upset all the plans; they were not yet settled but they really needed no further complication. I got married.

Typically impetuous, I first saw her in a nightclub. Sonia was a dancer, not one from the troupes of blondes making their debut in Cairo at the Metropolitan Dugout, but a member of the Danish ballet. I shall never forget her entrance. She was stunningly beautiful, with hair the colours Titian loved to paint—dark red with glints of gold. Her companion was a distinguished looking, grey-haired, meticulously attired gentleman. She was much to young and beautiful for him.

We danced, we talked—he was her father—and we did all the things instant lovers do. In a fortnight we were married.

Naturally my father disapproved, but neither did he increase or decrease my allowance. He always referred to her as 'the acrobat' or 'tight-rope dancer', and he never allowed her to visit him. You see, I had upset his plans for my marriage, and perhaps if he had not settled on some friend's daughter for me, he might have accepted Sonia. My choice made him lose face in the eyes of his contemporaries, and we were an embarrasment to his authority.

'You'll have to manage on what you get', he said. 'A man must learn his responsibilities even at the expense of his luxuries.' He advised me to take my acrobatic wife on a tour. That way, he said, if we were to raise our own troupe of street acrobats, we would at least know our way around the cities of Europe.

Sonia had to finish her tour at the Cairo Opera House, and then she planned to follow me to Athens. If I reached an agreement with the Germans, we would visit the Worlds Fair in Paris and then go on to Copenhagen before I made my way to Berlin and the training period in Germany that would be necessary in due course.

According to the instructions I had received in Beirut, I was to telephone Rohde on my arrival in Athens on 20 July, and he would then give me the address where we would meet. 'I will send you a driver. Let's meet at my place; we can talk there without being disturbed.'

The porter called me down to the lobby when the driver arrived. I was then driven down the King George Avenue to the end of the park, where the car turned right and stopped in front of a house that could just as well have been in Munich, if it had not been for the Acropolis visible over the roof, making it unmistakably clear where one actually was. As I walked up the garden path, Rohde greeted me from the door, studying me closely. In another moment the door had swung to behind us. He walked two paces in front of me as we entered a study.

He sat down behind a meticulously tidy desk and offered me a chair near the window—a large pleasant window, overlooking the sun-drenched garden. The room was tastefully furnished, immaculately clean. Everything was quiet except for the noise coming from the busy street at the bottom of the garden.

Rohde leaned back in his chair and said: 'Now we shall just go over the offer I made you in Beirut. After that, I shall explain the work of the secret service to you in as much detail as possible, so that there can be no misunderstanding. You know I prefer to work without complications. If you then have any doubts left, please tell me frankly.'

I lit a cigarette and told him that I had some questions, but that by all means he was to speak frankly. I could take it that nothing worth doing could be done without taking some trouble over it.

'As I see it', he continued, 'if you are to join our organization, I will want you to work by yourself at first. I won't want you to get to know anyone except me. Then you will have to report to Berlin before beginning the training period. You may meet some people at headquarters, but they will be the sort who work in offices and laboratories rather than in the field. You will get your orders from me and you will be responsible only to me.

'From time to time we shall meet somewhere; otherwise we shall communicate through the post, through accommodation addresses. That will be the form until the officers in Berlin assign you to another superior; or it may happen that you will work entirely on your own. If I may give you a piece of advice, try and bring us something concrete pretty quickly; that's the way to get established in the service. You are not a man who is easily led; you work better on your own—a pretty bad character. I am much the same sort myself, which is why I can appreciate that some people prefer to work unencumbered. They usually produce better results that way. But we haven't reached that stage yet.'

Well, he certainly did not mince his words. So, I am as bad as that, am I? Stubborn, yes, I have never denied it, but the man seems to think I am incorrigible.

'We've thought it over—you realize. I am only a link in a chain, and it has been decided to establish you firmly in the Middle East. After your training period has ended, that is where you will begin your work, provided of course that the political situation remains what it is today. You have a first-class cover and you don't need any cover story. Your work will consist exclusively of collecting military intelligence. Keep out of politics, it has nothing to do with our kind of work. We are soldiers, not politicians. Leave politics to the Foreign Office in Berlin and to the various Party organizations—we have nothing to do with any of that. This is an important thing to remember—only military secrets are wanted.'

'There has been one change in my situation', I said. 'I've recently married and would like you to know this, if we are to play fair with one another from the start.'

'I know', he said quite calmly. 'You were married on 25 June at the Danish Consulate in Cairo. We haven't been snooping; it came to our notice because the Danish Consul mentioned it at a reception he attended with a German colleague. I was a little surprised and thought—surely that's a bit early. But obviously love will find a way. At least I hope that's why you did it. For that matter, I am a married man myself, and so are many in this business. It would be better if it were not so, but then we are all men, and women. It's a good thing, though, that you haven't married a little home-body who wants nothing but a lot of children and a little house somewhere and all that sort of thing. If you had, I would have sent you word through the Attaché to forget the whole thing; it would have made things too complicated. We made inquiries—you appreciate that we had no alternative—and we have no objections. There will be a monthly allowance for your wife, the amount of which is decided in Berlin. As far as she is concerned, you will have a lot of business trips to make. In addition to your pay, you will also be entitled to expenses. These are to be settled with me. Regarding expenses, we can afford to be reasonably liberal since I can hardly expect you to submit receipts. In our work there are not many receipts to be had. For that reason relations between us must be based on trust.'

Then I told Rohde about the groundwork I had done in Cairo, without, however, mentioning any names. He lit a cigarette, produced a cloud of blue smoke and clearly had difficulty hiding his astonishment. He said nothing for several minutes, drew on his cigarette and gazed out of the window.

'All that will cost a packet! Orientals are not shy when it comes to wanting money—from the most idealistic of motives, of course! I am a realist, I don't believe in Father Christmas; but you've started something you can build on.'

I thought, He'd rather break a leg than admit he was surprised. Cool as a cucumber.

'O.K.', I said. 'But there are a few more things I want to ask about. I must insist that I am not to be asked to work against the interest of Egypt. The same applies to Denmark, as I don't wish to work against my wife's country.'

'Agreed.'

'I told you in Beirut that I don't have to do this for my bread and butter. I don't expect to receive vast sums, that would be crazy, but all work has its price. I don't consider spying as just a series of adventures, at least not only that. Nor do I see it as heroic. To me it is a very cold and calculating business, which will require all my time and energies. Let's leave sentiment to the amateurs, otherwise I would have to think of some decent people I know as dishonourable, for I am convinced they are spies—perhaps not by way of their principal occupation, but spies all the same. To me spying is just a dangerous job, without a safety net. If you 'fall', there is nobody there to catch you, but then there are a great many other jobs where this is also true.'

'You get 1,500 marks a month, for a start. Expenses—that's another matter. And they can come to a tidy sum', said Rohde.

'It's not a matter of tidy sums, leave those to others. Tidy sums are not interesting. The question is—do I accept your tidy sum? Because I want a contract as well.'

'You will have to discuss that in Berlin. They'll fall about with laughter when you tell them; they'll never have heard of anything like that!'

'As far as I'm concerned they can die laughing; I couldn't care less. Without a contract I won't even go there. If you want my services, those are my terms. I've always understood the risks I shall be taking, but I am willing to accept them on a contractual basis. I don't believe in Father Christmas any more than you do. Should I be unlucky and fall through the trapdoor one of these days, or should I find myself somewhere in a box six feet underground, there must be a sum of money that would be paid to my wife. Should I turn up at the end of the war, perhaps a cripple as a result of interrogation, I don't want to find myself on a street corner singing a patriotic song, because in that case I would starve to death.'

'You've thought of everything, my dear chap. I like it. At least I know where I am with you.'

'You're asking a far higher price than that from me—my life, should things go wrong', I said.

'Since you only have the one, I suppose you want to sell it as dear as possible?'

'No, I just want to sell it on a reliable basis.'

We did come to an agreement after some hard bargaining. If one were on the level, it was inevitable that Rohde's terms would be acceptable, no matter how outlandish those terms might appear to an outsider. He was an obstinate man who made one obstinate but not unreasonable, because that was what he was like himself.

We had had a marvellous lunch at the Alex Restaurant, and when I first saw the delicacies spread out on the tables, I felt reassured in dealing with someone who appreciated good food so much. Afterwards we returned to the room where we had begun negotiating that morning. During the second half of the day Rohde did all the talking. The sun was now shining through the other window, behind Rohde's desk. A high garden wall cut us off from being seen by anyone in the house next door; the heavy dark green velvet curtains were half-open and helped to filter the hot July sunlight. They had not been drawn in the morning, so I felt sure that there must have been someone else in the house. Perhaps on the other side of that door, behind the desk, there was someone eavesdropping? But there was no need to be cautious. I would not have changed anything had I been the eavesdropper himself. It was more likely than not in this trade that there was probably an ear listening somewhere. I should have to remember that.

Rohde continued his explanation where he had left off in the morning. 'The course will give you the final polish for this profession; hard work is the only way. Without the technical skills acquired during the training period, no agent can get by these days.

'Our opponents will describe as illegal the methods you will use to obtain information. We have the same attitude towards them. One side will call you a criminal, the other a hero. Nothing but words! In fact, no agent is either good or bad; he is, like all other men, both good and bad. You must make a point of not being found out. Once you make yourself known, you are finished. Make no friends.

'Should luck bring you some unusually important secret, you can be sure it will enhance your standing in the department. But carry on as if you had not accomplished anything special. Coming up with top-secret information means that you will have made a number of your colleagues jealous. Jealousy is more dangerous than a whole company of the enemies. Trust no man; use him, but never trust him, or he will let you down. You too will be treated with nothing but mistrust and a certain amount of hostility—even by colleagues and perhaps by your superior officer, if you have one. Never forget that the man who knows a secret holds power. A Chinese proverb says: "If two men want to keep a secret, one of them must die."'

What a splendid prospect, I thought! So far I have heard not a single encouraging word about this job. Any more of this, if I were sensible, I would change my mind.

Rohde continued calmly: 'Secret service work requires the ultimate in self-discipline, much more than military life. Never dream that you will be noted or praised for your achievements. Every now and then, if you are lucky, one of the bosses of the service might let fall some casual word of encouragement, but it won't go any further.

'Nowhere will your name be mentioned—except possibly in enemy circles, which is precisely what you must avoid.

'The name of your most dangerous adversary is the British Secret Intelligence Service. Its various departments and missions will be something you'll have to spend a lot of time over during your training course, so we can forget about them for the moment.

'Your first contact with the enemy will be with the Naval Intelligence Division, and in particular with Geographical Section South 3, which operates in Turkey, Egypt, Syria, Arabia, Iraq and Persia—the countries where you will do your early work. The others are of no interest at the moment. The people likeliest to be on your trail belong to the Security Service—MI 5. They are tenacious, those boys; once they have picked up the trail, they will not give up the chase.

'But nothing in this world is infallible and your future adversaries are no supermen—any more than we are, for that matter. The best advice I can give you is don't draw attention to yourself.

'During your course they will drum information into you about conditions in the various countries where you will work, until you are sick of it; but all that is really of no use to you whatever, because you are more likely to be noticed in Germany than in the country where you will be sent to work. In Germany your manner of walking, talking and even dressing will brand you as a foreigner. In the countries where you will work nobody will pay any attention to you.

'What will matter to you in the training course will be details of all the technical devices that are essential today for a successful intelligence organisation. All the other information—details of clothing, how to behave yourself, the customs of the people of the country where you will work—you can afford to skip, because you know more about it than the man who will try to teach you. Therefore, concentrate on the use of invisible inks and chemicals, radio-transmission techniques, codes and special photographic techniques. These things will be of the greatest possible value to you.

'There will also be a short military training course. Take it seriously and go through with it; and you have my word that you will then have acquired everything a good agent needs. For a man with confidence in himself, there is pleasure in adventure. A loner, not one of the herd, a man who knows his own strength—and who is bright—I think will find this a definitely interesting job.

'And that is the answer to any suggestion that the work has nothing to offer but disadvantages.'

Well, he had filled me in. I could take the next step and find out more in the north.

On the day we were due to leave Athens I had a last meeting with Rohde. He called at the hotel after breakfast and invited us both to lunch with him at the Alex. That meal gave us another chance to get to know one another a little better, and it provided him with an opportunity to talk with Sonia.

The luncheon was a great success, Rohde and Sonia taking to each other at once. The talk was lively and wide-ranging, and the three hours flew by unnoticed. Sonia suddenly realized it was past four and she would be late for her appointment at the dressmaker. We dropped her near Constitution Square and went on to Rohde's house. There he spoke for nearly half an hour, giving me the details of when to report at the Abwehr headquarters. As he said, at lunch we could of course mention nothing about my future assignment.

Chapter 5

School for Heroes

I arrived in Berlin on the evening of 15 August 1937. I slept well that night and left my hotel, thoroughly rested, at 9 o'clock in the morning to make my way past the Bahnhof Zoo towards the Kurfurstendamm. It had rained earlier that morning and the town had cooled down, but the sun already felt very hot. Outside the Café Kranzler, opposite the Kaiser Wilhelm Memorial Church, tables and chairs stood on the pavement clean and in straight lines like soldiers.

I had time to sit down and look at the Kurfurstendamm. This was the first time I had ever been to Berlin. I had the feeling of a very lively city, and as yet saw nothing of that famous Berlin earnestness about which foreigners so often spoke. Paris was more beautiful and light-hearted, and it had a certain magic, attributable probably to its architectural harmony and to the beauty of its women; nevertheless, Berlin seemed to me an attractive and friendly city.

The great looming four-storeyed building in front of which the taxi put me down and whose façade reminded me of a law court, was certainly anything but beautiful. Only the trees across the street, mirrored in the sluggish canal water, the sunlight playing through their branches, somewhat dispelled the depressing atmosphere.

I was at No 80–81 Tirpitzufer, the headquarters of the Abwehr.

My curiosity gave me no rest. At the gate I hardly had the patience to answer the commissionnaire. He made a telephone call from a little room adjoining his lodge, told me the floor and room number I needed, and gave me the freedom of the mysterious premises. A smart-looking officer sat behind the desk. Rising when I came into the room, he shook hands with me, introduced himself, and asked me to take the chair opposite. From the first moment I had the impression that he knew exactly what he was after. In front of him, on an otherwise bare desk, lay a file; on it were some symbols meaningless to me and a number. That was undoubtedly my dossier.

His questions made it clear that everything, down to quite fine details, was in the nice new file. He had already put together a general profile, and it was obvious that this was a matter of routine. He explained briefly that a certain Major Maurer from the Office known as 'Meldedienst-I' would look after me, and that after our interview he would be handing me over to him.

'Then—shall we say the day after tomorrow?—you will be going to Quenzgut to get a briefing on explosive techniques. You won't need anything of that sort in your work, but you must be in the picture.' He then stood up and led me along the corridor a few doors down to Maurer. Here everything was 'One, two, three!' My guide seemed to know nothing about human emotions or the pleasures of life. He knocked on Maurer's door and we entered.

Never in my life would I learn to get out of a chair with the same angularity as the Major. We southerners are feeble chaps compared with these deadly earnest gentlemen in their martial uniforms, buttoned to the chin—they must sleep at attention! Everything went by numbers and all remarks were rattled off like orders, even when no orders were being given.

It was explained that while I was going through the various stages of this mammoth organization, I would be looked after by a young lieutenant. After my training I would be posted to a unit that would teach me the basic notions of soldiering. 'Only what is necessary', said the Major, quite brusquely. 'We have no time to make you into a perfect soldier, but after all we can't just have you as a civilian in fancy dress. What would people think?'

After a while the Major simmered down somewhat—he had got a little carried away in the heat of battle, as it were. He reached for his telephone, asked for a number and said into the mouthpiece: 'I've got Rohde's man with me; I want you over here immediately.'

Hardly had he replaced the receiver than there was rap on the door and a handsome man in mufti came towards me, not before first making a barely perceptible bow, and said tersely, 'Mütze, Helmut Mütze', at the same time giving me a brisk handshake. Now 'Mütze' means 'cap' in German, so I said to myself that he was no more called Mütze than I was called Schultze. I had taken to heart Rohde's lecture about keeping names secret, to the point that during the whole of my time in this métier I assumed that any name I was given was a false one. Long afterwards I discovered that all three had given me their true names. The security was in fact a great deal less watertight than they made out.

A few minutes later Maurer ordered Mütze to show me round Berlin that night. We were not to make too much of a night of it, but no need to be too solemn either; and next morning we were to report at the Quenzsee near Brandenburg. But first, that afternoon, we were to call in at the Army Survey Office—the Heeresplankammer—after some lunch with him at Ewest's restaurant in the Friedrichstrasse. He would have a table booked for us immediately.

'A good agent never trusts his luck, but should he have any, he will know how to make use of it. Mark that well and always bear it in mind', said the Major. He gave me a friendly pat on the shoulder in the doorway. We were dismissed.

My training proper began that afternoon. We started at the Heeresplankammer, with maps to a scale of 1:10,000. On hundreds of sheets covering the Middle East, however, there were many blank areas. Nevertheless those cartographers had not been idle; the maps even showed details like an old tree standing on a prominence. Distances, width of streets, contours, frontier crossings—both official and forbidden—nothing was neglected. The condition of the roads, their suitability for the movement of troops, landmarks, large rocks, hillocks, even isolated houses all were shown. If I were to be asked to augment this material, I could see I would have to rush about Asia Minor with a measuring tape.

The following morning, after a night half of which had been spent in various Berlin night-spots, Helmut Mütze and I went to the Quenzsee, 65 km west of Berlin, to a camp called Quenzgut that lay in the most marvellous country know as the Havel. For the next two weeks the sky was a cloudless blue and it was hot. Sweating like a pig, every bone in my body aching, I crawled about on my belly through the marshes. I set explosive charges under dummy bridges and learnt how to blow up railway lines. I spent hours at the range, and learned how to crawl up to and then rush a position. I was frightened out of my life by being thrown off a 5m high board into a pile of sawdust and then bullied through a series of ground exercises. Forward rolls, backward rolls, a whole afternoon of nothing but somersaults—how I got to hate somersaults!

After only my second parachute jump and before I had time to unbuckle my parachute, Unteroffizier Schäfer, known as 'Sarge', rushed up to me all out of breath, shouting: 'You landed like a potato sack falling out of the sky, Sir. If you ever have to make a real jump and you break every bone in your body when you land, don't imagine there will be anyone waiting to help you stick them together! Land softly, like a cat!'

Him and his bloody cats! I'd damn well like to see him jump!

But the fat Schäfer did jump—and like a cat! He touched the ground as softly as a feather. I was green with envy. All this time I knew that Mütze was writing his report on the first part of my training. He told me so quite frankly. One evening I told Mütze without expecting an honest reply that I was quite sure they had attached him to me as a sort of male governess—in case I got lost.

'Of course not', said Mütze. 'At each stage of your training I am supposed to make out a report on your aptitude, both physical and psychological. I must describe your general attitude, official as well as private; your relations with the opposite sex and your ability to hold your liquor. In addition I must give my opinion about the best way to use your services when the time comes!'

'Since we are being so frank, which will also appear in your report, I would like to make something straight: service in the Middle East only. Sabotage—nothing doing! The work-out at Quenzgut was enough for me, thank you. Parachute jumping—only if absolutely necessary, though it's fun. But blowing things up is out. I am no anarchist. Let *them* blow things up. I was told all I needed was a rough idea, and I've got that now.'

'I should imagine you would stay under Rohde, at least for some time. The fact is, his word carries weight and he doesn't want to lose you. He said as much quite unequivocably in his report.'

That was enough for me. It fitted nicely into the framework I had built up for myself. I could now start training to be an agent. It was now quite clear there was no more baling out and somersaulting for me. Soon after that I left for Streigau, with the faithful Mütze in tow. The mysterious games of hide and seek of coding, decoding and writing invisible messages were to be taught me. I could hardly wait. The most striking figure we encountered at the Abwerstelle was a tall haggard-looking officer, who walked past us, his monocle stuck in his left eye as if it had been welded there. He wore riding boots the like of which I had never seen before. His uniform hung untidily about his frame. He was two heads taller than I—and Mütze, who was by no means short, only came up to his shoulder. The officer stuck his arm out in an angular salute, somewhat stiffly and cursorily, as well he might, since my companion was a mere lieutenant and I, a civilian, simply did not exist. Following the instructions of the guard at the gate, we crossed the great quadrangle.

'Was that the Great White Chief, that man who's just passed us?' I asked Mütze.

'That's Rittmeister von Hoesch—real old officer caste. He doesn't talk to any old Tom, Dick and Harry. When tight, he thaws out a little—otherwise, he's an iceberg.'

We arrived at the building that contained the cipher room. The Feldwebel (Serrgeant-Major) sprang to attention: 'Stabsfeldwebel Sitterlin, Herr Leutnant! Permission to show you to your quarters, Sir!'

We were installed in a pretty little house on one side of the square, one of a neat row of little villas. It was quite homely, and it was reserved for those taking part in the radio course. Mütze had been here before, in the same function of mentor-investigator.

'What a strange language you use here, Mütze! We wouldn't speak to Allah as abjectly as that. Herr Leutnant here, Herr Leutnant there, everything in the third person. You're out of your minds!'

'Discipline, my dear chap. But don't bother your head about it. There is only a fortnight of it for you.'

When it came to discipline, no area was left untouched. The Rittmeister asked us to his office, gave us another stiff greeting, spoke in staccato sentences, gave a few crisp orders to the signaller who was to instruct me, sent him to one of the cubicles to prepare the first lesson and coldly invited us for a drive into Breslau for a bite of supper there. That was all. Dismiss. We had hardly stepped inside his office than we were out again.

'If that's how he treats his wife, and if that's how he enjoys his conjugal rights, I pity the poor woman', I said to Helmut Mütze as we walked towards the instruction cubicle.

'That's what they call a Prussian officer. But there could be another explanation, such as duty is duty and schnapps is schnapps.'

For the next fortnight it was nothing but ciphers, callsigns, horizontal and vertical columns, frequencies, transmitters, receivers, wavelengths, directional aerials, condensers and calibrations, shortwave beams, monitoring stations, and God knows what else—enough to addle the brain of any normal man. But it all had to be got through, somehow. What my instructor in Streigau drummed into me was to come into very good stead later, and I learned to play hide-and-seek pretty thoroughly.

Then, with my head no longer throbbing with all I had learned, I was summoned to Berlin. It was exactly a month since I had last been there. Passing through sentries and guards and down corridors accompanied by Maurer I was at last given entry into the office of one who held great power.

The Admiral was tiny. Another like yourself, I thought. He seemed tired, and his expression as he looked at me was markedly sad, pessimistic and withdrawn. He spoke slowly and softly. The features of his face were regular, and despite the two deep furrows, from above his nostrils to below his lower lip, his expression was not an unfriendly one. What struck one most were his blue eyes.

The story was that Admiral Canaris was of Greek origin. His name could have been Greek, but there was nothing Greek about his appearance. He was said to be a bit of a cynic, and something about the look in his eyes confirmed that description. One would never confide one's closest secrets to him. He was opaque, devious and a good hater. I dislike haters. I was not allowed to address him, only to answer him. He asked me a great many questions and wanted to know what Rohde was doing. I knew nothing and, besides, what business was it of mine? It would be better, Herr Admiral, if you did not ask me such questions, because the only answer I can give is the Oriental one of silence.

'Piki', he said to Piekenbrock. 'We'll stick to Eppler. Forget about Gaafar. See to it that we straighten out his Arab origins. You know they don't like that sort of thing at the top. They would say he is tainted with a Semitic brush. So he'd better sign one of those "To the best of my knowledge and understanding . . ." things, to make the whole thing seem right.'

The Admiral got up and walked over to me. I thought, He can't be more than five feet tall—so much for your Aryan superman!

'They tell me you got top marks in your course. Well done! And give my regards to Rohde. He knows his business. I like him.'

'Herr Rohde will be pleased to hear that, Sir.'

The Admiral smiled a languid smile. He was miles away somewhere.

The printed form I was given read: 'I hereby declare that to the best of my knowledge and understanding I am of Aryan origin.' Signature and date. That's all there was to it. That made me into a genuine, 100 per cent, circumcised Aryan. It only needed a word from the little Admiral. Not that it bothered me very much whether I was Aryan or non-Aryan; but it did seem to bother the Abwehr. They seemed to set great store by it.

Major Maurer grinned. 'Now I can go ahead and sign your first contract. Everything in proper form. Wouldn't be in order without one, would it?' I never found out what making me an Aryan had to do with proper form.

Clumsily the tanks came out of the gateway. As they turned, their tracks grated and squealed jarringly. The rear of each vehicle waddled jerkily into alignment. Rosy young faces looked out of the turrets, apparently quite unaffected by the drizzle that had been coming down ever since my arrival for my military training course in Sagan near Frankfort-Oder.

The top brass had an inexplicable predilection for the eastern regions of Germany. This was the second time that they had sent me to the eastern frontier. First I was posted to Streigau in Silesia to learn to be a radio operator, and now I was in Lower Lusatia. Here at this hero-factory I was to learn soldiering. It was a complete mystery to me how they reckoned to make a hero out of me, but in the next few hours I was to begin my glorious career—the very embodiment of calm and composure, and fully aware of my honourable duty. Suddenly I heard a roar behind me rising through a number of octaves, a roar that reduced a young man who was walking a little way in front of me to a frightened jelly.

'You there, chimney sweep', the corporal continued. 'Yes you, you chimney sweep! With that bag you pinched. I mean you!'

I seemed to be the only one with a bag in the immediate neighbourhood, and since I had not stolen the thing, I turned round.

'You can take back that word "pinched". I don't go around stealing people's bags.'

That was as far as I got. The owner of the voice planted himself before me, and stared at me speechless for a few seconds with bloodshot eyes, trying in vain to force another sound out of his wide-open mouth. Then, suddenly, I was engulfed in a torrent of abuse, of which all I could understand was that I had lost all sense of reason. 'What the hell are you doing here?' asked the corporal in a fractionally less unpleasant tone of voice.

'I am supposed to report to the tank corps. I saw some of them driving through the gate just now, and assumed I was in the right place. Sorry if I'm not. Could you perhaps tell me where the Hindenburg Barracks are, please?'

'First of all, while I am talking to you, you be quiet. Get that?'

'I don't think that is a very good idea. Firstly I've never done anything like that before, and, secondly, I don't see any general's stripes on your trousers to make me want to try.' That did it. I thought he would fall dead any moment.

'To the guardroom!' he yelled, fit to burst. He turned about and marched towards the little building near the gate. What could I do? I trotted along behind him.

Identity card, travel papers, calling-up papers, all lay spread out before him on the desk.

'What's that funny bag covered with? Hotel stickers? Are you a spy? Come along, we have just the place for you here. I think I'll stick you in there for a start.'

He picked up the telephone and gave an account of this, the greatest sensation of his life. He had caught a spy! With a wealth of colourful NCO imagery, he explained to his comrade at the other end of the line: 'What do you think? The bloody cheek! Little feller. Nosing around on army property. Ten to one he's a spy—sure—lots of papers, no flies on me. Into the guardhouse he goes. Lock him up straight away, right, and then report up the line!'

There was a pause. Although he was sitting down, he clicked his heels: 'Yessir . . . Yessir . . . Yessir!' That was all. He put the receiver down, stood up, came round the table, took my bag in his left hand and said, very nicely: 'Would you kindly follow me, please.' I followed him, but not without inviting him to go before me through the door. A hero, I thought, must always mind his manners.

When we got to Company HQ, the Stabsfeldwebel tore him off a strip and told him to mind his own bloody business in future.

My first day at Company HQ was very pleasant. I was allowed to make myself nice and cosy in a room with bunks for ten men, was given an upper bunk and shown the bath facilities in another room, which was lined with wash basins. It was just like a hotel, only there was no hot water. I was given a huge wardrobe for my clothes—only they called it a locker.

'Private Eppler', said the Sergeant, who was quite invisible behind mountains of clobber, 'look out!' No sooner were the words out of his mouth than various items of equipment came flying through the air: one dog tag and chain, a cap, one battle-dress blouse, three army-style neckties, trousers, etc, etc. Then came a greatcoat. I took the liberty of trying it on.

'Sergeant, it doesn't fit.'

He made it fit in a trice. 'Turn around!' he said. I turned like a mannequin. 'What the hell are you grousing about? I tell you it fits!'

'But Sergeant, the arms are too long.'

'Well, you'd better hurry up and grow into them, you won't be here all that long!' Even though the locker assigned to me was huge, I had been issued so much free clothing that my own gear had to stay in my bag.

Basic training started the following morning at 6 o'clock. As the greenest recruit, it was my job to fetch the coffee. Outside the barracks I joined the other men who were heading for the kitchen, armed with great billycans, to fetch the 'coffee'. Having tried it once, I decided that coffee was bad for the heart. As we finished a lordly breakfast of hardtack, I heard somebody shouting orders outside in the corridor—what, I could not make out. The door flew open, and in came a soldier complete with tin hat. He roared out my name. Startled out of my wits, I reported present.

'Forgotten to wash your ears out, have you?'

'Sir . . . '

'Stabsgefreiter (Staff Corporal) is what you say to me—Herr Stabsgefreiter!'

'Yessir.' I had already learned that one just said 'Yessir' to anything and everything. The simple word 'Yes' had been expunged from the language as far as soldiers were concerned.

He told me to accompany him to the orderly room, where I was introduced to a Staff Sergeant-Major of the old-fashioned sort.

'You're lucky you've come to us; we'll make a tough man of you here. Like Krupp steel, that's how hard you'll be when you leave us. Follow me.'

I followed him to the great square, where my company was

assembled. Then the Captain marched into the yard.

'Heil Hitler, Company', he said.

'Heil Hitler, Herr Hauptmann.'

The Captain introduced himself to me and welcomed me in front of the rest of the men. In a whisper he explained that he had been put in the picture, and was supposed to make a soldier of me before I departed to undertake my dangerous duties. He felt honoured to have been given this assignment and hoped that I would always remember his training course. There had been a leak somewhere; he should not have known anything about my future work.

After I had thus been enlisted, one NCO after another took me in hand. One entire morning was spent practising salutes—the little finger of the left hand on the seams of the trousers, the right arm stuck up at an angle. The Corporal found me a slow learner and I practised the whole morning long.

Then there was song practice, and singing is not my strong suit. At school the teachers had always sent me out of the room when the others were singing because I completely threw the choir off.

'So you won't sing?' said the Corporal. 'OK, I'll play Fancy Dress Ball with you—then you'll sing like a lark.'

So we played Fancy Dress Ball. I was the actor and he the producer. 'At the double—march! Down on your stomach! Crawl! Up you get—at the double! Now!'

We went on like that until I learned to sing a couple of songs of comradeship. As the weeks went on, I was forced to learn a few more.

There was also latrine duty—'scrubbing the thunder boxes'. The Corporal wanted to make sure that I understood what a clean latrine looked like, 'because, of course, where you come from, you just shit out in the open—nothing but niggers there'. I ignored him. It would have been useless to explain to him that we had WCs when his ancestors were roaming the forests. He would have put me in the guard house.

Because I had already learned to fire a rifle at Quenzgut, I was given the Captain's permission to go straight on to the 'Hitler violin'—code name for the '42 machine gun.

For five weeks I endured this Prussian training, until October 1937. One rainy morning the Stabsfeldwebel turned up on the parade ground. He approached me in a particularly friendly manner, and gave me a hard biff on the shoulder as if we had known each other all our lives. He seemed a changed man.

He told the NCO on duty to carry on and asked me to follow him to the orderly room. When we were alone in the barracks, he explained that a car would be along in a moment to take me to the railway station. There would be no need to hand in my uniform and rifle—he would look after all that. I was to report in Berlin the next morning wearing my civilian suit. My training was over, and he would drive me to the station. Once we had got there he brought me a drink and said that after the telephone call from Berlin he had at last understood why the Captain had talked to me so confidentially.

'Very top secret, strictly confidential!' he said. Never would a word cross his lips, he assured me. He knew what top secret meant, all right.

Major Maurer looked like a family man. He wore no monocle—I presume because it would have interfered with the disguise—and compared to his colleagues his haircut was not completely military. With a little imagination one could almost say he had a well-shaped head, and except when he was agitated, very kindly eyes. He examined me without saying a word for quite a while. Suddenly, he said: 'I've had a telephone call about you from Hauptmann Krumm, who says he is satisfied with you. You did well with his company. Well done, my dear chap!'

'Thank you, sir. I have cleaned thunder boxes and serviced 'Hitler violins'. I have pumice-stoned and kept my 'bride' clean so she would shoot in any emergency—and so on. But, sir I've never even seen a tank, except for the very first day, when some of them drove past me.'

'What on earth are you talking about? I can't understand a word of it.'

'It's hero's German, sir', I said, meaning soldiers' talk.

Maurer threw back his head and roared with laughter. 'For God's sake, forget these ghastly expressions immediately and speak proper German. Come, let's have a decent meal at Ewest's; we can have a good talk there. What I have to tell you is important. You are about to be sent on your first mission. Rohde needs you. You will see your wife for a few weeks. You must prepare her; explain that you are going on a business trip. Meanwhile your papers are ready; but we must have a word about your name. There will also be a cover prepared for you, and then you'll be off.'

'Since Herr Rohde wants me, it will be in the Middle East', I replied. 'What do I need with a cover or papers, sir? I can go with my own, there's no better cover than that. My being there is the best cover story there is.'

We agreed—the Major was all for it. It suited him well. That way there was nothing for him to do.

I took the night train via Warnemünde to Copenhagen for a brief holiday with Sonia.

Chapter 6

Meeting the Grand Mufti

That December my first mission for Rohde was to begin. I was to go to Istanbul after spending a few days getting instructions from him in Athens. It was the beginning of a sort of endurance test.

We travelled south from Athens to Cape Sunion, where we sat under the columns on the broken steps. The air was clean and smelt of seaweed. Rohde explained: 'We have reports that Hadji Mohammed Amin el Husseini, the Mufti of Jerusalem, has moved to the Lebanon to get away from the British. You must get more exact details. You must talk to him.'

'What you mean is—I'm supposed to find him.'

'Yes, that's more or less it. But I also want you to get in touch with him. You must go about it very carefully, without committing yourself too far. Get him to seek contact with us; it should come from him, not from us.'

I could not help smiling. Just how did he imagine we would outwit the old fox? Moreover, I thought, Rohde would be all right whatever happened. If I pulled it off, he would be the bright boy in Berlin, and not a soul would know about me!

I knew this would be a difficult assignment. The Mufti would be wary of someone playing him for a sucker, and would try to outmanoeuvre me. Rohde acknowledged that he was cunning. 'You will just have to be more cunning.'

I listened with a sort of amused indulgence. The man who had pulled off the trick of leading the British by the nose, and making them endorse as genuine the non-existent title of 'Grand Mufti', was to be persuaded to seek contact with *us* when it was *we* who actually wanted to establish relations with him.

About a year earlier he had begun a guerrilla war and tried to turn it into a holy war. Nobody would endorse that, but it was enough to drive some of his enemies out into the cold, and even to silence them altogether. But then he went too far for the British, and they tried, in their best tradition, to get rid of him by banishing him to an island until they wanted him again. But before they could do so, he made himself scarce. That was all I knew. Apart from the impression that Husseini had prospered, we knew nothing else that had happened to him.

The sun sank slowly into the sea. Darkness was falling. There was a chill in the air, and it was almost cold. All of a sudden one could hear the beating of the waves more loudly. I thought, looking out over the water, that Rohde was unduly silent and thoughtful until he finally spoke.

'It's only for information.' His tone was almost apologetic. 'We don't want to get mixed up in it, but in our trade we have to be as well informed as possible about everything. The pogrom has meant that as the Jews wish to protect themselves, they are trying to emigrate, at whatever cost, particularly to Palestine. The number of Jewish immigrants is rising by leaps and bounds and will continue to grow. For us it is really a matter of secondary importance where they go, but we do need information out of Palestine—we want to know what's going on there.

'A conference recently took place between the Hagganah [Jewish Defence League] and the Jewish Socialist Workers' Movement. At this conference they set up a new organization—the Mossad Lealiyah Beth. Its primary purpose is to provide a response to the British White Paper proposing to divide Palestine between Arab and Jew; and the secondary is to do with illegal immigration into Palestine. An office has been set up in Geneva whose job is to provide emigration information and reception centres in Germany. It is through these centres that the Jewish emigrants receive assistance. Naturally the centres also serve an intelligence purpose.

'None of that bothers us and we shall not do anything about it. Before long, and this is new, another information office is to open in Istanbul. You will go there. I need particulars how and where the lines of communication from Istanbul lead.

'I had the report from an informer, a rather unreliable one; some of his information is correct, but much of it is idle gossip, offered to earn a penny or two. Your job is to find out exactly what is going on.'

Slowly we walked back towards the car.

'When do you feel like making a start, John?' asked Rohde in a voice that sounded as if he was in no particular hurry.

'Shall we say the day after tomorrow, since it all seems settled?'

'All right. All the arrangements for your trip will be made. The informant's name is Dimitriy Petkov. I'll show you a picture of him.'

'You mean so that I may avoid him? Don't worry, I don't mix in his sort of circles. I won't go near him.'

During my stay in the wonderful city of Istanbul I lived a crazy sort of life in Askaray, in the old city, and commuted every day to Beyoglu, also known as Pera. The Galata Bridge, which I had to cross, was packed with people and vehicles at all hours of the day. For a fortnight I made the same journey every morning and every evening. I preferred living in the old quarter, as it made my presence less obvious. In Pera secret police were always snooping around, in fact the place was crawling with them. On the northern shore of the Halics, as the locals call the Golden Horn, there were and still are many rich Europeans and Turks. It is there that the consulates are to be found and foreign businesses have their offices. I needed a fortnight to find out about the Zionist office and the name of the man at the head of it. I discovered that Moshe Shertok, head of the organization, made frequent journeys between Palestine and Turkey; so then I traced the two agents who were establishing the first lines of communication through the Balkans, which extended back to Germany. This was just what Rohde wanted to find out.

I spent the evenings in the company of Turks in local coffee houses, and the nights either in one of the many dives playing cards, or sitting on one of the terraces overlooking the Sea of Marmara, in the company of the many students in Istanbul from all over the Middle East. I wanted to get to know this town, because I was sure to come back. It was an excellent opportunity to make useful contacts.

Rohde got word to me, through a courier, that the information I had been sending him would do, and I should turn my attention at the earliest opportunity to the Mufti, Amin el Husseini. Even before I received these latest instructions from Rohde I was on the trail of the Mufti.

One of the students who frequented the terrace cafés had struck up an acquaintance with me. Early on, during our second chance meeting, he had told me of his admiration for Antun Saadah, the founder of the Parti Populaire Socialiste. Saadah's idea of the creation of a united fascist Arab state stretching from Syria to Jordan was utterly unrealistic; and in his attempt at achieving this, my friend told me, Saadah had contacted Amin el Husseini. The Grand Mufti, it seems, was in Lebanon. My friend said he would get word to Saadah and give me a message from him. This was just the lead I needed. This student wanted to put me in touch with his 'Fuhrer'.

For some days I had noticed that a man in plain clothes was following me. However, I always had been able to give him the slip, until the evening in Narlikapi on the southern outskirts of the city, when I was sitting in an old café waiting for the student, who was to bring word from Saadah telling me when I could look him up in Beirut. My 'shadow' had to go and pick this particular moment to sit down at my table as bold as brass, and to ask even more coolly who I was supposed to be working for. He did this in the way only secret policemen do, confident that they can get away with it with a stranger.

In Turkey at that time, no matter how innocent you were, one thing was absolutely vital—money. If you gave officials enough, they were prepared to turn a blind eye. I had money, and lots of it, so I played him awhile. Bribery was possible because the Turks were wretchedly paid, but most of them would do nothing that was against the national interest.

The man told me that he had been on duty outside the Jewish office and had watched me there for days. Then, when he was sure, he pounced quickly because he knew that he had found someone who could be shaken down. After he had calmly pocketed my banknotes, he said into the air over my head that he knew that I worked for Germany. Then he began the boring old story every Turk tells every German, that the Germans and the Turks are the best soldiers in the world, as they had proved during the last war. I had heard all that nonsense often before, and that evening I really had no time for it—the student was due to turn up at any moment, and was bound to shy away if he saw me sitting there at the table with a stranger. Here was this petty spy ruining my golden opportunity! I could have strangled him.

With my money safely in his pocket, he was brazen enough to invite me to a 'princely' meal—'between colleagues.' The most infuriating thing was I could not even punch him. I just had to sit there quietly and let him drone on. His pathetic mouthings continued as I looked for my student friend, who suddenly appeared and hovered on the fringe of the café. Whether or not he recognized my companion as a spy, he took no chances and kept away from the table. Then he drifted off. Still the secret agent droned on, until at last he caught sight of someone else—another victim?—and he was off. As if by a signal, my young friend reappeared, sat down, ordered some arak and said as calmly as if he were talking about the weather: 'Antun is in Beirut and wants to see you.' After a sufficient time spent in idle chatter, he rose and left, to be swallowed in the by-ways and alleys.

With this information I made haste to leave Istanbul. The next day I packed most of my clothing and had it shipped to Alexandria. The rest fitted into a small valise, which I carried with me to the Hayder-pasha Railway Station in Scutari on the Asiatic side of the straits, and hired one of those lumbering American cars to found there. These huge machines were popular as taxis. My idea was to get to Smyrna as quickly as possible, and Turkish trains, though cheap, paid no heed to timetables and were the slowest in the world.

The roads of Anatolia were not exactly the best, and the ram-shackle old taxis had lost every vestige of comfort in the course of their long and strenuous careers. It apparently never occurred to any Turk to replace a worn-out shock absorber. What on earth for, he would ask when the car would run without one! Nevertheless, the driver, more acrobat than chauffeur, was proud of his Chrysler Airflow, implying that it was the finest and handsomest machine in Üsküdar. His pron-unciation of the words Chrysler Airflow would have made any Ameri-can fall down dead, but, to make up for it, he showed a fine disregard for death as he tore along, hitting one pothole and ridge after another. However, he did deposit me all in one piece and in good time in Smyrna. I gave him a large tip, while making up my mind that this would be my first and last journey by taxi in Anatolia.

Smyrna (or Izmir) has a picturesque harbour, but its inhabitants have no idea of the meaning of punctuality. I booked a cabin on the *Derb*, a coaster that made up for her lack of youth by a plentiful supply of rust. I chose her after I had made some enquiries around the har-bour. Most people told me that if I wanted to get away, and no ques-tions asked, to go with Damazos. So on Damazos' broken-down old tub I went.

It was no use expecting a great deal in the way of cleanliness. Even her decks, never mind her cabins, were revoltingly filthy. Her hull was crying out for a fresh coat of paint, and the best you could say of her superstructure was that it may have been white at some time in the past. She was of some 750 tons, fairly long and excessively broad. It would have been a waste of time to look for any lifebelts, for there were none. But, by and large, the ship made a fairly substantial impression. She had been plying the same route since time immemorial, starting in Smyrna and calling at every likely port on the Turkish coast, whether large or small. There was always a load to be taken on or put ashore. Her hull was full to overflowing with merchandise. The crew seemed a disciplined lot and needed little supervision, and the captain seemed in no hurry. He was a repulsively hideous man, but showed his passengers the most distinguished courtesy and helpfulness. Pirates, I thought, when I first caught sight of him coming on board, must have looked like this Damazos.

I could not have chosen better. It turned out to be a refreshing and unusually instructive trip, and an inexhaustible source of invaluable information for me in my work. We made friends the very first morning of the trip. Damazos was a steady drinker. We lay under a tarpaulin rigged up on the after-deck. The light was sparkling, the offshore wind had abated and the sea was calm. By lunchtime we had put away half a dozen rakis each and I had a lot of useful addresses and names of people who were ready—for a consideration, of course—to render certain services of a confidential nature. Damazos acted on the principle of one hand washing the other and both together washing the face. I had understood. But there must be something in it for him, otherwise one or another of his 'people' could prove to be unreliable.

'Do you like truffles?' he asked.

'And how!'

'And you know how they find them?'

'By giving a pig a little sample, putting him on a lead, and taking him for a walk under oak trees; then, if there are any, the pig will root them out of the earth. . . .'

'. . . And all you have to do is to collect them', interrupted Damazos. 'Don't forget, my friend, life is full of truffles!' In other words, let someone else pull the chestnuts from the fire.

We were to make two more trips together, and 'his' people continued to find truffles for me. My primary task had been to establish useful contacts in the area, contacts who were reliable sources of information on troop and matériel movements; Damazos' friends were just the ticket and made this part of my first mission a success.

The Lebanese women are stronger than the men. They have created their own sisterhoods. The legendary Djamila, so the story goes, commanded a pirate ship with an all-female crew that made the Sea of Kandia dangerous to all traders in the area.

A long time ago a Lebanese woman who had killed her husband was summoned before the Kadi and was ordered to be branded, for having dispatched to the eternal hunting ground a Lebanese hero. She answered haughtily: 'I'm no Lebanese—I am a woman!' And al Chama, the renowned mediaeval poetess, one day described her husband as a lion in the house but in battle—a mouse. Ever since, Arab husbands have had this couplet repeated to them several times a week.

According to another Arab proverb, one Lebanese is worth two Armenians, and one Armenian is worth three Jews. That's how fast a Lebanese earns money!

When it came to women, Elissar, Antun Saadah's wife, was no exception. I had hardly managed to say good morning when she slammed the door in my face. I would still be trying to meet him if I had not caught a glimpse of Saadah wildly gesticulating behind her back and trying to indicate that he would meet with me later on. My poor student informant in Istanbul, thought I, would not idolize his 'Führer' if he had seen his wife.

For an hour I sat in a café listening to Saadah, who overwhelmed me with an avalanche of brain-numbing propaganda slogans. I had heard all these before, and they left me cold. Speaking like a cross between Mussolini and Hitler, he assured me that one day all Asia Minor would shout 'Heil Saadah!' But, as so often in life, things went awry. Years later, in 1947, he tried to translate his dreams into action, and his ungrateful people killed him for his pains.

It took all my patience to listen quietly, but I wanted something, so listen I did. Finally Saadah ran out of wind. If my mind and ears were exhausted, my patience was rewarded. He stopped talking about grandiose schemes for the resurgence of the Arab world, and resumed his role as intermediary. He spoke of his importance to the Mufti and then confided at last that the most Highly Learned Pilgrim Hadji Mohammed Amin el Husseini, the self-styled leader, would like to see me. At last, I thought, we're getting somewhere.

Husseini would like me to visit him in his French-donated hideout in Bohaar. When it serves their purpose, the French can be very hospitable! M. Colombani, the Prefect of Police, had put up his friend Hadji Mohammed Amin el Husseini in a most princely fashion. He was only following instructions to embarrass the enemies of France, no matter who they were. In that way he kept control of all the strings with which he manipulated the Palestinian puppets. No one would bother Husseini in his refuge, especially not the British.

On the way to his villa we passed through the town at the time when the muezzin was calling the faithful to prostrate themselves before Allah. Then, having left the town, before us we could see Kharneel perched on a hillside amid vineyards and mulberry trees.

He was short and amazingly his eyes were a vivid blue. As befitted a humble but pious Moslem, I kissed the Mufti's hand.

'Ahlan Wah' Sahlan', he said, as if he meant it.

He begged me kindly to make myself comfortable on the divan, clapped his hands and called softly for coffee. He made a fine figure sitting there, with his splendid djellaba falling in picturesque folds to the floor, and on his head a snow-white eh'ma. Self-possessed, pious, learned in the law—how the people loved him! Trustee of charitable donations and orphanage funds, spiritual leader and Hadji—whose hobby was rebellion! He was far too clever for an inexperienced young stager like myself to manipulate easily. A cunning politician, he knew perfectly well what I had come for; nevertheless my visit fitted in with his plans perfectly.

He told me that the last time he had been in touch with Jerusalem was before his flight. He had had contact with the German Consul-General, but always through intermediaries. So I told him that I had come only to meet him, to make his acquaintance and to establish a discreet channel of communications.

During the conversation I realized he must have had a first-class intelligence service at his disposal. It was the only way he could have escaped from the British in Jerusalem. It was nonsense to suppose that the British connived at his disappearance or that, through intermediaries, they helped him to flee the country. His escape, however, had been quite an easy matter. Having learned through his own channels that things in Jerusalem were becoming too hot for him in late October 1937, he walked out of the Omar Mosque in disguise. Calmly but swiftly he proceeded to Jaffa, where, unobserved, he boarded a boat for the small port of Doumar, only 20 km from Beirut. At the moment of our meeting it suited the French to let him stay at Kharneel. There he was safe—safe until for some reason or other the French were to change their plans yet again. From then on his days would be numbered.

Our talk proceeded evenly, I thought, with no overt pressure from either of us. We wove our sentences and appreciations in delicate arabesques until suddenly Husseini paused and said in a wily voice: 'I could do a great deal for the German interests in the Middle East, you know!'

This was going too far. I had been warned frequently that under no circumstances was I to talk politics. That had nothing to do with me and that was not why I had come to see the Mufti. I pretended not to have heard him, and, using the florid but meaningless phrases that come naturally in Arabic, explained that my duties were merely to establish a means of communication. In doing this he could be sure of our discretion in all matters by recommending some other people whom I could approach, and without further bother I could disappear. Had I fallen into making some sort of response to his remark, a response I had no authority to make, I would have been left holding the bag.

What I did do was to propose plans for transmitting intelligence, should my chief, Rohde, want a network set up; a system would have to be arranged that would work even if the Mufti had to leave Kharneel. The channels must remain unimpaired. For that reason it would not be advisable to have the contact run through Saadah, because, with his loudly expressed ideas, there was no way of knowing when he would be under lock and key. The safest man would be one called Noujaim. He worked for money, his job made him virtually uncatchable, and, provided one paid him regularly, he would work regularly. He would forward information, since he had no other axe to grind. He was, moreover, a Rohde man, known only to the two of us, which would of course make him a safer contact.

The Mufti would be given the code name of Hedshra. He was, after all, an emigrant, so the name fitted. The name would be an Open Sesame should he wish to get in touch with Rohde or Noujaim, or should Rohde wish to contact either of them.

He furnished me with addresses, which were later to be very useful. He was generous, but, being a sly fox, he must have had his reasons.

He did nothing except for a good reason.

The meeting with the Mufti was over. I had established contact with him and given him the means of keeping in touch with us. It was time for me to leave the Lebanon as unobtrusively as possible and make my way back to Athens. I had not had to show my papers to anyone since I had left Smyrna. Few knew that I was in the country. Apart from my contacts, nobody had been told I was there—and that was how I wanted it to stay until I had left.

Noujaim suggested that we should use Mitri Petrakis's boat. Petrakis normally forwarded Noujaim's 'mail', and at the moment his boat was moored in the harbour at Tripolis el-Mina. Noujaim explained that Petrakis was an amiable man who would sell his mother-in-law for money. He would arrange all the details of how I would get quietly aboard his caïque, a lovely little 15m auxiliary cutter. The boat was ready fitted out with a lugsail and jib, and had a 110 hp engine in her belly. A sort of superior cruising yacht, she was sturdy and had a nice turn of speed, which you would never guess by looking at her.

Shortly after midnight, we were off Limassol. On the horizon, by the light of the full moon, we would make out the black outlines of the coast of Cyprus.

Petrakis explained that during the day we would sail at half speed because he wanted to arrive at Syra when it was dark. 'We will spend a day there at my house; then I'll inform Rohde of our time of arrival at Cape Sunion, where he'll be waiting for you.'

Towards evening we sailed through the Karpathos Straits. A brightly lit passenger ship passed us to starboard, making for Rhodes. Just before dawn it had grown very dark again, the moon having set, and the island of Syra came up over the horizon slowly, like a great phantom in the dark. I am an uneasy sailor and always glad to feel terra firma under my feet. The day of rest at Petrakis's house was just what I wanted. He put me ashore at Cape Sunion and said: 'Should you need me again, you know where to find me on either coast! Kali mera sas.' He disappeared in his tender, swallowed by the night. Out to sea, not far from the island of Makronisos, we could make out the silhouette of his caïque, gently rolling on the waves.

I then joined Rohde waiting for me in his car. On the way back to Athens I explained the details of my meeting with the Mufti. Then we said goodbye. It was the last time I was to go on a mission for him.

Those that lay before me would be performed alone, without my superior officer.

Towards the end of January 1938 I returned to Abwehr headquarters for further instructions, and from then until May my mission was a topographical one carried out for the Army and Abwehr II, in the area extending from Erzurum in Turkey to Tabriz and Kermanshah in Iran. The following month I went to Baghdad to make contact with the chiefs of two tribes—the Kashgai and the Bachtiaris. This mission proved particularly valuable as preparation for my journey with the Ghulam Barakatullah, which began in May 1939.

Chapter 7

Into Afghanistan

The road ran from the shores of the Caspian Sea over flat country, but the plain narrowed as we began to climb into the Elburz Mountains in northern Iran. Twisting and turning, the deep rutted track made by the caravans over the course of time ran up through the bare rocks strewn about the hillside by the spring torrents.

I was walking beside my grey donkeys, which were so heavily laden that they could not possibly have borne a rider as well. It was more of a climb than a walk. The slender legs of the donkeys trembled whenever they climbed over the broken rocks that blocked the track. Their necks ran with sweat, and the loads on their backs shifted as they struggled to avoid a sudden slip into the precipice below.

For weeks since leaving Erzurum in eastern Turkey I had been dossing down in caravanserais without a bath or a shave, dressed in the Turkish fashion—baggy trousers, motor-tyre sandals and loose turban. I looked as if I had lived in these desert parts for a lifetime. Garlic and onions had done their worst to me.

It was the best cover I had been able to think up; but I did not exactly feel at home in the disguise. Somewhere in the mountains, in a safe place, I had to spend the night in the open, and towards the evening of the following day I was to meet Ghulam Barakatullah in the mountain town of Masuleh. His journey would have been even longer and more difficult than mine—from Herat, across the Afghan border, and then across the mountains of Kuh-e Shah Jehan to our rendezvous.

My being sent on this mission was a result of my good planning or my good luck; for it had been only a month ago (April 1939) that the German Foreign Office had entered into consultation with the Abwehr on strategy in the event that war with Britain became certain. Among other schemes put to Admiral Canaris was one to make the necessary preparations for an eventual German-Russian attack on India, which would serve to keep the British forces there rather than being released overseas. To effect this, detailed maps were to be drawn, radio-transmission posts established and, most important of all, sympathetic collaborators sought out and paid. Among the foremost of these was the powerful tribal chief Ghulam Barakatullah.

Planning or luck on my part? When I first went to Istanbul for Rohde in December 1937, I made contact with Amir Azurnuch. At our first meeting in the Takzim Bar, although from the sound of him it seemed as though money ran through his fingers like water, I had the feeling that he was not just a mindless spendthrift. After several encounters I found him to be keen, intelligent and ready to take risks. Then, when I learned that he was a Kashgai, a tribe of scheming warriors always in rebellion and reputedly one of the fiercest in all Persia, I felt that my judgement of him was confirmed. I hoped I had stumbled on the right track in picking him; besides he could be trained as a first-class liaison man. Nevertheless a certain caution was indicated; I had to beware of letting my optimism get the better of me; and, as it happened, Amir Azurnuch's brother lived in Masuleh. He would meet me there.

So here I was, on my way to meet Ghulam Barakatullah. This man, Amir had told me, was very quick on the draw and knew how to use his curved dagger; and even if he was one of the fiercest guerrilla chieftains in all Afghanistan, he was also one of the most reliable—a first-class shot, a leader of men and a seasoned warrior, who had fought with Betshe Saq'au, the Wazirs and the fanatical Mullahs against Amanullah. Furthermore, he had many contacts in the Hindu Kush as well as with the tribes of the Northwest frontier. He was a true rebel and, like all true rebels, he was not above accepting money to further his love of adventure

If this were so then he was exactly the man I needed to further the plan of rebellion masterminded in Berlin. Later on he might organize uprisings in various places, and then other agents sent by Berlin could arrive and carry matters further. All I was expected to do was make sure Barakatullah was the right man, equip him with the basic necessities and thus set the stone rolling.

I broke camp at first light. At sundown the previous day I had set up my tents by a great rock, and by morning the donkeys were well rested. They had devoured some of the scattered clumps of sedge that grew in the sandy soil. The pith of this plant stores water, which makes it possible for animals to survive. For the final day's journey to Masuleh the donkeys might be without water, and I would have to manage with the small reserve left in the rank-smelling goatskin.

The remains of last night's dew helped to moisten the atmosphere a little, but the narrow track we followed was still uphill all the way. As far as the eye could see in this rock-strewn ravine there was no sign of life except for three great bearded vultures that had circled above us ever since we had set out. It was the first time I had seen these magnificent birds at such close quarters. There must be carrion about somewhere.

Suddenly, as we reached a plateau, Masuleh came into view. Clinging to the steep mountainside, it was more a large village than a town. It hung on the mountain like an eagle's nest, with four- and five-storey buildings. They all had the same bare frontages, with many large windows let into the walls. It was a peculiar sight to come across right in the middle of a rocky wilderness, more than 3,000 ft above sea level. Between the houses stood a few straggly thorn trees, a mountain ash here and there, and a sycamore or two; otherwise there was nothing but boulders, sand and rocks. The place seemed cheerless and lifeless as my pack asses turned into the first steep village street.

Amir Azurnuch had seen me coming out of the ravine and across the plateau. He came towards me down the hill with long steps, smiling and waving his arms.

'Ghulam turned up last night. Didn't I tell you that you could rely on him?' he said, as he took the reins of my donkey and retraced his steps uphill by my side.

Ghulam Barakatullah had a short broad moustache. His hands were immense. He had on a clean grey kaftan, and a wide leather belt round his waist. He wore his turban like a crown. Seated by the only window in the room, he eyed me cautiously. He was not alone. Some way away in a corner sat a second Afghan, wearing a long striped shirt split at the sides, and long tapering linen trousers. On his bearded head sat an untidily wound turban, and between his knees lay a rifle.

Ghulam stood up and offered one of his huge hands in greeting. 'You stand in the shadow of my shoulders. No harm can come to you while you are with us!' He was at least two heads taller than I. As is the custom in this part of the world, I had to answer in similarly flowery language. We then sat down on low wooden stools—Ghulam and I by the window from which my gaze could sweep the inhospitable countryside.

I mentioned that I had heard he had taken part in the rebellion with Betshe Saq'au—in such a way that he could see that I was impressed. His eyes burned with fanaticism as he explained that in 1932 Betshe had controlled the eastern and northern part of the country for quite a while, and had even had himself proclaimed king under the name of Habibullah Khan. However, being a Tadjik, he had had difficulties with the other tribes mostly because he was receiving arms and ammunition from the GPU. As a result he had made some very bitter enemies among them, for they were afraid that they would be controlled by the Russians.

According to Ghulam, Betshe had accepted the Russian arms sent to him, and he had used Ghulam to transport them. Despite the advice Ghulam gave him, Betshe had wanted above all to maintain his contacts with India by holding the road to Peshawar at any cost. Then Ghulam told me that he would accept arms from the Germans but would not pay for them by becoming their bondsman.

I had to try to get every possible detail out of him, and find out where I stood before I could come to any firm understanding with him. There was too much at stake to leave anything to chance or instinct; other agents would follow me and they would have to be able to work in safety.

I explained to him that Betshe's strategy of keeping the road open to his friends in India was the correct one, for me. By this means we would know that the Khyber Pass was still controlled by the British, and that was essential information if the Germans and the Russians were planning a military advance into India. Ghulam assured me that his contacts with the Afridis, who controlled the pass, would never be broken. He nodded and indicated his friend sitting in the corner of the room, an Afridi named Medji. I had understood aright. This would cost money and arms. Probably their contact was Hadji Mirza Ali, the Fakir of Ipi in North Waziristan; and, in fact, Ghulam then suggested that the Fakir could prove particularly useful to me. That would suit me—and money and arms, should they be necessary, could be supplied—provided things went as I wanted them.

While we had been talking, and almost unnoticed, darkness had descended on Masuleh; soon we could see on the other side of the plateau the outline of the distant mountains etched in the moonlight.

Amir Azurnuch's brother brought in a sputtering, stinking oil lamp, which filled the room with smoke. It gave off no more light than the full moon in the clear sky outside.

After a while Ghulam explained that Betshe Saq'au had been captured in the mountains by the Shah Wali Khan, taken to Kabul, and killed, together with some of his own people. Although I said that Betshe Saq'au deserved a better fate, my real opinion was that he had received an appropriate end.

What had saved the chief from a similar death was that he had been up in Kushka on the frontier, to fetch a supply of arms from the GPU. With that bit of information I realized that Ghulam had plenty of weapons hidden somewhere in the mountains, because he was hardly the man to leave himself defenceless. He would rather go without clothes than travel without a gun.

'Ghulam, you forgot to mention that the counter-uprising was organized by Lawrence', came a deep voice from the corner of the room. 'Had he not been running everything from Niransha, we would have got to Kabul; and Betshe would today be Emir of Afghanistan.' It was the bearded Medji speaking. I was told that he and his people credited the failure of the post-war uprising in the area to Lawrence. This was nonsense. The legend of the mysterious and multifarious activities of Colonel T. E. Lawrence will live for many years yet throughout the East. It was a waste of time to fight it, and better to sort the wheat from the chaff later on.

According to Medji, during the third week of November Lawrence arrived at Kandahar not far from the frontier. Later he was captured by the Emir, whereupon he disappeared, just as he had come—without a trace! After that Nebi Khan received shipments of British machine guns, and quite suddenly he seemed to have all the money he wanted. This was long ago, but Medji still remembered it all, and he made this explanation quite definitively while Ghulam sat next to me by the window without saying a word. He gazed out into the night.

Although he had been dead for four years, the ghost of Lawrence still haunted the imagination of the Moslem desert and mountain tribes. What a man he must have been!

They see him reincarnated, travelling over mountain and desert in countless disguises, hiding among cave-dwellers, brooding and scheming how and where to unleash the next uprising. They see him haunting the valleys of the foothills of the Himalayas—this mysterious Colonel T. E. Lawrence, the true proconsul of the British Empire in the East; the man who had fabulous amounts of money and countless arsenals at his disposal; the greatest, the most mysterious, agent on this earth. No-one could ever tell these mountain tribes anything else. They would quite simply take no notice.

Was Colonel Lawrence mixed up in the Pathan rising after all? Whether he was or not, the legend will certainly live on. He will mastermind many a rebellion yet, dead though he is. The legend was, moreover, quite handy for me at that moment. It suited my plans, because the mountaineers of the Hindu Kush are fond of mysteries.

Our meal of shashlik, hot and seasoned with mountain herbs, was served by our host. No word was spoken during its lengthy progress.

Then, rather late at night, I decided it was time to set up the generator to make a contact by radio, and thought perhaps Medji, with his love of stories about agents, was just the man to help. After assembling the collapsible bicycle frame in the room next door, I called him. He stood astonished in front of the machine, quite unable to grasp what I wanted. Explaining that he now had a chance to do something not even Lawrence could have done, I showed him how to work the apparatus and motioned to him to sit on the bicycle seat.

When I erected the aerial and found the correct direction and frequency, Medji began to work the pedals a little anxiously and somewhat clumsily. After testing the set, I began to transmit the call signal. It was only a short report. Without giving a location, I explained that I had made contact with 'my man' and would call again in seven days' time. There was no need to wait for a reply, as all I needed was the 'Understood' signal from the receiver.

Then Medji got off the bicycle, still looking amazed. He had never seen anything like it before. It was the ti-ti-ti ta-ta of the morse pips in the earphone that intrigued him most.

'Is that your language?' he asked incredulously.

'They call it radio', said Ghulam, who had been standing by the door throughout the proceedings. Since there was no word in his language for a radio, he had to explain what he meant with a wealth of gesturing, how it all worked without wires, simply by flying through the air, 'quicker than the eagle, as quick as lightning'. I was surprised that Ghulam knew all this, but he explained how Ishan Aliev used to send radio signals when they had collected a delivery of arms from the GPU.

Medji was so intrigued by the radio that every evening, as soon as the bicycle was assembled, he wanted to get his feet on the pedals. It was obvious he considered himself indispensable to the operation, even though the signals were beyond his understanding.

On the morning when Ghulam and Medji were to take me from Masuleh to Semnan, we saw the dim light of 5 o'clock creep slowly over the horizon, and a cold north wind made us shiver as we loaded the camels. The evening before I had made a present of my donkeys to Azurnuch's brother in repayment for his hospitality, having already bought myself two good camels in the village. They were sleek and their humps stood hard upright. They would be fit for hard work for a good while, until their humps began to droop like old rags. Before we left, I unpacked some presents for Ghulam and Medji, a Luger for the former and a neat little Sauer for the latter.

Medji performed a little dance of joy when he saw the Sauer, and then he took Ghulam's Luger and weighed it expertly in his hand. I could see that he was itching to fire the gun, but of course he would never have dared to without a sign from Ghulam. Then Ghulam took the gun from him and tucked it with a little gesture of ownership inside his belt, in such a position that it could be drawn out in the winking of an eye. Indicating that it was time to be on our way, he walked the few spaces to his riding camel and gave the signal for the protesting beasts to be goaded into standing up.

Later we rode forth to the plateau.

Ghulam thought we could reach Semnan in a week. The northern slopes of the Elburz mountains are among the few areas of Persia with adequate rainfall, brought by the winds from the Caspian Sea. That is why this region is covered in thick, almost primeval, forest full of majestic trees covered in a rich profusion of climbing parasites.

We rode all day without a stop, with Ghulam setting the pace. Before night fell and we had set up camp in a clearing, Medji went off to hunt in a ravine. He had spotted a urial, and brought back a ram with the most beautiful spiral horns and a wonderful long thick coating on its chest. Ghulam baked flat bread rolls in the fire to go with the roasted sheep. This first day of our long journey had brought us a good way forward, and now it was suitably finished with a marvellous supper. Replete and tired, we crawled under our blankets.

Any feelings of excitement I felt for the adventure ahead were soon cooled down by the icy cold and the penetrating wind. I was awake long before daybreak but feeling rested and ready for our last day in the mountains.

We descended the southern foothills towards evening and beyond them was the Dasht-i-Kevir, the great desert, which stretches well over 300 km to the east; it was the northern neck of an immense, parched, salt-covered marshy highland, which was bleak and rocky, with icy nights and earth tremors. Medji had decided that the dangerous and lonely desert route was the only safe way to avoid discovery.

We set up our camp at the foot of a flat-topped rock, so that I could make the radio contact I had promised five days earlier. Medji sat in his saddle and pedalled away, as I crouched by my 'piano'. I clicked away and listened for a reply. My aerial was correctly aligned—but there was no word from the other end. I thought the bastards were away knocking back the beer while I was sitting in the middle of nowhere, drinking brackish water from a stinking goatskin and wearing my fingers to the bone on the morse key. Five minutes, then ten, my callsign went out on the air without any answer. At last, after fifteen minutes—there he was! Then came the 'message begins' signal, and the operator at the other end began an almost endless clatter.

I cursed and Medji gave me an anxious glance from his treadmill.

'End.'

'Message received and understood. OK, you can go and fill your guts with beer now; I'll be back to you in another ten days.'

Meanwhile Ghulam had lit a fire. What amazed me was where he could have found fuel in the bleak wilderness.

I fetched my code book, *History of the Mongols*. Having followed the plan of turning over three pages a day every five days, even if I had made no transmission, I found page 29, paragraph two, and the third word, 'Genghis, as one . . .' A great mass of bumph. What was the point of all this stuff when I have not even reached my destination yet?

In my left hand I held a piece of dry ewe's cheese and an onion—I was becoming allergic to the onions even when they were wrapped in wonderful fresh bread rolls baked in the fire by Ghulam. In my right hand was the coded signal. My companions stared at me intensely, as if they expected me to read the message out to them!

WITH IMMEDIATE EFFECT ALL TRAFFIC TO NEW COMMUNICATIONS CENTRE, VIENNA. NIGHT FREQUENCY 11258. DO NOT RPT NOT GO TO KABUL. NEW MAN ON WAY THERE. OTHERWISE MISSION UNCHANGED. CENTRE OF GRAVITY INDIAN NORTHWEST FRONTIER. DETAILS OF MOUNTAIN TRIBES. CONTACTS. NO RPT NO ACTION AGAINST RUSSIAN AGENTS. NOT ENEMY. HOWEVER, ALL AVAILABLE INFORMATION ABOUT THEM. IN NO RPT NO CIRCUMSTANCES INTERFERE IN AFGHAN AFFAIRS. MAKE HARD AND FAST ARRANGEMENTS ONLY FOR SAFE ADDRESSES AND CONTACTS. FIND AND SECURE PARACHUTE LANDING SITES. CONTACT HAMID SUBANA IN CHITRAL AND AGENT OF HIS. PREPARE BOTH AS RESERVE AGENTS. YOUR FUNDS SHOULD SUFFICE. OTHERWISE FURTHER SUPPLIES FROM KABUL POSSIBLE. ALADIN.

Reserve agents—all very fine—but why financed by me? I decided to give them retainer fees—as little as possible—for I had a long journey ahead and was bound to encounter all sorts of unforeseeable contingencies. Aladin could provide more money from Kabul. Such were my immediate reactions when I had read the message. Who were these people I was supposed to appoint as reserve agents? Here was Ghulam, and they had not even mentioned him. They had it all worked out, back there, at their desks. Aladin was a very careful man, though; he too had his orders, and had to carry them out. I needed time to think things out quietly before making a decision. The ride across the desert would be a long one; I would have plenty of time.

A normal day's march, without tiring the animals and ruining them for the whole trip, was 30 miles (about 50km); though, handled expertly, a particularly strong camel could manage 40 miles. Of course, we could have pushed on in case of an emergency, but on Ghulam's wise advice we stuck to 30.

Once properly watered before a desert ride, camels can go without drinking for several days. Our three pack camels carried fodder. On each animal was piled about 9 kg. of millet meal, a water skin and a bag of dates as hard as stones. Two radios and two generator sets were distributed between three of the camels; and each of us carried in our saddle bags garlic, onions and some rock-hard goat's cheese. Even if we were unlucky and found no game along the way, we could manage with the food we carried, supplemented by the wild salt-land herbs. These last were certainly available and would also provide nourishment for the animals.

The fangs of time had gnawed away at these highlands year after year, for an eternity. The merciless sun and the torrents after the spring rains, had created a dead salty landscape.

On the second day out one's lips were covered in a fine layer of salt and began cracking. Despite the headcloths drawn as protective veils, the skin on the face began to tear. We had made narrow slits in the headcloths through which to see but still our eyes seemed to be shrinking in their sockets.

Medji rode behind me, reciting verses from the Koran in a nasal voice, while Ghulam led the way through the country he knew so well. He rode in silence, keeping the same posture he had assumed when we set out in the morning, hardened against any feelings of hunger, weariness or thirst. He was a man completely confident of his instinct and intuition, a fierce tough rebel, who had killed many men in combat, and knew that few men could boast of having more than one friend in this world and that in an emergency one could rely only on oneself.

To keep from nodding off during the endless day I had to concentrate my thoughts and reconsider that latest radio message. Above all, I could not show any signs of flagging.

It was our third day in the salt desert. We had been riding four hours, and the going had been fairly easy. Towards noon, as we were passing between some hills, Medji suddenly galloped past me and signalled for me to look behind us. A few hundred yards away—it was difficult to make out details in the distance because of the heat haze over the salt flats—a dark figure was following us across the blinding greyish-white expanse of the plain. When I looked a second time, I could make out some details of the man riding a camel. He wore a burnous that fluttered behind him as he rode. The animal was moving at considerable speed, following our tracks exactly.

Medji and Ghulam had meanwhile closed up and were riding on either side without saying a word. Ghulam reined in his camel and seemed to be waiting for the man, who was slowly gaining on us. He had taken his carbine out of its holster and had laid it between the ears of his mount. Then when the stranger who was riding towards us was a mere hundred yards away Barakatullah took aim. I saw Medji raise his carbine with a lightning movement and in the same instant heard the echo of a shot reverberating from the hills on either side. The figure fell from his saddle. His camel veered off at a tangent, then stood still a few metres further on, as if riveted to the ground.

Medji spat and muttered: 'A Hesareh, filthy traitor.'

Everything had happened so quickly that I could not grasp what had taken place. I would have been unable to make out whether he was a Hesareh or to what tribe he might have belonged. I thought I had excellent eyesight, but it was obviously nothing as good as my guides'.

We rode up to the body. Medji's bullet had hit him exactly in the centre of the forehead, there were no burn marks on the skin—just a clean hole, out of which blood was running.

Then Ghulam explained that no one else should see us with the body, as if killing a man were the most natural thing in the world. He took the rope that was wound round the pommel of his saddle, tied the Hesareh's arms together, and fastened the end of the rope to his saddle; he mounted and rode towards the nearest bit of high ground, dragging the corpse behind him. In about five minutes he returned, having left the body lying behind a rock.

Ever since the revolt under Betshe, they had had some quarrel with the Hesareh, who at the time had fought on Amanullah's side and had wrought havoc among the Tadjiks, the tribe to which Ghulam belonged. They also accused the Hesareh of living by treason; and Ghulam did not in any circumstances want to be seen by an Afghan on Persian soil so far from the Afghan frontier.

I felt extremely weak at the knees as I clambered back into my saddle.

Medji had caught the Hesareh's camel and had hitched it with a leather strap to one of the pack camels. Then his own mount got to its feet with a roar and, growling, broke into a trot. We rode on until nightfall without exchanging another word.

I had a lump in my throat for the rest of the day. I had seen a dead man before, but never before had I seen a man's life extinguished in a flash like that.

It was almost two weeks later when we arranged to separate a day's ride away from Meshed. Ghulam and I would proceed to the sacred city while Medji and his pack animals would wait for us in the Hari-Rud Valley near the Afghan border. Then we would ride together by horse over the Paropamisus range, crossing it by the Khabody Pass, and proceed to Talig-an in the Hindu Kush where I intended to make my base. It would be a good hideout because it was in the area controlled by the Tadjiks, near the Indian border and among people who liked Ghulam and were his countrymen. I would be safe.

Ghulam and I decided that Medji would accompany us only as far as Zebak, a place midway between Talig-an and our destination Chitral, where Hadji Mirza Ali, known in Europe as the Fakir of Ipi, was waiting for us. We did this for security reasons. Chitral, in the Nuristan region of Afghanistan and India, is deep in the country and right on the border, so that, if we should not return by an agreed date, Medji would be not far away and could go to Nuristan with some of Ghulam's Tadjik relatives and some of his own Afridi tribesmen to look for us.

Ghulam and I rode our horses the long day through the valley of one of the small rivers that rises in the Upper Hindu Kush and joins another at Chitral, the first place of any size on the frontier. From the confluence the river flows to Kunar, until it finishes in the Kabul-Sin.

This remote and mountainous region of the Northwest Frontier is outside the monsoon belt, and has mainly fine weather. There is not a cloud in the sky all summer. The seasons of the year are very clearly distinguished from each other. At these altitudes much of the precipitation is in the form of snow, but it can also be murderously hot and the area buzzes with disgusting flies and mosquitoes, all of which sting.

The river flowing south of Zebak into Nuristan ran behind a screen of leafy poplars. Ever since we had begun to ride parallel to its course, we could hear it rushing along but not see it.

The cold wind howled down from the snow-capped mountains.

We crossed the narrow western end of the Wakhan Corridor, created by the British before World War I so that British India should not abut on the Russian frontier. They arranged things so that the Afghans, who in those days were under their suzerainty, would share a common frontier with China, even if it was only a very narrow strip controlled from Indian Dardistan, where the British themselves were established. It was possible to cross the Kilik Pass into the Yeherhch'tang valley and the southern corner of Sinkiang only for a few months of the year, and even then with a great deal of difficulty.

About 1915 a German officer had penetrated into China at this spot from Mesa-i-Sharif in northern Afghanistan. His mission had been to organize a revolt against the British, but nothing came of the plan. The old men of the region were still telling stories about it; and some of them, whom I saw in Zebak, even had carbines dating from those times, which the Germans must have distributed.

The giant mountains of this northwestern frontier are the homes of the Hunzas. In this dramatic landscape, with its gleaming peaks reaching almost to the sky, they live to be a hundred or more years old, are white-skinned, and belong to the Maulais, a very pious Moslem sect. They eat only very little meat, live off vegetables and fruit, gather herbs and drink soured milk. Their great chief, the Mir, was a good friend of Ghulam's.

The rocks began to crowd in on us; the path became narrower. We had to leave the river valley. In the narrow ravine before us there was no room even for the narrowest of tracks.

Ghulam knew his way here; he rode without haste, his pack animal behind him, his reins tied tightly to his saddle, negotiating the broken rocks that lay more and more thickly on the road. Then he led the way on foot, leading both horses behind him, across the wooden footbridge that had been built to provide a crossing over the ravine. It was of rough-hewn logs laid over beams and lashed with ropes, across the water, which was now a narrow torrent.

The road-bed of twigs and small branches moved with every step; they had been thrown loosely over the logs, and the ropes holding them together were old, so that the whole thing swayed with every step. The animals scrambled, eyes wide with fear, legs trembling, from log to log. Ghulam went on whistling an odd little tune to them through his teeth the whole time we were on the bridge. They were much quieter than my mount, whose nostrils I had to cover with my hand to prevent him from becoming too restless. I was walking beside him, as if stepping on a tightrope of timber, while the water roared below.

An icy wind blew down from the flat rocky plateau above. The rock rose sheer from the very edge of the path. Somewhere in the ravine there must have been a waterfall, as the rock-face was wet up to quite a height and the trail was slippery. We walked through the Scotch mist for a good way past the rocks, where the path again climbed steeply.

The sun was sinking fast behind the high jagged peaks. The plateau at the end of the climb, which narrowed towards the east and to which our trail was leading, was quickly enveloped in shadow. We had to make camp here, before it became quite dark.

Ghulam had unsaddled the stallion and was busy with the load carried by the pack horse as I arrived at the flat rock fringed with stunted scrub that he had chosen as our camping place. The pack horse went on ahead of the stallion to a small mountain pond that lay at the foot of a steep rise. When my horse had been unsaddled, he too trotted along behind the other two. Slowly they lowered their heads and drank the clear water of the pond contentedly. The following morning I too would dive in, I promised myself. It would be a wonderful opportunity for a cold refreshing bath.

Ghulam went to find kindling for the fire, having already spread out our blankets on the flat rocks. It would be a little hard, but we would sleep well after our ride. We had no meat with us, but we ate rice flavoured with the coriander that grew everywhere, washed down by thick sweet tea—and we would sleep after that!

Total silence lay over the high valley. The fading light was of a rare beauty: the peaks glowed red, shading to a dark blue at the floor of the valley, where ancient gnarled oaks stood on the steep slope behind the little pond. The pond itself was already an eerie pitch black.

Ghulam brought the wood for the fire and was cooking the rice. The horses came back, neighing, and I went to fetch their feed bags. When I came back, Ghulam was sitting by the fire. The flames etched the lines on his face deeper than they were in reality. It was a face like a wild landscape, craggy and full of character. He sat by the fire like a lord.

Here the Northwest Frontier was only theoretical. In practice you could make it out only in the north at the Baroghil Pass, and in the south at the Khyber Pass. There you would find customs officials and large notices saying 'This is the frontier', but they counted for little. Bakshish remained the operative word in this wild region.

Between the two passes lie 500 km of territory as the crow flies, inhabited by Wazirs, Afridis, Tadjiks, Pashtos, Uzbeks, Turkmens, Kirgizes—and who knows what other tribes, which come and go as they please.

No outsider can control them. Anyone who would really like to try it would be well advised to keep his eyes peeled; they shoot pretty fast and they shoot straight. Their greatest pleasure is to kill a man. No one on this earth uses a gun so readily and so frequently as those tribesmen, who are always ready for a spot of brigandage or a fight.

In the towns and villages it is unusual to see a man walking in the streets without a gun under his arm, or slung from his shoulder. Using archaic tools and instruments, they manufacture their own very accurate rifles and pistols—and even machine guns. If you watched them at it without knowing what sort of people they were, you would think them mad, but they soon make you change your mind.

When an Afghan buys a rifle, which he can do in virtually any town of any size—in much the same way as we buy bread—he will step outside the shop into the street with the gun and let loose a noisy fusillade; and should the gun not suit him, he will repeat the performance until he has found the one he is looking for. No one will interfere. Passers-by won't even look round. Every free man, and they all consider themselves free, carries some sort of artillery about his person, rather as we have a packet of cigarettes in our pockets. The trousers and shirts covering their bodies are in rags, their diet is meagre, but they all have guns. First comes a man's gun, second a camel or horse, and only then a wife of his own.

Hadji Mirza Ali was waiting for us among the 'infidels'—the Kafirs. These people have their own way of life. They are not true Moslems, having inherited their customs from their forefathers and preserved them. They were supposed to have been animists until forcibly converted to Islam in 1896, which is why, and only why, true Moslems call them 'infidels'. Some ethnologists insist that they are of Greek origin, owing their presence here probably to the fact that Alexander the Great spent some time in these regions on his way through the Hindu Kush, before he marched on to the Delta of the Indus with his army.

To this day the Kafirs have a truly democratic form of government. Every year twelve representatives of the people are elected in every Nuristan town and village. These Uorirs then select a Jagir, who is supposed to be the wisest and bravest man in the village, to be their village headman. All decisions affecting the village are made by the village assembly or Jirga, which decides such matters as the distribution of water, defence matters, the marketing of livestock—everything down to the smallest detail that affects the village. Thieves must pay seven times the value of their loot as compensation, and murderers must extinguish the debt of the blood they have shed by paying a sum of money, the amount to be determined by the elected village representatives. The fine for adultery is one fat cow.

The strongest and bravest young man is appointed to be their shepherd. In the spring, maidens of the village accompany him to the mountain pastures singing and dancing around him and the flock; and he is brought home in like fashion when it is time to drive the animals down for the winter. He stays up in the mountains for six months with his rifle and his flute, walking ahead of the village animals, protecting them against danger and marauders.

The women wear magnificent head-dresses, which fall down over their shoulders and to which are stitched shells, bright metal ornaments and little bells. When they are pregnant, they are brought to the 'House of Solitude', of which there is one in every village, and which is richly adorned. They stay there for three weeks, waiting for their confinement, since, according to Kafir custom, they are 'unclean' and must give birth in total isolation.

It was noon as we rode down from the terraced hills and past the first huts of the village. The women had just taken one of their pregnant sisters into the isolation house. The streets were full of them. It was a small place, but as important for the inhabitants of this region as a big city is for us. There was a bazaar, where one could meet people when one came down from the mountains and when it seemed too far to go on to Chitral, which was of course bigger. In this village everything was as it had been in the Middle Ages—a meeting place for nomads since the beginning of time.

Many of the Wazir huts were stuck on to hilltops or built between rocks. They looked like small fortifications. Near the village stood the tents of the nomads. The market place not far off was full to overflowing with people of all the tribes who haunt the area. It had the colour and atmosphere of all North Asiatic markets, teeming with people and animals. We had difficulty forcing our way through the throng.

Suddenly a Wazir appeared by the side of Ghulam's horse, took it by the reins and, without a word, led them out of the market, down to the banks of the fast-flowing river Kunar. He stopped before the porch of one of the few stone-built houses. In front of the door stood an armed Wazir who welcomed Ghulam Barakatullah like a long-lost friend.

The man who had brought us there led the horses through a gate behind the house. Immediately, the armed man turned and went through the door before us.

In a large room, at the far side of a short passage, two Mullahs sat, lost in thought. They were playing with their strings of amber beads, passing them between their index and middle fingers and, like all

Moslems, murmuring verses from the Koran. It is a simple method of taking exact note of what is going on without letting on that you are.

These Mullahs, the arch-conservative divines of the Moslem world, are always game for a plot. Nothing of importance can happen without them—they must always be in on everything. They had chased Amanullah from his throne, and had done the same to others before him—or had them murdered! They are sinister people who interpret the laws of the Koran as it suits them.

A middle-aged man had just entered the house from the garden through the open door. He was tall, a giant compared with most of the men who lived in this part of the world. His long and well-formed nose sat in an intelligent face. A well-groomed man, he, with his light complexion, could easily have been taken for an eccentric Englishman who had taken it into his head to receive his guests in Wazir clothes.

After the obligatory introductions and greetings, even the Mullahs, who had been sitting in one corner of the long divan which occupied the whole of one side of the room, drew nearer. I remember Mirza Ali saying somewhat ironically: 'Being a secret agent, you are bound to know all about me. It's part and parcel of your *métier*, is it not?' His English was excellent.

I had to acknowledge that I knew him to be the chieftain of North Waziristan, much loved for his courage by his followers. I also knew that his men were not over-fond of the English, except possibly their institutions, which he had got to know in England. He admired their style of life back home; otherwise, all he wanted was that they leave the area as quickly as possible.

He understood and saved me the trouble of saying anything more. Laughing, he clapped his hands together, whereupon a servant appeared instantly, with a tray of hot, sickly-sweet and revoltingly strong tea. By now I was used to the stuff, but never had I drunk tea as strong as that, not even on this trip.

People began to arrive. The great room filled up. Not one man came without his rifle. Each man had two full bandoleers, worn crossed at the chest over shirts that were anything but snow-white. There was enough ironmongery here to wipe out an entire company.

I hoped that Ghulam was not being too optimistic, and wondered if he really knew the Hadji well enough to sit next to him as calmly as that? He knew him very well indeed!

The great palaver began when the room was full to bursting. Men were sitting on the divan and on the floor, and standing in corners—as wild looking a bunch as you were likely to meet anywhere. There was so much noise you could hardly hear yourself speak. The Hadji signalled to me and I leant as close to him as possible. 'You know the custom, we shall have to eat all together; but after that I would suggest that we adjourn to the next room.'

It was now time for the great blowout.

The food was carried round on immense brass dishes. The throng packed together even more tightly, the men wiping their fingers on their shirts, ready to pounce. There was mutton, chickens, pigeons, beef, rice, vegetables, and mountains of flat bread.

I seized a chicken leg—its owner must have been a marathon runner, judging by the size of it. But that chicken drumstick in curry sauce with chapatti—a pancake baked in an amphora oven—soon reconciled me to the conditions. It was a delicious meal. Only it's better on these occasions not to ask what it was cooked in until later. The amphorae are made of mud and cowdung. When the pot has thoroughly dried, dough is spread in the inside; and when the dough has been baked over the embers, it is peeled off with a wooden spatula. The resulting taste is superb. There were chutneys, curries and other sauces in plenty, plus saffron, ginger, red pepper—enough to set one's palate ablaze!

And to wash it all down? Buttermilk—ugh!

What I would have given for a lovely glass of beer! But that is the price of having dinner with a Moslem!

The assembled company belched very loud and very often, audible signs of appreciation and a great compliment to the host Mirza Ali. The latter came up to Ghulam and myself, with his adjutant, a grim-looking, bearded Wazir, armed to the teeth.

The guard took up a position behind his master that clearly indicated to every man there, One false move from you and I will shoot you as full of holes as a sieve.

That chap nearly got on my nerves, not so much because of the arsenal he carried about him, but because of the nasty look on his face. I asked Mirza Ali if his bodyguard had ever smiled in his life. The Hadji gave a well-bred grin, turned round and said a few incomprehensible words and the Demon King left the room, glowering.

In a few seconds two other men took his place. They were unarmed. One was dressed in a snow-white kaftan with a meticulously wound turban surmounting his clean-shaven face. The other must have belonged to the Hadji's personal staff; he wore a grey flannel suit and over his well-laundered shirt a perfectly knotted black tie. He looked as if he had just flown in on his private aircraft from some nearby city.

He spoke English with only a slight accent, rolling his rs heavily. Otherwise he was neat and tidy and obviously had a good education. He knew it, too. He must have attended one of the English Mission Colleges in Karachi or Bombay, or one of the other innumerable colonial schools scattered through the vastness that was British India.

'Sadar Afizullah', said Mirza Ali, introducing him. 'He will maintain liaison with Ghulam Barakatullah. They know one another. Sadar is in any case my most trusted man as far as our mutual affairs are concerned. You too can trust him implicitly.'

I replied that perhaps it would be best if I came straight to the real reason for my presence there. I wanted to establish certain contacts, and I would like to leave a radio transmitter/receiver and generator with him. It was meant for the radio operator who was to come later. I did not know when, but Ghulam would be told in sufficient time because he was to be our contact. There might be others but for security reasons I did not know who they were. My job was to establish this particular contact. Thanks to Ghulam I had done just that. The Fakir knew the rule in intelligence services that one knows only what one is supposed to know—just so much, which was precious little.

Politics were not my affair, I told him, but I did know that before long he would have a visitor who was to have the appropriate plenipotentiary authority, possibly including political authority, which I did not have. To be precise, I concluded that in me he saw only a man who, when he returned to base, would give an account of the military aspect of his experiences but of that aspect only. On my way I had made certain military-geographical observations that could be of importance to both our sides. He no doubt would be contacted from Kabul as well.

The Hadji seemed satisfied with our meeting. He thought the world of Ghulam and made no secret of it, telling me quite frankly that without him our meeting would have been out of the question. However, he had been trying to establish contact with us for some time, provided it could be done in circumstances of total security. He had no wish to compromise himself, that would be far too dangerous. The British would stand no nonsense whatever when it came to such things. You could see their point of view.

I had said no more than was my brief, since my mission in effect consisted of finding out exactly what possibilities there were of coming to an understanding with him as a contact for information. Everything else would be done by others who would come after me. Their task would be the more responsible one, but it would be easier now that contact had been well established.

Of course, I knew that the idea had occurred to someone in Berlin, and probably more than just the idea, of making difficulties for the British on the Northwest Frontier. I had understood as much, from a conversation at which I had been present. The idea was to incite the mountain tribes to rebellion. It was early days yet for that, but I realized it was a possibility.

In carrying out these manoeuvres Berlin would even have Moscow's blessing. But all this was not my responsibility; I was to secure my contacts and then ride back the same way I had come with Ghulam, finishing the remainder of the journey from Zebak, or going on to Faydzabad by myself.

Ghulam had suggested leaving after dark if possible, so as to get away unmolested. Accordingly we rode over the hills in the late afternoon, just before the sun set.

Sadar had given us an escort of three men, to accompany us halfway to the plateau. He was a careful man and made a point of never moving without wearing both belt and braces. I had noticed this trait in the course of our conversation, after Ali had left us. It was reassuring, because it meant that our association would be more enduring.

Ghulam was visibly pleased with our success. For the first time, as we were riding into the mountains, he spoke about our days together since Masuleh. Our conversation was at times almost merry; we had many good laughs about the three Wazirs with us and about how seriously they were taking their job. During the whole ride they had us in the middle, with one of them riding a few hundred metres ahead, spying out the land. Sadar Afizullah must have put the fear of God into them.

When we reached the heights it became very cold again. An east wind cut like a knife through the mightiest mountain complex in the world. We spent the first night in a hollow at the bottom of a huge moraine, which we had crossed in utter darkness. We camped under some mountain ash that still grew at this altitude. In the morning we awoke to find that our bodyguards had disappeared without a sound. We had not heard them go. Then we rode on, alone again.

The next night we spent on the same flat rock we had camped on coming, by the same little pond. The icy wind had lost nothing of its edge. It was going to be a cold night. We made our camp fire over the ashes of our previous one. It was still dark the following morning when we rode away towards the mouth of the valley where the great grey Tirich Mir stood, marking the natural frontier.

After that the track sloped very steeply downwards. We had to lead the horses behind the overhang because it was very slippery and the track had become very narrow. We could already hear the waterfall in the gorge. Up above, the wind was still howling, but in the lee of the rocks there was no stirring at all. We could see the first rays of the sun reaching into the valley.

Suddenly Ghulam hesitated for a moment, as if he had heard something he had not liked the sound of; but he continued downhill, leading his horse by the reins. We rounded a bend, and the precipice directly in front of us fell sheer into the valley far below. We had to grope our way past the rocks; the stones lying on the trail were liable to slide away suddenly, dashing down into the valley, smashed to pieces in a trice.

How much easier the journey had been when we were climbing! The horses had been a lot calmer then. Now they had the sheer drop in front of them, and they were nervous. Horses hate steep slopes anyway. But we managed. After the difficult descent, we were standing once again amid the fine spray before the cleft from which the river issued. In front of us lay the half-rotten footbridge that led over the water.

Ghulam wanted to be the first to cross. Once again he began his funny whistle, intended to calm the horses. He took his riding horse by the reins, and started on the footpath of logs thrown across the beams. Then he made a sudden jump to one side of the bridge. I could just see his head and shoulders.

His horse shied, sprang backwards, and ran down the short embankment on which the tree trunks forming the bridge lay, dragging the pack animal, which was tied to its saddle, along with it. The two of them came to a halt near the poplar trees by the river, ears pricked stiffly upright and nostrils flared, utterly bewildered.

It all happened as in an old movie.

'Behind the great stone', I heard Ghulam say very softly, although judging by his face he must have been yelling it. The roar of the waterfall in the ravine drowned all other sounds.

I had no idea what was supposed to be behind the great stone, which was just to the left of me; but I slid behind it, and immediately I knew. Exactly over my head a bullet came whistling. It must have come from the rock wall. Peering over the edge, I could just see Ghulam's head and shoulder.

Never in my life did I see a man snap a rifle to his shoulder faster than that afternoon. I learned then and there and for the rest of my life that in those areas a rifle does not hang by a saddle bag but slung across one's shoulder.

I had been too lazy. But not Ghulam. He had torn his from his back even while jumping for cover behind the bridge, where he was now lying, and I could see he was pointing the barrel into the ravine.

What a bloody fool I was! I now had to lay my hands on my gun when I could easily have had it with me. There it hung, on the right flank of my horse, just nicely positioned to give that bastard over there, scanning the entire valley, a chance to pot me like a rabbit.

The beast was about to trot downhill to join the other two. I whistled; the horse halted in her tracks, pricked her ears—and went on a few paces. Then she thought better of it and again stood still.

If the ambushers had bagged my horse, because they could see the artillery dangling from its saddle, then I really would have been in trouble. The horse wandered slowly back and came to a halt no more than two yards from me. The gun was slung on her far side. To get it, I would have had to run round the creature; in which case they could take their time and bag me neatly in one shot.

But they were concentrating on Ghulam. Wherever I looked, I saw little puffs of dirt fly up; they were firing at the footbridge.

My horse was once again preparing to join the others. It was now or never; I had to make a jump for it, otherwise she would be away, and my gun with her. There she was, turning her back towards me. I leapt at just the right moment. It all went so quickly that I had no chance to think. Seeking cover behind the horse I tore the rifle from its saddle-holster, and with the other hand I seized the revolver, which was in a saddle-bag strapped to the pommel. I took the three bandoleers I had hung in front of the saddle round the animal's neck, and which I gripped with my thigh while riding. All this took but a second or two. The horse began to get restless and walked a few paces forward; then she was away, tearing down to the bank of the river at a gallop.

By this time I was already squatting behind my little bit of rock. I had lost one of the two bandoleers on my way back. It lay just out of reach among some flowering mountain poppies, which blanketed the whole valley. Then the horses quickly disappeared out of our field of fire, trotting along the valley.

I said to myself, You fools! The horses were perfect targets, and you have let them go. If it had been me, I would have got the horses first; that would have improved the chances of finishing us off. The horses had rather quickly calmed down and were grazing somewhere lower down in the lush meadows by the river. Once it was dark, we would be able to round them up and creep away. And, I thought, we had another chance as well. We were two days overdue because we had stayed too long at Sadar's. I had wanted to do everything thoroughly so that we could come away with nothing to worry about.

Medji! I hoped he was worried that something had happened to us and was already on his way with his people. By nightfall the whole situation could have changed, because the ambushers might well have succeeded in getting us before we managed to reach the horses.

I had heard no shot, but in a moment I was to know just who it was who had fired.

From a good twenty yards up the wall, about half-way up the rock, a long filthy shirt and a pair of fluttering white trousers tied at the ankles fell through the air. Over the collar of the shirt I saw a bearded head that had lost its turban, now sailing behind him through the breeze. The body performed a cartwheel before it fell with a plop—on to a ledge on the rock, after which it turned again and fell, this time with its face towards me and turning on its own axis before me, with a dull thud on to the path in front of my cover. The fellow lay there, his face towards me, stretched out on the path. His skull had been cracked by one of the small rocks with which the path was strewn. He must have had a bit of a shock. The gun shot could not have been fatal; Ghulam must have hit him in the shoulder. I saw the point of entry of the bullet right in front of me; it was through his armpit. It must have been the impact of the bullet that had thrown him off balance out of the crevasse and on to rocks.

He was beginning to look pretty awful. His face was the grey of cigar ash, the blood was running down his unkempt beard and his brains were spreading out. I peered over the top of my rock towards Ghulam. He laughed and signalled me to jump back on to the bridge.

I stayed behind my rock.

Ghulam was signalling to me again, this time somewhat more impatiently. I was shit scared. I knew I ought to grab the edge there and jump down, but I remained squatting behind my stone.

In front of me, somewhat to one side, there was a slope which ran down on to the meadow. All I had to do was to move pretty smartly; then they would not see me.

I hung the bandoleers about my neck, took the gun in my right hand and slid down the little slope. It was all right, no one saw me. I began to crawl, keeping very close to the ground. As I did so, I managed to collect the bandoleer I had lost on the way up. Then I sprang up; and I was not the only thing to be running. The shit I had in my trousers was running along with me—and running pretty fast at that.

Another leap, and I was lying beside Ghulam. One of the ambushers was firing out of a fissure in the rocks exactly above the entrance to the ravine. The bullet slammed into a tree trunk right next to me.

'How the hell did they get up there?' I asked.

'Simple. Just crawl on to that ledge over there just above the entrance to the ravine. It's not the first time they've done it. They come over the Kilik Pass, whenever it's open. They do a bit of smuggling and a bit of stealing and fire at whatever moves, then disappear over to the Chinese side. They're always in groups of five or six. They attack any caravan and whatever else comes their way.'

'And now it's our turn!'

'Why didn't you jump at once', asked Ghulam.

'If I could die just for a little while—say for a day or two—I would have.' And I thought, What a bloody question! A fatalist, I am not.

One of the bandits—I could actually see his slit eyes and droopy moustache—crawled out from behind his rock cover on all fours, his rifle in his hand, his head almost touching the ground. He was trying to reach the next projecting rock, where the angle was better for him to aim under the bridge where we were lying.

Ghulam raised his rifle, and I mine; one of us would get him the moment he came a little more into view. It was impossible to miss him. There! He clutched his head with his hands and started back, the rifle fell from his hand and he plummeted into the river.

We stared at one another in amazement. Neither of us had fired!

Then a rock flew straight past my face. It had come from the opposite bank. Behind a poplar tree stood Medji, gesticulating to us. Three men I had never seen before ran to the footbridge on the far side, where they lay flat on the ground and fired away into the rock wall. Medji sprang over the loose logs on the footbridge, which flew about in all directions in his wake. Then he lay next to us.

Silence fell over the rocks. Nothing moved. There was no more firing. I was sure they had figured out that there was no point going on and had crept away somewhere. My idea must have struck Ghulam and Medji as idiotic. They glanced at one another, but said nothing.

Then, suddenly, there was one of the killers coming towards us in his long kaftan and huge turban. The free end of the headcloth was hanging down to his shoulders. He was walking slowly along the river bank, holding his rifle over his turban. When he was no more than five yards away, one of Medji's men shot him in the belly. That was the last shot I heard.

The whole business was sickening. After all, the man was trying to surrender, and to gun him down in cold blood like that was barbarous. But it did not seem to bother them at all.

From behind us two men came up across the flower-strewn meadow with our sopping wet horses. They had waded across the water somewhere far below us. Medji decided to wait it out in case some other characters were in the area. Ghulam Barakatullah, his gun slung over his back, swung into his saddle. This time I had mine slung across my back too.

In the evening, when Medji arrived with his people, Ghulam said I was not to ask questions; so I realized what was up—the others were all dead.

After Ghulam and I said goodbye the following morning, Medji accompanied me for the 400 km trip to the immense orange-coloured rocks of the valley of Banyan, where stands a Buddha sixty feet tall. The marauding hordes who have marched through this valley have made a sorry mess of him, thoroughly mutilating his smiling face. Beneath the thousand caves dug into the rock-face by monks and highlanders I said good-bye to Medji—and then I was on my own. Three weeks is a long time for a solitary ride, but sometimes it's good to be on one's own.

Thanks to my work with Ghulam, contacts were established to relay information on military and political movements to the Abwehr. During most of the war German political agents tried to break the British control in the Middle East; as a result Iran was a hotbed of Nazi intrigue. From time to time, encouraged by German shekels, the tribes, particularly the Kashgai revolted against the Persian government, causing diversionary movements and impeding the Allied progress of the war.

Chapter 8

Interlude in the Balkans

Whenever I returned to Abwehr headquarters in Berlin for further instructions, I would also spend a few days in Copenhagen with Sonia.

It was autumn; the flowers had faded in the Tivoli and the terrace of the Wivex had been cleared for the winter. We had had to eat in one of the dining rooms. It was late, as it always seemed to be when I said goodbye to Sonia. We had spent the morning strolling along the shores of the Baltic. Now we loitered about the Radhuspladsen for no better reason than that whenever we said goodbye we always came here. The Town Hall was illuminated in the early darkness, and above us, on the façade of the newspaper office, the news flashes, just as in peacetime, spelled out the latest reports—only now they were not reports of peace. We strolled along in the drizzle. In the evening Sonia would be dancing at the Opera, and I would be asleep on the boat train crossing from Gedser to Warnemünde.

In November 1939 Copenhagen was still a friendly place. By the time I was to return there would be no more passport control; immigration officers would have been replaced by soldiers. From then on the city would just vegetate, joylessly and hopelessly. No town is a cheerful place under enemy occupation.

My visit to Berlin was brief and businesslike. I went to the Kleiststrasse, and packed a set of old suitcases that had been sent from Istanbul to my flat, taking particular care only to carry things that had been bought in the Balkans or in Turkey, and preferably clothes with labels bearing the names of tailors who worked there. I drank a beer on the corner at Nettelbeck's, and sent off the suitcases. Then I had a splendid meal at Ewest's in the company of a bigwig from the Tirpitz Embankment, pocketed a letter to Colonel Paschöll in a sealed envelope, and was driven to the airport.

According to the instructions I was to follow Paschöll's orders and then proceed to Bucharest for my next mission. The chief himself had taken a hand in this matter. Canaris had had a meeting with the head of the Siguranza(the Romanian secret service), and had made certain arrangements that did not concern me—this was stated very explicitly in my orders. Should anybody from the other side draw the Siguranza's attention to me, and should I then find myself in prison, I must not assume that I would receive any help, despite the harmonious cooperation between the two outfits and between the chiefs—Canaris and Morozow. It was in other words a routine secret service job, according to the familiar precept—I knew nothing, had never heard of it, and was somewhere else at the time anyway. It was enough to know that I was going on another assignment.

Paschöll was a painstaking officer, and hated all Prussian haste. He was a true son of Vienna. He never failed to send a car to meet me at Aspern airport. One should, if at all possible, run a pleasant war, he would say in his comfortable way whenever we met.

In his office he followed his instructions, giving me money and a fat envelope that did not interest him in the least. I absorbed my new instructions, gave the papers back to him, and he burnt them in the enormous ashtray on his desk.

'Your contact will wait for you at the Fenstergucker at 8 o'clock. He arrived yesterday. Now, let's quickly have another cognac before we have to say *au revoir.*' The whole thing took only half an hour. He asked me neither what I was up to nor where I was going—nor what my business was with Isidor Klatt.

The car drove slowly through blacked-out Vienna to our rendezvous.

There was no one in the whole world who could behave as unobtrusively as Isidor Klatt. You just did not see him, even when he was standing right under your nose. Nor was there another agent in the Balkans with his connections. His sources were obscure but by far the best anyone had. Most of them were downright sensational. Isidor had many enemies and few friends. A few of the Abwehr officers liked him, but many of them hated him. Envy and intelligence do not thrive side by side.

'Why don't you go and visit a good optician?' asked Klatt, tugging at my jacket coolly, while holding a pastry with his other hand and looking up at me with his innocent brown eyes. I took a vacant chair opposite him. He sat there calmly eating pastry and drinking coffee, and joking. A clock in a tower somewhere struck nine. Isidor demanded the bill and paid it, got up, took me by the hand and we rushed into the railway station. Ten minutes to go before our departure on the very punctual Orient Express, we went through the gates and Isidor said: 'I've seen to everything, Johnny, tickets and all. We shall be alone and we shall have good berths. The service will be first-class. You know how I do these things. I insist on luxury, especially in hard times.'

In the compartment he told me that we were going on to Sofia of all places because someone was waiting for us there. There was nothing about it on my bit of paper, but I had to meet this man. This was quite a big job. So, if any fun was to be had, it would be in Sofia—there were some smashing women there! I was frankly amazed at the way Isidor just took things into his own hands.

We had a good table in the restaurant car. An elderly woman sat opposite us. Since Isidor did not think any delicate old lady pursued our profession, he felt we were free to talk. He asked if I had lots of money on me—really lots. When I asked him if he didn't, and what business it was of his anyway, he told me that the man in Sofia worked only for lots of money—but was worth it.

If he said so, it was true. The man was a fantastic chap. But I had to wait until we got there, and see for myself.

Over our after-dinner coffee Isidor became a little more communicative. For a while he had said nothing. He was being most cautious. But then he decided to fill me in. I remember he told me the situation in words something like this. The Italians had occupied Albania that Easter but it was nothing really new—they'd had considerable influence there for a long time. The day they marched in, Zog ran for it, together with his personal adviser and friend. Zog was now in Alexandria—that was the point. It was his adviser and friend whom we were meeting. He was of no further use to Isidor, but could be very important to me.

The man had been working for Isidor since 1938—but he cost a packet. Isidor advised me that if our contact should prove too expensive for my pocket, I could easily raise the money by using my friends on the currency black market. Most importantly he admitted that the sources he told the Abwehr about were all false. Extraordinary results required unusual methods. How right he was! I appreciated the fact that the Abwehr would have got rid of him long ago if he had disclosed his sources. As he was a Jew, they would have put him behind bars long ago and then made use of his sources themselves. He certainly knew what he was talking about!

'There are plenty of possibilities in Alexandria', I said to him, and asked why I should use such an expensive source.

He explained that our friend, the ex-king, was under Faruk's wing and a frequent visitor to his house. The same went for Zog's friend and adviser, which was why he was so expensive. His information, Isidor found, was always 100 per cent safe. He was now in Sofia, and had had to slip across the frontier for a few days, probably to get money or jewels for Zog; then he was to return to Egypt. None of this had anything to do with partisans. That he left to other people; it was not his cup of tea. He did not think much of shooting—chasing women was more in his line. But he got around everywhere and had a finger in every pie, including some no one else could get near.

I agreed on going straight to Sofia, but for one day only. I had to get to Bucharest, where I had some business. We could meet again if necessary.

He did not reply immediately, but when he did, he said something I have never forgotten. 'It would be best, Johnny, if I went along to Bucharest too. I'll have a word with some of my people there. It's a good thing some of the chaps at the top don't know some of the things I know. It gives one a certain feeling of independence, knowing that they need one. They've probably sent you to find out what I have up my sleeve and what I can find out in Bucharest before you do. Therefore, my boy, we must come to an arrangement. Given good sources of information, you can always make good any mistakes you might make. The chaps on top only hear the grass grow; they've never actually cut any.'

So that was how things stood. The Abwehr were puzzled by his first-class sources, but he was far too clever to let them put anything over him. Far too shrewd, was Isidor, and above all absolutely right. The setup in his case seemed to be—you let me have my freedom, Abwehr, on condition that I supply you with good information.

That was fine, a business deal like any other; and one of his sources was this friend and adviser. Wouldn't the Abwehr have liked to know!

Isidor Klatt and I had got to know one another at Quenzgut, and from the first moment had realized we had a lot in common. As confirmed civilians, we would sit drinking our beers in the evening in one of the ill-lit taverns, marvelling at the presumption of the soldiers, who led a dog's life because they were not prepared to struggle for their daily bread. It was only then at Quenzgut that I had begun to understand that struggle, spoilt as I had been among the fleshpots at home. It was there, largely under Klatt's influence, that I had finally ended the 'daddy's boy' period of my life. The gentry had joined the army because they could not cope with everyday life. That was why they had posted themselves to that haven for the inadequate, where their food, clothing, work, spare time and thinking were all prescribed for them.

We had not extolled comradeship in high-flown words, as they did, but we had established a comradeship all the same. It was one that was to endure through those days and many others to come.

There was much else that the Tirpitzufer officers did not know. In fact, they knew nothing beyond what every Tom, Dick and Harry throughout the Balkans knew. They knew that Romania was a rich country bursting with oil, grain and timber, with corrupt politicians all jostling and shoving away at one another. They knew that two months earlier a French engineer had arrived in Bucharest, accompanied by a senior officer, in an attempt to repeat what they had done twenty years earlier. After all, he was the same man who had pulled off the trick in Bucharest in 1918. They assumed that this man would try to block the Danube. It was not difficult—simply sink a few barges laden with cement in the channel, and there you were! The idea may have been excellent, but it was only an idea.

It was to be my first trip to Bucharest, but I was sufficiently briefed to realize that at that time Romania had many facets. It had the Iron Guard, which was a fanatical Fascist organization, founded by Corneliu Codreanu. Then there was the mistress of Carol II, Mme Lupescu, whose name meant 'Mrs Wolf'. That did not sound quite so romantic, but it meant the same thing. She was half Jewish and a Roman Catholic convert, with auburn hair and very beautiful. The most important thing was that she had the King under her thumb. From her palace she could walk straight into the royal gardens through a gate at the rear. She went everywhere with the king—even when he went to Sinaia, his mountain retreat, she worked on him all alone and as long as she wanted to. All secrets were discussed. Then there was the Siguranza. It was a first-class, and totally unscrupulous, intelligence organization, which flirted with all the others, and with the Russians in particular. In Romania everyone informed on everybody, and informers were everywhere. It was a very beautiful but rather dangerous country. And that went especially for Bucharest, 'Little Paris', the town of corseted officers and their beautiful women riding in superb open carriages up and down the Calea Victoriei, where a man wasted in riotous living the money earned for him by his peasants.

True to his Imperial Russian aspirations, Stalin wanted Bessarabia back, the Germans wanted oil and grain—and the Allies wanted to stop both of them. There were things already afoot in Bucharest and one had to watch one's step. Everybody mixed with everybody.

My orders were to find out how, if necessary, one could infiltrate a commando unit into Turkey, where it could lie low until it was needed to help the Wehrmacht secure the oilfields of Baku. My instructions were also to see what our colleagues from the Secret Intelligence Service were up to in Romania.

That's what was called strategy, and strategy was something I knew nothing about. I did not trust my eyes either, when I read about it.

At the hotel in Sofia Isidor assured me that he was expensive, this new man, as I would understand later that evening. I was all for getting the whole business over with straight away, but Isi insisted that we must be patient. We were to pick up our contact in a nightclub, where he would be waiting. Unfortunately we learned he had got into a fight over some women. But Isi pulled a few strings with the police, and we were able to save him a night behind bars and who knows what other unpleasantness.

He was so good looking that I immediately nicknamed him 'Handsome Jovan', greatly to Isi's delight. He was no Albanian but a Montenegrin from Podgorica—though he failed to fit the picture one has of these people. One imagines them mostly as assassins, anarchists or bomb-throwers—or dangerous savages who never emerge from the dark crevices of their native mountain forests without sticking out like a sore thumb. Jovan was far from being a backwoodsman. He was a man of the world, very elegant and well-groomed.

He was tall, charming and looked much younger than a man in his mid-forties. There was some grey at his temples, but otherwise he had dark wavy hair, the kind women like, and a delicate and finely chiselled nose. His eyes were greyish-blue, and particularly attractive with his tanned complexion. Altogether he made a pleasant impression. Women went weak at the knees when they met him and began to dream about him. And—he always got what they used to dream about!

Jovan had perfect manners and hated any kind of rudeness. He was charming to all women, no matter what class they were. He was cultured man, which was particularly appreciated by those who knew where he came from, for generally speaking culture is not what Montenegrins are famed for. How could they be, living as they do in some forest, up some gulch or beside some wild mountain stream? But Jovan had cast off the coarse mantle of his origins.

Men of his type either make true friends or—since jealousy among men is even more pronounced than among women—many enemies. The latter applied to Jovan. But he did have one true friend in Zog, the overthrown and fugitive King of Albania. Not as handsome as 'Handsome Jovan', he made up for that deficiency by being extremely wealthy. There was no jealousy between the two men.

Women love either handsome men or money. What they like most is a man who has both.

Zog had had first-class financial connections with Italy, dating from the days when he was the dictatorial president of Albania. But these connections were not as useful as the contacts and talents of his friend and adviser, Handsome Jovan. Jovan was therefore in a position to give his King ample help when Mussolini was developing an appetite for Albania. Since the Italian had for some time been financing Zog, without ever getting a penny of his investment back, he naturally wanted to lay hands on the country. Although the Albanian self-declared King seemed pretty well bankrupt, there were still plenty of reserves hidden in the capital, Tirana, and Zog was not prepared to leave them behind. Five years previously, Handsome Jovan had made sure that everything his boss had, down to the very last penny, was brought out of the country when the Italian fleet successfully threatened Albania into granting further concessions. But Zog and Jovan had overlooked one by no means negligible and well-hidden box of jewellery. It had been deposited in Zog's home when he had become president in 1925, and had been lying buried there ever since. Jovan Elmas wanted to slip over the frontier and collect this last morsel for his lord and master, who, by all accounts, missed it sorely.

Isidor and I heard all about this the following morning, when we had had a good night's sleep after that stormy evening and the visit to the police station. The three of us were sitting on the terrace of the Hotel Bulgaria, admiring the Church of St George, with its wonderful gilded domes, across the way.

Jovan naturally knew the way into Albania; it was not for nothing that he was a Montenegrin, at home in the world of the mountains. However, he had a good 250 km of Yugoslav territory to cover before he got to the Albanian frontier, and even then he would not be at his destination. Jovan was accordingly provided with excellent papers by Isi Klatt and went scrambling over the mountains to Albania. He returned three weeks later with his treasure.

That was my first encounter with the ultimately highly useful Jovan. Isidor as usual was absolutely right: knowing Jovan would eventually come in quite handy.

Meanwhile we had to get to Bucharest, and Isidor wanted to take a roundabout route.

'Leave it to me; you'll see, it'll be all right', he told me at the railway station, buying two tickets to Varna, which was nowhere near our destination. We had to change at Turnova, a junction of the branch line to the border town of Ruse, an utterly god-forsaken place and the railhead. On the other side of the river at Ruse the frontier is the Romanian Danube port of Giurgiu, where the rails begin again—to Bucharest. This direct approach was not for Isi. He wanted to travel to Bucharest from Galati on the eastern end of the country, and he had good reason.

From the railway station at Varna we made a beeline for the harbour. Isi seemed to be in a hurry, so, stepping out smartly, each carrying only a simple valise, we walked side by side without a word. A medley of vessels lay tied up at the quay. There were sailing boats, trawlers, cutters of all sizes, all mixed up together any old way.

Two coastguards kept watch by a single-masted auxiliary cutter, their rifles slung over their shoulders. As they saw us, they approached, chatting to one another, and greeted Isi in a language I could only partly understand.

A fisherman came down the gangplank of the boat to the shore and joined us. Isidor reached into his left pocket, fished out a wad of banknotes, counted them out into two lots and gave each customs man a bundle. They plunged the notes into their uniform jackets and, still chatting at the tops of their voices, disappeared.

BAKSHISH is written in the Balkans just like that, all in capital letters. It is the most important word in this part of the world; at least it was in those days. Today, I am told, it is of less weight, but then humour is another word that is now written very small there too.

'Let's go on board', said Isi, starting up the gangplank, which was just a thick board.

A second man, who had been standing on the stern, lifted the hatch cover under which the engine lay, and cranked it into life. With the muffled throbbing of the diesel under our feet, we sailed slowly towards the channel in the middle of the harbour and out into the Black Sea.

It was now pitch dark; you couldn't see your hand before your face. 'This could be a great mistake but, for what it's worth, I trust you. You must promise as a friend and comrade never to tell anyone who works for me what you have seen on this trip. Not a soul must know, Johnny, where I get my information, you understand? No one but you has come as far as this with me before, and there'll be no one after you!'

I had felt it in my bones for some time that we were about to do something a bit bent. At first I had thought it would be one of those shady deals that helped finance Isidor's contacts. I thought perhaps we were going on a smuggling trip. It did not bother me particularly. In every intelligence organization it was everyday routine to be engaged in some sort of illegality, if you chose to call it that. The main things, Mütze had always emphasized in Berlin, were that the ends should justify the means, and that one should not be caught.

Isidor was right: this way, he became indispensable and they could not drop him overboard, even though they might want to. They needed him.

Our boat passed Cape Galata close inland and headed out towards open water. We needed the whole night to make that secret journey, though the skipper did not waste a minute. The reliability of the boat and the engine I learned were due entirely to Isidor. He had paid the man to have it installed. During the swift passage over the churning water Isi told me we would be covering over 150 km to our rendezvous.

'Unless I am very much mistaken', I guessed, 'we are going to meet one of your sources, are we not?'

'Yes, the most important—Russians.'

He told me that they fished for sturgeon, and they did some smuggling. While they were at it, they brought him material from agents in Russia. It was all very well organized. It had taken him a long time and cost a mint of money—not to speak of the risk. Information could not always be sent on the radio, especially when working from this country, because its monitoring surveillance was first-class. So, he went on, he had occasionally been obliged to take a trip. Since all these reports cost money, they had to be forwarded somehow. They could not be sent by mail because of the censorship. To stay independent, he bought merchandise with the money the Abwehr gave him. Goods were appreciated much more than money by his agents in Russia, because there was practically nothing they could do with money—and, as far as ideals went, you could go fly a kite!

That was all I ever learned of his operation. Although we were good friends, he could hardly tell me any more. I would have done the same in his place, for one should never show all one's cards. According to him, Berlin was always astonished at the intelligence material he produced. They would have given their right arms to know how it came his way. They would have liked very much to lay their hands on his sources. For that reason some people suggested, in a roundabout way, that he was a Soviet agent, or rather a double agent, but that was not the case. His sources were reliable and he played fair. They had plenty of evidence that he was on the level. Nevertheless there were people in Berlin and elsewhere, at various outposts, who insisted that most of the stuff was nothing but fairytales, with the occasional genuine report thrown in for credibility. They were jealous.

'To give you an example', he said, 'I was the first to report the Russian troop concentration in Bessarabia. I gave the stuff to Paschöll only the day before you arrived, when I was at his place, and before that I had spoken to our man in Sofia. He laughed in my face and told me not to exaggerate. When I was in Vienna, Schmalschläger wanted further details, but I played hard to get. That's because I don't want to expose my people to unnecessary risks and it is getting very dangerous now to maintain permanent contact. When we meet them this time, I will put the accent very much on lying low. The Red Army has already cut off the whole Dniester Estuary, and my fishermen could come only at the greatest risk to themselves. The Red Army sets exact times when sturgeon can be caught. They have another catch in mind—it's Bessarabia they are hoping to net. The Russians are determined to have it back at all costs. They've never really given up.'

I told him I did not know what they said about him—I hardly saw anyone. When I spent a few hours in Berlin, I only saw the man I wanted to or had to see. I talked to him only about my work. I did have an idea, though, that they did not realize how well we two knew one another—and I preferred it that way. The last time, when we were at Ewest's, I was with Major Stolze of the South-East Department. He gave me the letter Isidor knew about, and that was all. As I said, he may have had no idea at all that we knew one another. Perhaps he did not even know of Isidor's existence. They isolated their people from each other. My contact man there would hardly have been likely to mention me at all, partly out of jealousy and partly out of fear that he could lose me.

Paschöll, Isidor told me, thought the world of me and Paschöll was the man I trusted. Otherwise I was extremely wary. Even Schmalschläger, under whom I was supposed to be, and who naturally behaved as my immediate superior, I trusted no further than I could have thrown him.

The weather was settled and the cutter made good progress. The bigger of the two Romanian fishermen, Dumitru, was manning the tiller. The other one, the one who had come ashore, was sitting with his back against the mast. He was visible only in outline.

We sailed on through the night. Towards dawn a wind began to stir. It must have carried the sound of the engine a long way. The fisherman at the mast had the same thought, because he throttled back the engine. The sun came up and the air began to warm a bit. The man at the rudder set course westwards, up one of the arms of the Danube. We were running into the delta. On either side of us stretched low-lying sandbanks and islands covered in tall reeds.

Suddenly a bullet smacked into the water. I threw myself flat on the deck next to Isi. So suddenly had the firing broken out that I had banged my head. And, then, all was still again.

The helmsman had also thrown himself flat on his face, thrown the clutch out and killed the engine. He let the boat run aground amid the tall reeds of the sandbank. I saw the other fisherman crawl across the deck, seize the grapnel and throw it in a high arc on to the sandbank, without, however, throwing it too high.

Then we heard the second shot.

I said to Isi as I lay next to him: 'And I suppose you never heard of rifles—you know nothing about them, you buggers? I suppose we just sit here and let them drill us full of holes?'

'Under the forward hatch cover, on top of the sacks, there are two carbines, some ammunition and a few hand-grenades; but if I were you, I'd let them lie there. Hang on a bit; you can always get them later but they are hardly likely to close in on us with artillery. A few shots can't do much harm.'

I was worried that they would hole the boat, that she would let in water and then all they would have to do would be to wait until she sank. We would drown, even if their bullets missed us. That was not my style—if I had to go at least one of them would have to go with me.

Isidor hung on my arm and whispered to me to stay still. You see, we were exactly where he had arranged to meet his Russians—if not, this would be the first time his plan had misfired.

That was a great consolation, I told him.

A few metres away from the boat a flock of water birds had risen from the grass after the second shot. A little way further out, where there was no telling whether you were still in the river or out at sea, a pelican dropped quite serenely, almost perpendicularly, out of the sky. Lying on the deck, we could see it disappear below the side of the boat. A few seconds later the bird reappeared, a fish in his beak, and climbed steadily.

I crawled on my stomach to the lee side of the boat and lifted my head over the deck rail to see what was going on. There in the bullrushes stood a man pointing his gun at us. A giant! I have met many men but never one with such an immense barrel of a chest. His face was yellowish and a lock of blond hair hung down his forehead. It was difficult to guess his age but he was not ugly or evil-looking. But there was cunning in his features.

I signalled to Isidor, and he crept to my side. He too looked carefully over the rail at the giant. Then he jumped into the knee-deep water. There followed a lively argument in Russian. I stood up and saw two other Russians rise from the grass, each with a rifle under his arm. They were wading through the reeds with some difficulty towards the other two.

The helmsman had forgotten to make the agreed sign, Isidor

explained to me. They would have blown us out of the water if it had been dark still. The idiot was supposed to have hung his little paraffin lamp on the bow—if he had done that, Ulean Stanka would not have fired. The helmsman seemed quite shaken still, the fear of the fusillade still in his bones. Isi had forgotten to see whether the wretched thing was hanging there or not, and I was in no position to know the arrangements. The whole thing had pretty nearly ended in disaster! It was Isi's fault, for, after all, he was the boss.

Dumitru began to busy himself with the forward hatch cover and to fetch bags out of the hold. He put them on the shoulders of the Russians, who meanwhile had waded up to the boat.

The helmsman had recovered his nerve. He was unloading his bags, whistling a little song in the cold morning air. But I was turning the near disaster over in my mind.

Death is somewhat—conclusive, 'so permanent', as the English say. It was worth giving the whole incident careful thought. One should try to die as late as one reasonably could—quite apart from which, there would have been no end of a rumpus had the man killed us. Sooner or later they would have found us, for sure; and then there would have been a flutter in some pretty high political dovecotes.

'There could have been a right old balls-up', I said to Isidor, when I told him what had been going through my mind.

'I can't help it if you are a lily-livered bastard', he said.

He had received some good intelligence material, and had done well out of his smuggling. Everything had worked out fine and he was cock-a-hoop.

By the afternoon all four of us were again on board. The Russians had gone through the reeds to the opposite bank where their boat lay moored.

It was getting cool—the sun was hidden behind clouds and the wind was rising. The delta, with its islands, sandbanks and immense areas of swamp, lay grey in the afternoon light. We made our way to the Sulina arm of the river, which runs the whole length of the delta. Isi had to pay his Bakshish to the customs men towards the morning in Galati.

When he had finished decoding the messages he had got from his Russians, he told me that our people would be amazed when they saw the stuff. He had details of the Russian side: everything between Bilyayevka, Tiraspol and Kamenka, including regiments, garrisons and names—and some details of their equipment. He had a list of the whole invasion horde, which was as yet only standing by but would presently descend on Bessarabia.

'I should like to see the other agents supposed to be in this country produce any better information. That lot they've got sitting here aren't worth a shit. All they get is what the man they infiltrated into the Embassy brings along. And even that can't last. They get some stuff from Urluzianu, the Major. But he only lets them have what he and I have previously agreed he should supply them with. The rest, the important stuff, comes to me. There's nothing to it: I offer him more—and Urluzianu needs lots of money!'

'Nasty little man, aren't you?'

'No, I'm not. You know how they work. Keep bringing it, bring lots—as if it were all that easy! Moreover, as a Jew I must keep my position strong. What's more, I live in the Balkans, where people think differently from the way they do up north.'

'Why don't you chuck the whole thing and simply go to Turkey? You could live there just as well, perhaps even better, and certainly more safely.'

'Because I am not alone, Johnny. I still have an old father; and he can't uproot himself any more. But they don't know anything about that.'

A thick mist was coming across from the Sea of Jalpug just as we sailed into the main stream of the Danube. Isi was always lucky, I thought—now he can slip up to Galati unseen.

The Alea Vulpache is a street in one of the smarter suburbs of Bucharest, and No 3 an attractive villa dating from the twenties. The front garden was beautifully kept. Four gently rising marble steps led to a heavy, richly decorated front door, which opened into a spacious entrance hall in whose middle hung a crystal glass chandelier from a ceiling of fine plasterwork. One had the impression of being in a house which must have belonged to a man of refined tastes, who had filled it with treasures from every corner of the world, but maintained an essentially Balkan atmosphere.

The first living thing to greet me was a friendly, handsomely spotted Dalmatian. After a little while the butler, a man of medium height a little inclined to stoutness and dressed with exaggerated correctness down to his snow-white gloves, appeared to receive me. He was just a tiny bit too haughty, I could not help thinking. It was the Balkans all right—slightly phoney. I hoped the master of the house was a gentleman.

He was, and he greeted me with measured courtesy. I can still remember him—tall, slender and impressive as he came down the heavy oak stairs. He did not walk, he progressed. He was immaculately dressed—open-necked shirt, impeccable silk scarf with subdued pattern, quilted smoking jacket, grey flannel trousers and, of course, made-to-measure ox-blood shoes polished so you could see your face in them.

Domnul Urluzianu was the gentleman's name. He had a fine face, a waxed moustache and a reassuring air about him. This was no foppish elegance; Urluzianu was truly a gentleman and could almost have been an aristocrat. All he lacked was that touch of degeneracy.

We went into the drawing-room, and, after the first whisky and the mandatory formalities, the Major came straight to the point.

'Hm', he said, 'Mr Isidor Klatt, a friend of mine of many years' standing, told me on the telephone that you were coming. That makes everything perfectly all right. You can trust me absolutely.'

Up to a point, I thought, but I replied: 'Unfortunately Isidor is tied up at the moment; otherwise he would be here as well.'

'Yes; and I believe it's an unpleasant affair, which is liable to give him some problems. But we can relax—he is an outstanding chap who always falls on his feet. He will find a way this time too.'

The Romanian Secret Service had taken one of his men, and Isi was trying to arrange his release, the question being of course how much Isi was prepared, or able, to lay out. This case was about oil. Isi's man probably had done nothing too serious, but his name had come up in connection with a parachute operation. Someone had split on him. The Abwehr had wanted to put a section of the rail line out of operation so that the oil that had been promised the Poles would not reach them. Isi had just found out that his man was in stir together with some Ukrainians, who were also implicated.

'Klatt told me that you have come about a special matter.'

'Yes indeed, Herr Major; but I would like to know your price first. I always think that once the money side of a thing is settled, everything else goes a great deal more smoothly.'

He pretended he had not heard. What he did make clear was that he had two relationships: one with other Abwehr agents, the other a special arrangement built up over the years with Klatt—and the latter suited him better. But, because Klatt had told him that ours was to be a 'once only' affair, that was a different matter.

I understood. As a once-only customer in this business of buying information, I would naturally have to pay more. He would give a rebate to his regular customers.

'If you give me reliable information, my friend', I said, 'I will pay you like a Lord, subject to certain safeguards, of course. And then it's quits.'

The handsome Major of the General Staff and vendor of intelligence information was in no hurry. He let his butler serve us two more drinks, talking the while about the weather and the political situation in the country; he told me that he had the best possible relations with 'the lady next door', by which he meant Mme Lupescu, and that the lady had a particularly soft spot for Domnul Urluzianu. She set great store on his advice and had presented him to the king several times. In other words, he was hoping to make his story as fascinating as possible, and thus to raise the price. He frequented the house in the Strada Romana where Lupescu had her own intelligence service, and was therefore able to supply me with some of the most reliable information to be had in Romania.

No, he assured me, nobody had so far inquired about the activities of the British Intelligence Service. I was certainly the first, at least as far as he was aware, but by coincidence only yesterday he had found out that they were busy bringing explosives into the country. They had brought many boxes of ammunition and explosives in Danube barges up the Delta via the Sfintu Gheorghe mouth of the river and into Lake Razelm.

Well, well, I thought, the great concept mentioned in my briefing is beginning to take shape! The Allies are going to try to block the Danube. Funny only two days ago we had been quite near the mouth of the Sfintu Gheorghe. We had seen nothing.

But that was no reason why I should dismiss his information as false. We were not the only ones who had seen nothing unusual; other agents, who were supposedly in the area at the same time, had reported nothing to us either. Of course it had been pitch dark when we had sailed past that spot. Isi would be able to check this report.

After some more haggling, the 'Gentleman' agreed to disclose his information for 6,000 lei—a perfectly routine business transaction, much as one buys a pound of oranges. I paid, on condition that should this information prove to be a *canard*, Isidor Klatt would deduct the same fee from his next bill. Urluzianu immediately agreed to this condition, and 100 per cent genuine his information proved to be—we checked it.

Before a year had passed, on 6 September 1939 his King, just another Balkan ex-monarch, together with his beloved—I mean the lady who had taken the Major so completely to her heart—travelled into exile without the 'Gentleman,' but with ten heavily laden railway trucks.

When I returned from my talk with Urluzianu, Isi was sitting in the lobby of the Athenée Palace Hotel in the company of a number of distinguished-looking people. They were lost in earnest discussion.

The Romanians are a jolly lot, colourful and easy-going. They are no bomb-throwers but people of mixed blood, who enjoy life to the full. In their veins runs the blood of Gypsy Tartar, Greek and Bulgar. Some of it even is Turkish. But they are of Latin origin, and very proud of it. Their forefathers came with the Emperor Trajan to what was then the Roman province of Dacia. I mulled all this over as they sat around me in their elegant clothes and made their lively if somewhat agitated gestures—rather like Italians.

'Tonight, Johnny', Isi said, interrupting his animated talk, 'we're going out, do you hear? The hotel has a fantastic nightclub. In the meanwhile sit and have a drink with us.' He was almost too earnest in his attempts at sincerity with his Romanian friends. He seemed to be trying to assure each of them that only for them would he put his hand in the fire.

When they eventually got up and left us, Isi explained that the business of the Brandenburger unit which was to be infiltrated into Turkey—as my standby commandos—had all been settled. Furthermore, Isi's man had been released by the police with profuse apologies, of course, and was joining us that evening.

He looked around the room and then indicated a chap sitting in a leather armchair near the window. It was Dianu of the security service, a man who had his finger in every pie, including some in which it had no business to be in. His influence was everywhere, including the Iron Guard—and that was saying something! He was the one who had sprung our bird.

1918, the garden of the Alexandria hotel with my mother and two of our Sudanese houseboys

Somewhere in the desert with my uncle Abdel Kader and his youngest son and a falconer

The day of Sham-el-Nesim 'the Smell of Springtime', when families picnic on the Nile

Rohde and myself on the day I left Erzerum for Afghanistan

Hadj Amin el Huseini, the Mufti of Jerusalem, near the Brandenburg Gate in Berlin, after his escape from Iraq

1942 in Tripoli; Sandy and our 'booty' Ford station-wagon just before Operation Salaam/Condor

Operation Condor: on mission, photographed at the Heluan railway station in Cairo

Major A. W. Sansom of Field Security in his Cairo office, 1942

At the Capea in the Calea Victoriei, we had dinner washed down with lots of Tuica, that marvellous Romanian plum brandy. Afterwards, feeling fine, we wandered across the wide square just to stretch our legs—past the Royal Palace and across to the other side to carouse the night away at the nightclub of the Athenée.

I remember the band playing Gypsy music, as my antennae were starting to warn me that something was afoot. They were strong warnings, but I ignored them, and glanced around the room. I dared look only a moment.

I bet she's good in bed, I thought when I caught sight of her.

She seemed to know what I had in mind, and blushed. I tried to think of something else. She was fascinating and yet—just a little common. She had something that charged my own sexuality, and she had this something to such an extreme that I became quite distracted and conscious that every fibre in me was alive and aching for sexual release. There was a crying need for caution, yet, so strong was her attraction, that all I wanted was that fantastic piece of woman. I wanted to reconnoitre, to find out what was under that evening dress with the deep *décolletage*.

At the same time she was trying to make an impression on me by showing her shape in profile. I already had the message. She was gorgeous. There now began a sort of complicity. The attraction was mutual, so mutual it could not be denied any more.

'This is crazy', I said, and Isi heard me. 'She isn't one of the locals, not one of the hostesses. Never seen her before. I must say she has a fantastic chassis!'

There was a pause in the music. Isi ordered a new bottle. We were hitting the stuff pretty hard. The enormous semi-circular room was dimly lit. It was like any other expensive nightclub in the world. Although the room was large, it had a sensuously intimate atmosphere.

'You don't come from here', I said in French, while we were dancing our first few steps. In the Balkans one could always get by with French.

'I come from Vienna', she said perhaps a little too casually.

I looked at her critically. Not in a million years, darling—you don't speak French with a German accent. For a Viennese her French was too harsh. While we were dancing, I could feel the softness of her hips and the suppleness of her body. Then came the silly chatter men fall back on when they are casting about for somewhere to start.

'Are you making a pass at me?' she asked, shortly before the dance was over.

'Perhaps; I don't know; yes, definitely.'

'You don't seem very sure!' she said, returning my look of admiration with a smile.

'Shall we go?'

'Right!'

We went.

But as we were about to leave, Isidor, making his excuses to her, took me aside and asked: 'Your room, don't you think? It's all the same to me, but—just in case.'

'Either mine or hers, Isi. See you at breakfast.'

A few moments later we were at her place, in the hotel where Isi and I were staying. She switched on the lights and locked the door simultaneously. With the grace of passion she walked across the carpeted room and turned on the light of a standard lamp next to a large couch. With a dancer's sweeping gesture, her light coat fluttered to the floor. She turned, smiled at me and turned again. As she walked to the cupboard her movement revealed the supple play of her back and thighs. I turned round toward the door we had just entered and switched off the main light, while she prepared some drinks. I took off my overcoat and carefully put it on an armchair nearby. When I faced her again, there was a glass of whisky in each of her hands, one of them outstretched towards me. She was standing next to the vast couch. When I took the glass from her and raised it in greeting, she slowly sank into the corner of the couch.

We drank the whisky and chatted about this and that, in the course of which she most obviously showed an interest only in one thing. I drained my glass and sat down next to her.

I felt the firm flesh of her buttocks and the warmth of her body.

She knows what's what, does this one; she's been around. I had sensed it immediately, even before we danced. But she is no whore.

She switched off the standard lamp that stood next to the couch, leaving alight only the table lamp on the cocktail cabinet, which cast a dim glow over the room. A trite enough little incident, really, which later on one would recount as an amorous adventure.

She was more than pretty—she was stimulating, she was keen and she loved it. Get it right, and both of us would have a marvellous time.

But still those warning tingles would not stop. I helped her to pull her dress over her head. She needed no bra for the delightful curve of those breasts, I thought, caressing the firmness of them with my hand.

She touched my cheek and stroked my hair. Almost imperceptibly her other hand wandered over my back. My skin prickled to her silken touch. We spent a good while on the couch, and then moved to her bedroom. She lay now in the wide bed next to me, the covers thrown aside, completely naked and content. 'Have you known that Isidor Klatt long?' she said, smiling at me.

Sensing my annoyance at her question, she bent over me. So my premonitions were right. I pushed her very roughly out of bed. 'And now, tell me nicely who sent you, sweetheart, or this little game will end up very badly.'

It was hot and sticky in the room; I could hardly control myself. I looked down at her face—at her eyes, wide with fright. Slowly, keeping my eyes on her, I went towards the passage that led to the sitting room. She took the opportunity to leap up and run to the wardrobe, but I ran fast enough to reach the cupboard before she could open the door fully.

'Take your hand off that wardrobe door!'

I seized her wrist and was holding it in tight. With my other hand I opened the cupboard door, and saw a neat little pistol lying on a pile of underwear. I took it, and slammed the wardrobe shut. She sat down on the chair again as she was, naked.

I threw her dressing gown at her from where it lay at the foot of the bed, went backwards into the next room, the pistol aimed at her, and with my free hand tried to put my trousers on. It was too difficult, so I just held on to them.

Meanwhile she was getting close to tears. She was shaking all over.

'Where is your super-nerve, woman?'

I picked up the 'phone and asked for Isidor's number.

'How was it, boy? She must have been quite something in bed!'

'Pull your trousers over your arse and come over here immediately. The door of No 87 will be off the latch, don't bother to knock, and hurry!'

I replaced the receiver before he could ask any questions, as he would find out soon enough what the situation was once he was here. I went to the door and pulled back the catch. The girl sat whimpering, collapsed in the chair. I gave her a cigarette.

'If your people have nothing but fools like you on the force, they won't get very far. Who are they, anyway?'

She began blubbering. I became uneasy.

'You've got some mighty expensive perfume here!' said Isidor as he came through the door, wrinkling his nose. 'And you either put those damn things on or put them down. If anyone rushed you, you'd trip on your own trousers.'

He sat down at the foot of the bed, looking at the little bundle of misery on the chair, then turned to me and said: 'What's the matter with her? You haven't been beating her, have you, Johnny?'

'She asked me how long you and I had known one another', I said, struggling into my trousers. 'What a bloody fool I've been!'

'Clumsy, clumsy, my girl! Rushing in like that, like a bull in a china shop. New to this trade, are you, my love?'

I opened the window, drew the curtains and saw that outside the sun was shining. It was 7 o'clock.

She had draped her dressing gown only loosely round herself and her lovely firm breasts were exposed. It was a curious sensation—to despise her and want her.

From the edge of the bed Isidor said to her: 'And now we'll have a lovely breakfast and a nice quiet chat. All nice and cosy, my poppet.'

I picked up the 'phone and ordered breakfast. While we were waiting, I would have a nice hot shower.

'You'll have to take her along to the bathroom; she's bound to want a shower and she can't go by herself, can she?'

So I stood in front of her and saw that she was not crying anymore. She was looking at me with those lovely eyes of hers.

'Come, Uschi, or whatever your name is, cheer up; we'll go and have a shower. I can hardly let you go by yourself.'

'I wish I had your nerve,' said Isidor. 'The cheek of the man!'

Then breakfast arrived. Pushing an elegant trolley, the room service waiter had brought a breakfast fit for three lumberjacks. Isidor sat in one of the chairs around a small table in the drawing room, pulled up another and pressed me to have some food.

'Come along, my darling', he said to the girl as we sat over coffee. 'You must tell us your fascinating story nice and quietly. Without that, you won't leave this room. The waiter will not return until I call him; I've seen to that.'

'I am Polish', she said, out of the blue, between two gulps of tea. Hence the hard accent, I thought.

'And you are called Uschi?'

'It is not actually forbidden to be Polish', said Isidor. 'You are hardly the only one. There are a few million other Poles.'

He was slurping his coffee; it was not a pretty sound.

'No; it's only that you told me I should tell everything nicely, one thing after another.'

'You should know that it's best to be a good little girl. You should never try to take two old hands like us for a ride.'

'But what's a Pole doing in Bucharest; and why did you want to know whether Isidor and I had known each other for a long time?'

'Because somebody wants to get in touch with Klatt.' She was even capable of blushing.

She had to be a novice at this game, she knew so little about it.

I drank my hot coffee, which was just what the doctor had ordered. That night had made me thirsty. I watched her closely. She returned my glance and quickly lowered her eyelids, tightening her dressing gown.

'Don't distract the little lady', said Isidor, who missed nothing.

Then he asked if it were the outfit in the Alea Alexandria, the VIP quarter—the Polish Deuxième Bureau. If those midgets of the Intelligence world wanted to contact him, they had better forget his name as quickly as they could. He said this as he put his feet up on the table and lighted himself a cigarette, looking more like an over-fed official of some kind rather than a first-class agent.

'His name is Nikizinski Usebisoid', Uschi said, 'and he has nothing to to do with the Bureau. He's a courier; moreover, that's his real name.'

'What next! You do have a nerve, my sweet! His real name, indeed! He must be a fine little arse-hole, this courier of yours. Chatterbox, isn't he, to give away his real name?'

It could not possibly be true. Either she was trying to play games with us or she really was as thick as two short planks.

'Do you speak Turkish, love?' Isidor asked her.

'No.'

'Was she good in bed?' Isidor asked me in Turkish.

'I was praying for a prick of steel. What a night! She just couldn't have enough of it. Why?'

'Because the stupid ones are always good at it.'

But she was no fool. She played her part very well. She was taking us for a ride, playing naïve; and she was getting just the results she wanted.

Imperceptibly she had regained her composure. Quite calmly she admitted that her job had been to contact Isidor. When she saw us together, she had thought that the best way to gain his confidence would be through me. And besides, she chose me because . . . Then she became flustered and looked down at the table.

'So I'm not your type, am I? Well, fair enough. I won't hold it against you.' Isidor said it laughing, but I saw he was not all that amused. 'Well, if one does have to make a contact, one might as well enjoy it.'

All of a sudden, the lady was playing a different ball game altogether. The simulated naïveté was cast aside in a trice. The trouble was, she looked so marvellous—and she knew it! She had hair as black as sin, and eyes to match, and her complexion was enough to drive a man wild. She calmly stood up and asked me to unlock the wardrobe.

'You can have the pistol', she said. 'All I want is to put on some clothes.'

She got dressed just as if there were no men in the room at all, then went up to the little cabinet in the next room, brought out a bottle of cognac and three glasses and said: 'Time to have a drink.' She poured out three hefty tots, gave us each a glass, sat down, crossed those incredible legs of hers, making it clear beyond any doubt that she had the finest pair in all Bucharest, raised her glass and tossed back enough to do credit to a real he-man.

Between the suburbs of Herestrau and Baneasa in the northwestern outskirts of Bucharest, where the lake makes a great bend, stood an old-fashioned looking house. It lay behind a hedge of shrub roses that must have looked wonderful when they were in bloom.

Shortly after 11 o'clock on this morning of 14 December 1939 we climbed out of a taxi in front of the rose hedge. Uschi had seen to everything. On the firm assumption that the timetable she had set herself the previous evening would work out, she had even given the waiting courier the time of our arrival—so he told us later.

Strangely, what Isidor and I had been sure would be a cock and bull story actually convinced us. It seemed that the man's name *was* really Nikizinski; he was a Jew, and a Polish national, but held a diplomatic passport from Chile and acted as courier for the Polish government in exile. He had returned to Bucharest from Warsaw a few days earlier.

In the past he had served as financial adviser to the Chilean Legation in Paris for a long time; and then before the outbreak of hostilities, had gone on to the Chilean Legation in Warsaw in the same capacity. After the fall of his country he saw no point in remaining in Poland any longer and went, armed with a diplomatic passport from the Legation, back to Paris, where he placed himself at the disposal of the government in exile. He was now being used as courier. Protected by his Chilean passport, he could make trips to Warsaw from Paris by motor car and later from Bucharest, and maintain contact between the government in exile and the resistance movement.

During a recent trip to Istanbul (a few days before he was to return to Warsaw again) he had been contacted by agents of the Zionist office in Istanbul, and had agreed to run errands for that organization in the course of his missions as a courier. That was Uschi's story.

We had taken her tale to some extent on trust, but could not figure out where Isidor was supposed to fit into all this. And he was keen to find out how his name had come up. Should the whole thing be a trap, he could rely on his back-up connections with the Siguranza to nip the whole business in the bud. That is why we followed up on her explanation. If it was a trap, Isi would throw the book at them. He would not hesitate a moment, nor would he reproach himself afterwards. His iron rule was, Put your hands round my throat and I'll beat you into the ground.

A well-groomed man opened the door of the house. His bearing and clothing were carelessly elegant; his face was striking. He led us into the library, offered us an armchair each and went straight to the point without any preliminaries. 'The events that have led to our acquaintance have been somewhat unorthodox; it was the only way to contact you. I have Delius to thank for giving me the opportunity.'

Isidor gave me an almost imperceptible wink. We said nothing.

To lend weight to his remarks, Nikizinski gave us particulars about Delius that quite obviously could not be known to Tom, Dick or Harry. Moreover, he gave us his true name.

He explained that he and Delius had been old friends who had fought side by side against the Bolsheviks in the Russian Civil War.

Their friendship stemmed from those days; and thanks to Delius he was able to travel to Poland as courier without let or hindrance. Although he did have a diplomatic passport, it was by no means easy to pass through the controls. But Delius had seen to it that, at least so far, everything had gone without a hitch; and Delius had given his approval to the present meeting.

When he returned to Sofia, Nikizinski added, Klatt could tell Delius that we had met and that he, Nikizinski, was grateful to him for arranging the meeting.

Still we said nothing.

'Anna, would you mind making us some coffee, please?' So that was what he called Uschi—Anna! Actually it really was her name. She was the daughter of a Polish family friendly with Nikizinski, and had escaped with his assistance.

'And what's all this about?' said Isi at last.

'You are a Jew, Herr Klatt.'

'So what?'

'So am I. A Polish Jew. Delius of course knows all about it. That is why I wanted to speak to you. As Anna must have told you, I work as a courier for a Zionist organization based in Istanbul.'

I knew the outfit. I had come across it two years earlier. I recalled how Rohde had told me quite clearly at the time that we would not meddle with it, and that it was building up a line of information centres and 'safe houses' reaching all the way back to Germany. Moreover Rohde had nothing against it, and had even made this quite clear, provided it went no further than that.

Nikizinski produced details that proved that he was genuine. There was no question of any trap. Isidor seemed to know a great deal more. He started an earnest discussion with Nikizinski, asking him how he visualized a collaboration between the two of them.

'I am prepared to discuss anything and we could come to an arrangement on condition that we discuss only contacts, transmission centres and 'safe houses'. Espionage is out of the question. On those terms, I am prepared to play along; free of charge, of course.' Isidor's tone of voice made it clear beyond any doubt that he was prepared to cooperate.

I was only a passive listener to that conversation, and could not help wondering why Isidor trusted Nikizinski so much. He could of course rely on my making no use of what I had heard, since, after all I had experienced, I had my own opinion of those ghastly pogroms.

Nikizinski spoke several languages, which he handled like a master. Everything he said made good sense. He appeared to have a profound understanding of the situation. In the course of his journeys as a courier he must have made some pretty thorough inquiries. He was like one of those Jews I had met during my training period in Berlin before the war, whose judgements were based on precise knowledge of the situation. They did not speak a single unnecessary word when one was talking to them; and everything they said made sound sense. What was astonishing, given these qualities, was their fatalism and their total lack of any will to resist. But that was not the impression made by the man who now sat before us. He was a fighter, who would not meekly allow himself to be done down. He was an interesting man, with a brilliant mind, a great deal of courage and a most attractive personality. His words had fire, and each word he spoke came without hesitation. He and Klatt understood one another perfectly. That Delius, an equally intelligent man, was his friend and had helped him in every way he could was not really surprising.

Subsequently Isidor was to build up a network of transmission centres and 'safe houses' under the nose of the SD. He applied himself to the business with his customary zeal, and he probably had the help of Delius as well. They remained active in the Balkans a long while.

As to Nikizinski, I never saw him again, although I later heard about his being in the POW cage from another agent. He was accused of collaboration with the Abwehr—an absolutely ungrounded charge—and was drowned by his own people. He was not the sort who would ever have worked for an enemy.

His friendship with Delius was quite genuine, dating from the time of a common struggle against the common enemy. Such friendship outlasts everything.

Shortly after 9 o'clock, as arranged, Isi was sitting in the breakfast room when I joined him at his table, having taken rather a long time to pack my case. I was astonished to see that his lower left arm was in a plaster cast. He noticed my consternation and stole a quick look in the direction of the only other occupied table, where a grey-haired lady sat, drinking her morning coffee. Having ascertained that nobody was listening, he whispered: 'It's not as bad as it looks.'

He raised the arm a little awkwardly: 'Sit down; the waiter will bring breakfast immediately; we haven't a lot of time. The train won't wait.'

I just did not understand. The previous evening we had gone upstairs together to our rooms and both his arms had been perfectly all right then.

'For God's sake don't make a scene. Take this and read it, and look as casual as possible', he said, pushing a unmarked green folder towards me. It's uncanny, the contacts the man has, I thought, as I opened it and began to read a dossier of the Romanian secret service.

A copy of everything worth noting in that folder was under his plaster cast. The documents showed that the Secret Intelligence Service had reorganized the oil protection organization it had operated for years, and was about to turn it into an outfit for destroying the oil wells. To judge by everything in the dossier, which had been assembled by someone who had just swept the papers together, the Romanians were standing by with arms folded, as if the whole matter had nothing to do with them. They were not going to lift a finger to prevent the oil wells being destroyed. They had collected everything their agents had learned in that file—and did nothing with it. Not until later, as a result of German initiative, and pressure, did things change; but by then I was over the hills and far away, and it was no concern of mine.

I might as well have saved myself the money I paid Gentleman Urluzianu.

The folder also contained reports on the possibility of an eventual Soviet invasion of Bessarabia, but without anything like the details obtained by Isidor from the Russian fisherman. Another report said that one member of the Government was negotiating for the arms through his Italian contacts—for the time being mostly about the amount of Bakshish he would get. There were Hungarian and Bulgarian intelligence reports about preparations by German transport units on the Danube and on the railways. There was also a lot of trivial informers' gossip.

The SIS Special Branch D wanted to blow up the refineries at Ploesti in the near future. This information was highly important because it came from the British Legation, where there must have been a leak planted by the Siguranza, the benefit of which Isidor reaped to the full. But there was nothing in the folder about the barges in the Danube delta everybody had heard about. So we were still in the dark on that score. Perhaps there was nothing in it.

Isidor later told me what had happened during the previous night. Apparently, after I had gone to my room, his contact had arrived with the file. After an agreed interval it was to be fetched back again. Isidor studied the documents thoroughly and copied down essential facts, and then rang an old friend who was a doctor. Isi went to him with the notes he had made, which were to be buried in the bandage with a bit of dry plaster, gauze, cottonwool and a couple of splints. To complete the handiwork, Isi took an indelible pencil and on the upper side wrote a fictitious date, indicating that he had broken his arm some days earlier. Then he had rubbed a little ash and dust over the cast as a finishing touch, to make it look a bit used.

As we were preparing to leave the hotel in Bucharest, Isi showed his cool cheek by putting the folder in an ordinary envelope and giving it to the porter for collection by his contact, who would fetch it. We got a taxi and drove to the station to catch the Orient Express for Istanbul.

Chapter 9

Interlude in Egypt

I was told to collect new orders in Istanbul at the Beyoglu Central Post Ofice. The letter I collected contained some harmless generalities, from an old friend in Budapest who did not exist. After the proper treatment, the secret message appeared and Isi and I read my orders together. I was to proceed via Palestine to Cairo, where I was to contact someone whom the Berlin officials wanted me to meet.

Apart from this information there was also a mighty rocket in the letter about my having gone to Sofia on my own initiative and not having reported it until I had got to Bucharest. There was not a word in the letter about Isi, so I took the rebuke as just more evidence of the fact that headquarters did not know that we had been to Romania together; nor did they know anything of Jovan Elmas, who had been waiting for us for the past two days in Istanbul at the Hotel Bulgaria.

In this letter my superiors grumbled about my shuttling between Sofia and Bucharest because they could not make head or tail of it. They wanted to know what I was up to, anyway; and wouldn't I be better engaged attending to my duties instead of chasing skirts? Well, I thought, you have a point there to some extent—but only to some extent! About my report concerning the loading of the explosives and other things, they spared only a few grudging words, as if the whole business was water under the bridge. Just routine . . .

'Good bunch of chaps, but a trifle cantankerous', said Isidor presently. 'Let's go to the bar and have a drink to welcome Handsome Jovan, because from here on I formally hand him over to you.'

Jovan and I were to go on to Cairo where I had to make contact with Abas Hallim.

The day we were due to leave for Palestine Jovan explained to me in a casual manner that his false passport, which had been given to him by

Isidor, had gone down the loo and that he was now using his real one, in which there was already a transit visa for Palestine. It came naturally to him to mention important things in a casual manner.

Before giving me a transit visa for Palestine, the British Consulate in Istanbul had demanded that I state my exact route. They had become a great deal more cautious, even regarding an Egyptian who was only returning home.

As we were leaving the airport building, there was a small incident. A fat and desperate-looking little man had tried to come along with us. He stood imploringly at the counter near the exit and kept repeating the same story over and over in a plaintive voice. For weeks now he had been on the run through Europe and had at last arrived here safe and sound, and now they were trying to send him back again. He simply had to make it to Palestine—and wouldn't someone please take pity on him and give up his seat? After all, there would be another flight in a few days' time. The Turkish emigration official had stopped taking any notice of him at all and looked as if he simply didn't hear him.

The plane leapt forward over the tarmac at Florya Airport. We were gathering speed; now the land was dropping away as we gained height. Our route was over Yesiköye. Turkey had had to cede a great tract of land to Bulgaria at the Treaty of San Stefano. To the left, lay Bakiköy, white under the sun, where many a Roman Emperor had camped with his troops in preparation for battle or for a victory parade in Constantinople.

The plane was full. In front of me, to the right, sat two Egyptians whom I had seen somewhere before, but I could not remember where. I was disinclined to meet anyone I had once known; but, in true Oriental fashion, they were so busy with their own affairs that neither of them took any notice of the other passengers.

Jovan had closed his eyes. His face was a sickly green. 'I hate this flying business', he had said, as we walked across the runway to the plane.

'Do you know Antonio Pulli Bey?' asked Jovan later, breaking into my thoughts.

'No, but I do know that he used to be intriguer-in-chief at the Abdin Palace and was then promoted procurer to His Majesty.'

It turned out that Jovan knew Pulli very well and thought that we would find him 'useful'. Pulli had Faruk's ear and his official title was Private Secretary. I was not keen about the idea of working with someone who was not noted for his discretion or honesty, and I disliked the idea of having to pay Pulli.

'You know how the saying goes', Jovan said. 'Only death is for free. We'll have to discuss the money side of our collaboration.'

'Please, no. Not here in this kite!'

'OK. We'll leave it for later', he remarked drily. 'But I shan't forget.' And he stared indifferently out of the window.

Against my better judgement, Jovan persisted in discussing the prospects of Pulli's working for us. I was able to shut him up, however, after he had told me that Pulli was working for the Italians.

As we were landing in Palestine, I steered the conversation on to innocuous subjects. The plane came to a stop at the end of the runway and the gangway was pushed up to the door. We walked a few yards to the airport building and the two exits marked 'British' and 'Non-British'. Jovan and I made for the Non-British exit, where most of the passengers had already gathered.

'Good-afternoon, sir', said the Defence Security officer, who stood at a barrier behind the Passport Control officers, inviting me quite unmistakably to hand him my papers. I stepped out of the line and went up to the barrier and gave him my passport, watching him suspiciously. Why pick on me for the dubious honour of out-of-turn service? He leafed about in the passport for a long time, looking interested, but made no move to return it to me.

'What's wrong with my passport?'

'Sorry, sir. Where do you propose to spend the night?'

'At the King David Hotel. And tomorrow I am going on by train to Cairo via El-Kantar. That's where I live.'

For a few seconds I had the feeling in my stomach one always gets whenever one crosses a frontier, even when one's conscience is perfectly clear.

'They were only doing a spot-check', Jovan later explained. 'They flipped through my passport quite cursorily.'

'You were lucky—it could have led to some questions. Now you can sleep in peace and that phoney King of yours won't have to bail you out. I'm sure he would have found it most inconvenient.'

The King David had not changed since my last visit. As always there were British officers in the lobby. Everything, or nearly everything, was still as it had been in peacetime. It would be some time yet, almost a year, before the Italian Army reached Sollum and then Sidi Barrani. The Italians were to remain on Egyptian soil for only a short while, until General O'Connor and his Western Desert Forces drove them back to El-Agheila, annihilating ten divisions and taking thousands of prisoners in the process.

The officers of the Arab Legion were drinking their whiskies at the bar of the hotel, enjoying a few days' leave before crossing the Jordan again to patrol the desert. The horrid old war had not yet elbowed its way into this place. The British were still riding about like Bedouin knights in their cross-country vehicles, some of them sporting the Arab burnous and riding fast meharis. The Legion was an élite corps, which had been started with a handful of Bedouins and fashioned at that time by the British into the most formidable fighting unit of the Arabian Peninsula.

Her name was Roberta. Of course, she had been to bed with the Albanian Casanova. The evening before, we had travelled from Qantara to Alex via Cairo. Jovan had made the arrangement by telephone, and we were supposed to meet her in one of the many cafés on the Yacht Club Promenade by the East Harbour, in Alexandria.

The city was entirely preoccupied with its own affairs. The prosperous men of the city would sit the whole day long together with other drones on the terraces of the cafés and clubs, watching the beautiful girls go by. Money and women, that's what life is about in this Mediterranean city. Virtue and vice go quite naturally hand in hand; it does not seem to bother anyone.

I was waiting with some excitement for the little number who would be coming along. To tell the truth, I thought this would be just another affair with some pretty young thing who needed money, or with some slightly shopworn, heavily made-up wife of a stinking rich pasha, who would want a little dirty adventure to amuse her for a few days.

I did not want to offend Jovan, so I had agreed to go along like a well-brought-up little boy, to kiss her hand, and take my leave a few days later.

I did not know Handsome Jovan well enough.

He sat, with the air of the regular customer, immersed in his *Messagero Egiziano*, and spoke not one word. He did not even bother to look up when an open coffin, covered only with a silken shroud and followed by keening women, screaming and howling, went past the terrace. The coffin wobbled precariously on the shoulders of its bearers, who were walking fast, because a nearby policeman was urging them on. The use of the elegant Corniche by funeral processions was frowned upon—even for a man who had been of some consequence in the life of Alexandria. A fez had been placed at one end of the coffin, as if the deceased were likely to put it on at some future time. The procession was preceded by three ulemas reciting verses from the Koran and two blind men with sticks singing in the deepest of base voices: 'Illaha illah illalah Mohammed and Mustafa . . .' Jovan was totally preoccupied with his newspaper.

If there is such a thing as an outstandingly beautiful woman, then Roberta could be considered to be one. No sooner had the funeral procession passed than I saw her stepping from one of those horse-drawn carriages of which there are so many in Alexandria. Perhaps she was a shade too tall, but, apart from that, she had a pair of well-turned legs, long hair the colour of ripe corn, very white skin and eyes—those magnificent eyes of hers—of violet.

Her clothes were quiet in style, yet almost distinguished. She wore just a touch of make-up; there was nothing common about her. She was a stunner; and there was something indescribably sensual about her mouth. As she stood there before us, I thought, All the men in Alexandria must have swarmed about her, like bees round a honeypot.

Jovan dropped the newspaper, and, in a trice, he was wide awake. There she was, standing and smiling. How could such a lady's man be knocked all of a heap like that?

Behind her on the wide pavement all Alexandria was promenading. Tipsy sailors, Arab fishermen, a Coptic priest, whores with provocative behinds. A vendor of syrups was clashing a small pair of brass cymbals together to summon his customers. There was a sheikh, Nubians wearing snow-white turbans, and tawny-skinned Bedouins with noses like hawks. Black-veiled Egyptian women, walking very close together, slipped nervously past the café terraces in case anyone should see their faces. There were Greeks, Armenians and Maltese, and whatever else the Levant had to offer by way of races. There were laden camels setting their soft hooves gingerly on the street, and looking down on the people about them, very much *de haut en bas*. It was, in other words, just another Egyptian day.

After the usual introductions and a few mumbled platitudes, Jovan let the cat out of the bag by explaining my presence to Roberta. His small talk had some semblance of meaning only because she was completely infatuated with him—and he knew it. I found it hard to suppress a grin at the sight of her feminine subjugation.

Having been told that she could have full confidence in me—a complete stranger until a few minutes ago—she began quite unrestrainedly to relate the sort of gossip going around in the country, and bored me to death. But there were some details that made me prick up my ears.

It was through her that Jovan had secured the connection with Antonio Pulli, the vilest creature in Egypt. Thanks to Pulli's special gift—genius, indeed—for intrigue, he had been elevated to the rank of Bey, much to the horror of the holders of that august title in Egypt.

Faruk, once such a likeable figure, had developed into a sexual monster, and required a daily supply of women on an absolutely monstrous scale. To satisfy this lust Antonio controlled a host of pimps whose job it was to supply the King with five or six women a day. The confidential secretary seemed to have no trouble at all providing this extraordinary quantity of merchandise; and, because the nature of his services gave him the ear of his Prince, quite fabulous opportunities were open to him.

The Servicio Internazionale Militare had tried to tap Pulli as a source of intelligence, putting it to him that in view of his Italian origins he should show himself loyal to his country. But he was far too clever not to realize that this could turn out to be a dangerous trap, since the Egyptian Secret Intelligence Service, far from being asleep on the job, was having him shadowed. He declined the offer. The field was therefore wide open for Jovan.

Pulli, fond of playing with fire but unwilling to approach it too closely, had struck up an association with Jovan following a sudden discovery by both of them of a 'cordial' inclination for one another's company. Naturally Roberta had played a part in this game. Jovan had received information from Pulli, and Isidor Klatt had paid him handsomely for it.

Roberta had also kept the King company in bed, but as the King had become so fond of variety, she was no longer asked to the Palace. She had been clever enough, however, to keep in touch with the *souteneur*. Evidently she was a bright girl—and perhaps the only one, since the others quickly vanished into obscurity and never dared mention that they had obliged the King, lest it prove unhealthy for them.

That evening, when I had finished my bath and was getting dressed, Jovan telephoned and asked me to come along to one of the night-spots on the Corniche. 'Pulli wants to see you, so hurry up!'

At first I was surprised that the business should have gone so quickly, but then I reflected that Casanova was always short of money, and realized that this was why he had fixed up the meeting so promptly. I did not want them to think I was in a hurry. Pulli, whose ill-disguised greed and ambition were quite obscene, was someone I did not normally want to be seen with. But he undoubtedly could be useful, and his behaviour was not that much worse than the blood hunger in Iraq. As I walked past the Abu Abas Mosque and out into the Corniche, it occurred to me that the war would one day creep across the sea, and that it would be a good thing to know something about the harbour defences.

If this pimp could supply me with such details as the number and locations of submarine nets, the entrance to the great harbour basin, what time the harbour boom opened and the strength of AA and coastal batteries already installed, or even details of the fortifications, it would be well worth coughing up some money.

Pulli seemed delighted as he shook my hand and we sat down at a table, which he was quick to explain was the King's. He giggled heartily as if he had just told an exquisite joke.

Then he told me what I already knew, that his insatiable employer kept a table permanently reserved in all the best hotels, restaurants, cabarets and nightclubs in Cairo and Alex. Since he could not be everywhere at once, but was likely to turn up at any moment, most of the tables were kept empty at all times.

'I keep a few men busy running around checking on the night-spots to see that the tables in fact remain reserved', Pulli said proudly.

'And should His Majesty happen not to be visiting various places of entertainment in your company, your friends can enjoy the privilege of sitting at a table like this one?'

'I enjoy the full confidence of the King. He knows that I occasionally allow close friends this privilege.'

Big deal, I thought.

Jovan and Roberta seemed so wrapped up in one another and heedless of all else that I was able to put my needs to Pulli, who by now was making me feel quite sick. It seemed, however, that his feelings for me were the very opposite of mine for him.

'Would you like to go for a little stroll between the Arsenal, the Gare Maritime and the South Pier? Nobody will stop us, since no one but the King gives me orders. There are some warships tied up there. They may be of interest to you.'

We went out for our little stroll. Jovan and Roberta stayed behind.

Next morning, as soon as I had dressed, I made a sketch of what I had seen in the course of my walk with Pulli. That done, I packed my case and went to catch the train to Cairo, where I had an appointment.

Jovan seemed to be a good catch. Naturally I had to see how things would progress, but for the moment I was satisfied. Once again Isidor had given me proof of his friendship.

I knew very well that money would play a large part in this affair. It was always the same old story. The gentlemen in Berlin were pretty mean with the stuff, while complaining that information was not reaching them in a steady stream. They obviously believed the whole world was just longing to swing into action on their behalf without being paid for it. Perhaps they even imagined that one of these days lines of applicants would appear on the Tirpitzufer. They seemed to imagine that Jovan and this Pulli, on neither of whom were there any flies, could not tell the difference between good and bad intelligence material, and its worth!

I arrived in Cairo shortly before 6 o'clock. I had some time to spare, so I went to drink a cup of coffee opposite the house in the Shariah Fuad el-Awel.

A good thing I did! None of my instincts had given me warning; I had no premonition whatever, and simply felt like a cup of coffee.

There was a man walking up and down in front of the house opposite. For a moment I could not recall his face, although I knew I had seen him before. But where? No matter how I racked my brain, I could not place him. As I got up, I saw that he was about to cross the street. He waited for a car to pass, stepped off the pavement on to the roadway—and then I knew who he was.

His name came to me at the same moment. It was Salah, whom I had seen with Zulfikar when I was getting ready for the meeting with Rohde in Athens in July 1937. It all came back to me clearly now. It was not particularly convenient to be meeting him, but I could hardly avoid it, since he was standing right in front of me.

'A good thing I saw you here, Hussein. You are going to see Botros, aren't you? Don't go upstairs.'

How did he know where I was going?

'Who told you I was going to see him?'

Salah pulled a scrap of paper from his pocket on which Botros had written that I should keep away from his flat since he was being watched.

'It's the people from the Midan Sheikh Yussuf', he said, walking alongside me down the street.

I knew this was the address of the office from which a watch was kept on students hostile to England. Only later did it become the HQ of the Field Security Service in Cairo. The two outfits were of course one and the same thing, but at this time it had a different name.

Just in case, Botros had arranged that whenever the heat was on, a towel would be hanging on the rail of the balcony at the back of the house. Everyone who was in on the secret would first go round the back of the building to see if the coast was clear.

The Sudanese gatekeeper was a member of the Moslem Brotherhood and therefore reliable. He saw to it that messages reached their destination. Botros had given him the note and he in turn had passed it on to Salah, who had thereupon started patrolling the street, waiting for me to turn up. So my journey to Cairo had been a waste of time. About a quarter of an hour later I sauntered into a restaurant to have a meal in peace before catching the evening train back to Alex.

The next day was Friday, when Egypt's long weekend began: Friday for the Moslems, Saturday for the Jews and Sunday for the Christians. Each day was sacred to one of the religious communities, who saw to it that their commandments were strictly observed.

As soon as I got to the railway station at Alex, I rang up Jovan, because I was anxious to meet Pulli again, as he might be able to give me some information on the surveillance of members of the Moslem Brotherhood. It was Roberta who answered the 'phone. Well, how about that, I thought—she was living with him already!

'Where is Jovan?'

'With his ex-King.'

We made a date. I thought I might try her out a bit.

I drove out to our family house, which at this time of the year was occupied only by the gardener and two domestics, who looked after the garden and the house respectively. Towards noon I had a shower, looked out a light blue shirt of the type that was then fashionable, plumped for a charcoal grey suit and a favourite club tie of mine and rang for a taxi to take me to the café where I was to meet her.

I did not have to wait. She was already sitting at a table in the sun. It was a perfect day, the sea was as calm as a millpond, a few seagulls were running about on the beach. For once there was hardly any noise.

I said in a voice meant to be complimentary: 'There is no doubt that Jovan is head-over-heels in love with you; and he must have been for some time now.' I sat down opposite her at the table.

'I know', she said, watching the effect of her words.

'Could you reach Pulli Bey for me?' I said, hating myself for calling him 'Bey'.

'Yes, I suppose so.'

'Then be a darling and try to arrange a meeting. I should like to ask him something.'

She stood up and went inside the café.

When she came back she said: 'We have an hour. He too would like to have a word with you; it came quite handy, my calling him.'

She then proceeded in that hour to tell me that she came from Reggio di Calabria in Italy, towards the toe of the boot, where she was born. One day, when she was twenty, she ran away from home to Naples—straight into the arms of a thoroughly bad chap. Wasting no time, he had immediately tried to ship her off to a brothel somewhere in the East. She had run away from him in Alexandria, and that was how she had got to Pulli. The rest I knew. There were many like her—it was out of the frying pan into the fire—but she had learnt how to stand on her own feet.

Then Pulli turned up in an immense Minerva. I knew the car—there were not many like it in Egypt. One of my mad cousins had one. First came a few yards of bonnet and then the driver, practically invisible somewhere inside. It was a sports job, of course—nothing but the best!

'I hope *you* don't drive around the neighbourhood in this ponce's chariot', she said, as Pulli was parking it ostentatiously smack in front of the café. Then she moved her wicker chair to one side to give Pulli room to come through to our table.

'No, *mes enfants*, we'll go right to the back of the place, to the reserved table over there. Nobody will bother us there. *Allons-y.*'

That man might be almost tolerable if he would stop showing off so much.

Roberta and I followed him. Our entrance was accompanied by bowing and scraping as the mighty Confidential Secretary proceeded through the establishment. Then Pulli seated himself, Roberta and me, and from his jacket pocket proceeded to pull out some papers. One of them was a list of detailed answers to all the questions I had asked him about the harbour fortifications.

I could hardly believe my eyes. But with disbelief came doubt. He could not be doing this for the sake of money or my blue eyes. He too wanted something.

'Presently, *cher ami*, you will go with this *bella ragazza* to the jewellers. And since she is such a lovely creature, only the best jeweller in town is good enough. You know the one I mean. There you will buy her that great big pearl necklace in the window—she has been longing to have it for some time. After that, we'll never talk of this list again. OK?'

She threw her arms around his neck. What a loathsome little man, he was! When a crook has a heart, it's as big as a barn door.

She got her necklace—and then she threw her arms around *my* neck. 'Ciao!' she said and was gone through the swinging doors that led out to the rue de France. She was going to show off her triple strand of pearls and make the fat bejewelled ladies of Cairo society puce with envy.

There remained only the settlement of accounts with Jovan. I was square with Pulli, but Jovan had to be considered. As the intermediary he was entitled to some money. Next morning he came to the station with me. I was returning to Qantara.

'Everything OK?' I asked.

Handsome Jovan smiled: 'When you see Isidor, tell him from me he is all right.'

We walked along the platform. The train was due to move off in a moment. I dislike railway stations; there is something depressing about them, something that goes against the grain.

Jovan was by my side, head bent slightly forward, as if lost in thought. Then he took my arm, looked at me and said in a bantering tone: 'If I should come unstuck one of these days because of what I am doing and end up facing a firing squad, I hope someone realises they've made money out of me. Just think of the profit made on the twelve bullets it will take to kill me: 72 pfennigs!'

'You can't even buy a whisky for that.'

The time had come for me to get into my carriage.

'What's the matter, Jovan—why the macabre gags?'

'Oh, everyone has thoughts like this sometimes. There's nothing to them. I suppose it's saying goodbye, not knowing if we shall ever see one another again, old boy. *Bon voyage*! And keep your pecker up!'

Alas, Jovan was not fated to die by the bullet! His own countrymen butchered him in the most revolting manner. It is a good thing no man can know what his last hours will be like.

Chapter 10

The Pan-Arab Dream

It had all begun in Ankara on 6 August 1940, when Osman Kemal Haddad, private secretary to that master of intrigue, the Grand Mufti, was introduced to Herr von Papen, the German Ambassador. The Iraqi Ambassador in Ankara who made the introduction was the brother of Rashid Ali el-Ghailani, the Prime Minister in Baghdad, who was pro-German.

Haddad informed von Papen about the situation in Iraq as follows. Italy had already given the Iraqi Government an assurance supporting the independence of all mandated Arab countries or those ranking as protectorates, and Iraq wanted a similar declaration from Germany so that she might on that basis revive diplomatic relations with Berlin. Nuri Said was to be removed from the Iraqi cabinet and a revolt was to be organized in Palestine from Syrian territory that should be of definite help to the Axis in the fight against Britain. Haddad assured von Papen that the Iraqi army was in real control of the country and that there was an agreement with Ibn Saud on the question of Palestine independence. The strength of Iraq's army and the problem of Arab unity were the subjects of further discussions. Anglo-Iraqi relations had been growing strained since Iraq had refused permission for British troops to pass through the country on the way from India.

Haddad did not always stick to the truth, because he needed German backing and saw no reason not to use anything that would do to gain his ends. In August and September Haddad had a number of talks in Berlin, and presented himself as the ambassador of the Arab world, informing the Germans that a coordinating committee existed in Iraq of all the Arab countries under the leadership of the Grand Mufti. The committee, Haddad said, wanted an Axis declaration in support of the Arab national demands. In return for such a declaration Haddad promised to renew diplomatic relations with Germany and to conclude an agreement with both Italy and Germany for the exploitation of Iraq's natural resources—particularly oil.

At about the same time as Haddad was meeting with von Papen I was in Istanbul, on the terrace of the Pera Palace Hotel. An Oriental beauty I had got stuck with from the previous evening, and who was now looking rather more crumpled than beautiful, was with me, and we were watching the sunset. While struggling to think of some way I could ditch the doe-eyed little darling, I noticed a man sitting at a nearby table signal that he wanted me to meet him in the men's toilet. I then recognized him as another Abwehr agent, and made my way to that place, where the gushing water provided us with an acoustic backdrop. As we faced the wall, he explained that the head of the KO (Abwehr office) for Turkey wanted to see me immediately.

So I was provided with a perfect excuse for leaving that little lovely waiting for me outside, and I might get away from the restless city of the Bosporus. The girl would sit there for a while, pouting and sulking about the ways of men, and then she would get up and leave the hotel terrace.

I pressed a banknote into the waiter's hand, disappeared through a side door, and two hours later was sitting in my seat on the night train to Ankara. It was not the first time I would visit the 'German village', as the Turks called the German Embassy. I tried to stiffle my feelings of unease, perhaps brought on because of what I knew about von Papen when he had been Military Attaché (in other words Intelligence Officer) in Washington in the years preceding World War I.

When he had left the States, after being expelled for espionage, he had ended up in front of British Immigration Officers in Falmouth, who examined his luggage while he stood by incredulous that they should dare remove from his case the German Embassy code book and several top secret documents, as well as the addresses of his agents in America. Herr von Papen had not been able to bring himself to burn everything before leaving Washington, and as a result 126 German agents in the United States were rounded up with the greatest ease.

That experience should have taught any normal man a lesson. Not so the Great Wizard. Shortly afterwards he was in Palestine, acting as Liaison Oficer with the Turks, when the British took control of

Jerusalem. Von Papen ran for it, and, because the suitcase was too heavy for his aristocratic arms, he left it behind. The British army officers, who were particularly inquisitive when it came to intelligence agents, found in that case the documents they had not managed to remove from von Papen's belongings at Falmouth!

I wanted to avoid if possible meeting the Great Wizard.

I dozed away the next few hours, dog-tired, having to sleep as best I could sitting up in the train compartment. Once in Ankara I went immediately to the 'German village' to meet Aladin, the man who had asked me to come from Istanbul. He was one of the cleverest Abwehr agents, and the cover name Aladin fitted him perfectly. I can still remember opening the door, and seeing him sitting in the deep armchair by the side of his cluttered desk in his pleasantly furnished office in one of the Embassy buildings.

He had a twinkle in his eye as he shook hands with me and said, 'So Assisa let you take the first available train without making a fuss. Is that how you managed to be here so soon?'

'I see; the chap who brought me your message has been telling tales out of school, has he?' I said. I was as angry as hell, and swore I'd fix that bastard when I returned to Istanbul.

But Aladin set things right, explaining that, because he had wanted to see me, he had had to find the surest and safest means. In the end it was quite simple. He admired my taste in hotels, cafés and women, so he had instructed the contact to seek me out at the Palace, and the rest had been easy. Then he dismissed the matter and suggested that we went for a run in his car, as he wanted to talk in private. As we were driving towards Chankaya, Aladin reminded me about the necessity for caution in our profession, where no one trusted anyone else—a reminder I had so often repeated to myself. He stopped the car by the side of the road, lit a cigarette and looked out at the view. We would discuss everything we had to in the car before I was to return to the small hotel in the Yenisehir district in Ankara and wait for Aladin to contact me again with all details regarding the new mission.

Then he explained that just a few days previously a certain Osman Kemal Haddad, the Grand Mufti's secretary, had been introduced to von Papen by the Iraqi Ambassador, and had made proposals to the Ambassador about a possible *coup* in Iraq. I replied that I knew Haddad, and that in my opinion Husseini, the Grand Mufti, had a finger in far too many pies in far too many places.

Aladin said that Haddad was very keen to go to Germany to negotiate, and that the German Embassy had issued him with a passport in the name of Max Müller. He was at that moment on his way through the Balkans, and should be in Germany by the next day.

When I warned him that Haddad looked like no Max Müller I had ever seen, and that he would never get through any British passport control with the assumed name and passport, I asked who had thought up the crazy idea. Aladin explained that certain people were keen for him to make the journey, and that Haddad wanted to talk to someone from the Reich Foreign Office in Berlin whom he had known from earlier days in Iraq. As for my mission, Aladin said that I was to go to Iraq and bring back any information that could be of interest; to find out what was going on and look into the situation in general. The Abwehr wanted to know about the people who were preparing this *putsch*, what the British stand was, and about the relative power positions—in fact everything. Politicians might play their little games, but we could do nothing with only vague promises to go on. That was the way to get rapped over the knuckles, which could be most unpleasant. 'I want you to go because you already know many useful people there', he said. 'You still have your transmitter—so Leverkeuhn told me. Any micro pictures can be sent via Hélou. He is safe. Frequencies are your business. I should imagine you'll keep your old ones since they weren't traced during your last mission.'

'Code? The same rubbish as last time will do: Wensinck's *The Muslim Creed*. I have two copies left. I'll send one to Berlin with the next courier.'

I took the book from him and leafed through it.

'Let's agree, Aladin. Page 4, skip a page a day, and always take the second paragraph. That book's thick enough to last us for the whole mission. It's the old key: "Donauschiffahrtskapitaene (Danube Navigation Skippers)". Let the radio operator know that he'll have to be patient. He mustn't switch off for the first few days but stay switched to "receive". I can't guarantee that I'll be able to send something on the very first day. It's a hell of a bore, but he won't be wasting his time. Anyway, he'll be sitting pretty. He can afford to wait.

'I shall cross the frontier openly, using my Egyptian passport. It's the best way for me to get through passport control. I've got an exit stamp in the passport and a Turkish visa valid for a few more weeks. That will tell the immigration officials that I have been to Turkey.'

'Now, about money', said Aladin. 'I'll bring you some to your hotel this afternoon.'

He pressed the starter and turned the car back towards the town. We moved off.

'Don't forget to bring me a few diamonds, just in case', I said, while we were driving towards Ankara.

I had booked into a small, quiet hotel where I had stayed several times before. It was in Yenisehir, known as the *Quartier Résidentiel*, at the foot of the hill on which the old city stood. Aladin knew the place because we had hatched a previous mission there.

The hotel porter was a cheerful fellow. There was something about the way he accepted his tips that told you that, provided it was big enough, he would not be interested in seeing your passport—this despite the fact that the Turkish Police enforced the regulations with exceptional severity. These regulations specified that the name, nationality and the genuine identity of the holder of the passport must all be in order, down to the smallest detail. Doubtless the porter had a brother, or even a son, well placed in the police station. In Turkey anybody who can possibly manage it makes sure that he keeps on the friendly side of any of his relations in the police force or in government, and that enables him to drive a coach and horses through any ordinance. Every hotel guest who gave a large enough tip would be addressed as Bey, whereas the uninitiated would be in for a hard time.

Aladin turned up shortly after 6 o'clock. He had parked his car away from the street so that it would not be spotted—there were any number of 10-piastre agents keeping an eye on the 'German village' for the British. The Secret Intelligence Service was bound to know who Aladin was—it could have been no secret to them—which was why he was a little late arriving, having made a few detours through various side streets before reaching the hotel.

He made his excuses: 'Moreover, I have had some news from Nadim Hélou, via Mahamat Gülay in Adana. It came in just as I was about to leave. One of his contacts, who works with the Kurds up in Dihok, has spotted an agent who is not one of ours but nevertheless seems to work for someone else in Germany. I cannot tell you any more; Hélou wants to keep any further details back until you are with him. Perhaps he is being careful. You know he is very cautious, and I can only approve of that. He knows you are coming. Gülay has warned him through the usual channels. I take it he'll be able to tell you more when you join him in Adana tomorrow.'

'That could only be a man from the Amt VI (Office No 6). They've always been interested in the Kurds. Somewhere in Berlin I bet there's a student of Kurdish affairs who's stuffing their heads full of all sorts of nonsense. They take it all in avidly and see themselves already standing at the foot of the Kurdish mountains grabbing the valleys of the Euphrates and the Tigris by a *coup de main*. Well, he's no friend of mine; I don't want to see him!'

'The word for that sort of thing in Berlin is "wild" (or freelance) espionage', Aladin remarked. 'That's because the SD and ourselves are at daggers drawn. I must say it's idiocy to have two intelligence services working at cross-purposes in one's own country, though there's nothing else for it—both sides are jealous of one another, instead of working together! There is no need for two parallel secret services.'

'I agree. When I am there, I'll give instructions to my agents to chase him over the mountains into Persia. But if he should be stubborn, I won't wait to make him harmless.'

Since I had to get going, I repeated my instructions that the radio operator at Stahnsdort was to start monitoring me on 25 August and was to hang on indefinitely until he heard me. I then saw Aladin to the door.

I left the hotel after dark. Without haste, I disappeared down the first side street, and then took another turning a few steps further on. Since I knew the neighbourhood, I knew how to get to the railway station unobserved. The porter had sent my case ahead in the afternoon. Until departure time I hung about in the poor light under some of the few stunted trees near the entrance to the station. When I heard the train pulling in, I turned up the collar of my raincoat, retrieved my valise and went, shivering, quickly to the platform. The moment the train came to a halt I disappeared into the first carriage. I was certain those blasted 10-piastre agents were hanging about here too, and I did not want to be seen.

A group of policemen walked past the window of my carriage, laughing and chatting. When the departure bell was rung, the engine whistle blew and a cloud of smoke drifted past the window; there was the clanging of buffers and linkages, and slowly the wheels began to judder.

There were unscheduled stops at stations in the middle of nowhere, so that it was dark when the train pulled in at Adana in the south-eastern corner of Turkey. Exhausted after a journey that had seemed unending, I took one of the ramshackle taxis that stood in front of the station and had myself driven to Mahamat Gülay's. He lived next door to his grain business, and the moment you entered the house you could smell the strong scent emanating from his sheds. A servant showed me to the comfortable Oriental parlour common to every middle-class household.

Aladin had sent word that I would be arriving, and Mahamat, despite the fact that he was a very shy and retiring man, greeted me effusively. We had met twice before, so there was no particular need for precautions.

Mahamat had close business relations with my contact man Hélou in Beirut. They must have been doing good business, because as time went on they both seemed to be amassing sizeable fortunes. Since my last visit Mahamat had refurnished his sitting room, and he was wearing a valuable ring I had not noticed before. It must have been a very profitable business being a contact man, especially when one had such a first-class cover.

He and Hélou, during their occasional visits, had worked out an impenetrable code, which had something to do with their trade. This enabled them to exchange news unobtrusively. They called me Barley. I found it funny, and it suggested to me that Rohde, who had recruited Mahamat, had given him a first-class lesson about cover names. There is no more elementary mistake than to use names that bear any resemblance to the real one. Mahamat had decided to use one which had a completely different sound and which moreover was frequently used in their business. I was only surprised that there was no confusion between the two men in the process, since they did deal in grain, and barley must have figured frequently in their correspondence. Still this was not my worry.

Mahamat told me that he had cabled Hélou, who would accordingly be waiting for me five days hence in Homs.

Mahamat was a careful man, and had therefore prepared a room for me so as to avoid carelessly drawing the attention of the extremely suspicious Turkish Police. In addition he had let it be known among his customers and acquaintances that an Egyptian businessman occasionally visited him and sometimes stayed one or two days or longer. In this way my appearance attracted no particular notice.

Aladin had told me nothing of all this. Perhaps he knew nothing about it. Although very talkative, Levantines are good at keeping secrets, especially if their safety and livelihood are at stake.

'Hélou has a surprise for you', Mahamat said as we went into the dining room. There laid out was a table groaning under the weight of delicious Turkish dishes, for pure Turkish cooking can be delicious.

'A princely repast, Mahamat!' I said, determined to have as little as possible. It was getting to be too much of a good thing. But Mahamat was equally determined to do the thing in style. He knew what he owed to his own standing as a merchant respected in the town.

'It's nothing—a trifle!' he said, fishing for more praise in true Oriental fashion.

We were sitting in the parlour, drinking coffee and smoking a nargileh prepared by the servant, when Mahamat told me that the German, and a companion who appeared to be Assyrian, who had turned up at Dihok, were trying to get in touch with the local Sheikh, Djafar. The Sheikh had immediately sent one of his people to Mosul to report to our contact man there. Djafar had kept the German in Dihok and he was still sitting in the desolate mountains of South Kurdistan.

The unnamed German had apparently made the mistake of telling some tale about an Egyptian he was supposed to meet there—that had immediately made them suspicious. The second mistake he had made (in the presence of his friends) had been to mention my cover from last year. Apparently he did not know the new one Hélou had sent just as I was leaving Ankara. As a result, Djafar raised the alarm with Hélou. One Kurd had been sent as far as Deir ez-Zor, to Prince Ramsis. Kurds crossed frontiers the way other people crossed the thresholds of restaurants. So our bird was still sitting there. Hélou was to give me more details. He wanted to have a word before he led the man into a trap. He did not fool around; he was far too careful. And no wonder—he had everything to lose.

I was sure that neither Hélou nor Ramsis would run any unnecessary risks. It was also quite certain that our man was a German. But these details were none of Mahamat's business. His only job was to maintain contact and to forward written messages. It was for these services that he was paid. He seemed to expect me to say more, because he realized that I knew more. But I had to disappoint him.

Twenty-four hours later I went on to Meidan Ekbes across the

Syrian border. Borders were beginning to be nothing to me.

The centuries-old, if not always harmonious, connection between Arab and Turk finally came to an end in 1920. It coincided with the upsurge of the Arab nationalist awakening in Turkey.

Intellectuals, army officers, and occasionally the British had made use of this nationalism, strictly out of their own political motives. The British did it by artificially manufacturing a sort of nationalism at a considerable cost in money. The people themselves were aroused through well-paid agitators and agents like T. E. Lawrence, calling on them to fight for their national freedom. In World War I they pressed a gun in the hand of every Bedouin, only to receive shots from these guns eventually.

Basically the Arab does not understand nationalism. There has been no such thing in his entire history. Generally speaking, the concept of the Arab world means those countries where the mother tongue of the population is exclusively or overwhelmingly Arabic. The Arabs do not make up a nation. It is Islam that binds them together—more or less.

However, for centuries there have been numerous secret societies, and there are still a number of them around today. One of the most famous was the Assassins, a secret society created by Hasan Sabbah. It was organized as a terrorist group and enjoyed the support of covert members throughout the Near East. It established itself in fortified places and unassailable redoubts all the way from the fort of Alamut in the Elburz mountains to the Lebanon.

The Grand Master of the Order, Sheikh al-Jabal, the Old Man of the Mountains, the brilliant leader of this secret society, secured the loyalty of his devoted members by inviting them to his beautiful palace hidden in the mountains. Here he entertained them lavishly and let them indulge in exquisite sensual pleasures, the chief of which were enjoyed when they were under the influence of hashish. Hence the name 'Assassin', or 'hashish-eater'. They shrank from no kind of murder or act of terror. The Crusaders even had a song about their atrocities. To this day the Arab retains a weakness for secret caucuses and conclaves.

But the most intelligent, unscrupulous, fanatical and baffling of all intellectual prophets of nationalism was Hadji Mohammed Amin el-Husseini, self-styled Grand Mufti. Moslems snickered when they heard the title Grand Mufti. There was a Mufti in Jerusalem, but it had no such thing as a Grand Mufti. Islam knows only Muftis.

His guileless blue eyes and his dignified demeanour made such a great impression that Berlin saw him as the majestic spiritual leader of the Arab world. In truth he was an intriguer, filled with enmity for everyone who was not on his side; an obdurate trouble-maker and agitator; and an implacable foe of both the Jews and the British. Opposed to all reconciliation, he dreamed always of revenge. Never was I able to discover who in fact he was working against, and what his motives were. Most probably he was simply against everyone who did not dance to his tune. He was, to coin a phrase, *coup*-crazy.

Husseini distrusted everyone, including myself, of course. Later in Berlin, because I did not take him for the great man some gentlemen there cracked him up to be, I had some difficulties to contend with.

In the course of a life of conspiracy Husseini had built up a well-oiled intelligence machine, and his undercover agents were devoted to him. I was sure that one or more of them was sitting in my own network too. They were bound to have reported my arrival in Syria, and it would not be long before a furtive meeting was arranged, in the hope that I would be bringing news or even help from Berlin Husseini could use any amount of gold without even bothering to say 'Thank you'. But since I was no diplomat who built bridges by chatter, I should have to disappoint him. All I was interested in was what he was up to in Iraq. Since my first meeting with Husseini, I had had no illusions about his personal ambitions, which were unscrupulous in the extreme.

The train pulled up at the border station of Meidan Ekbes. The screech of the brakes woke me from my reverie. An immigration official appeared at the door of my compartment, asked for my passport and began to leaf about in it. Without a word he went out into the corridor, and I saw him disappear into a hut on the platform. After a few minutes he came back, gave me my Egyptian passport, and made excuses, saying that from time to time it had to be submitted to a more detailed check. Whereupon he went off, without even examining my luggage.

Ten minutes later the train left the frontier station, and I had once again slipped through the net 'legitimately'.

At Homs I got in touch with Hélou to make several arrangements.

As usual, contact with this man was always an example of accuracy and discretion. As in my visit in Adana, so in Homs, I was taken for a business acquaintance of Hélou's, and stayed at his home as an honoured guest. Here we could exchange information in the utmost secrecy without anyone suspecting anything.

To clear the way for the important business I asked Hélou to get word to Prince Ramsis in Deir ez-Zor to send the transmitter ahead into the South Kurdistan mountain town. I made it clear that I would see him, but that first I was going on to Dihok to settle the annoying business of the other German agent.

The best way to avoid all complications was to inform the German agent via intermediaries before he became suspicious that the Secret Intelligence Service was on to him—in fact was hard on his heels. One would then offer him help and make him an attractive proposition by convincing him that there was nothing better he could do than to disappear over the frontier before it was too late. Should his mysterious companion go along with him, so much the better. If not, other methods would have to be resorted to. Djafar was just the man for the job, and capable of anything. But before he went over the border to Iran, I wanted to have a look at the man myself. I wanted to know what he was up to and who had sent him.

For this purpose he was to be invited to a farewell banquet without arousing his suspicions. The safest place to lay this on was up in the mountains, over the Samdi Dag range, at my friend Mustafa Abdul Hamdi's. His place was only a few kilometres from the frontier. I planned to wear a djellaba and turban, so that I could mix with the guests and, unobserved, get a look at him that way. I had to let Djafar know of my plan immediately, so that he could make the preparations as soon as possible; I did not have much time.

The following morning I left Homs, taking with me a Kurd as a guide. We drove along the track that runs north-east like a thin line as straight as an arrow by the side of the oil pipeline across the endless waste of the desert. Just before the Iraqi frontier we would turn off to Katounijeh in the Gebel Sinjar, and then slip through the mountains unseen.

For hours on end there was not a tree, not a bush—and no shade. In recent years I had spent so much time in the desert that it had lost its fascination for me. To tell the truth, I was sick and tired of the wretched wilderness. What was hardest to bear was the sun—that awful, merciless sun. I could not wait to get into the mountains, where it would be cool and green.

The first stretch of the journey was unbearably boring, but after a while the landscape began to turn hillier, with scattered plants here and there. Presently we were in the cooler valleys of the hills. We crossed the frontier during the night to a ravine behind el-Hol.

My Kurd knew the way like the back of his hand, but he was the most taciturn guide I had ever had. Even when we stopped, he barely said one word. He cooked black tea you could stand a spoon up in, with which we washed down the dry flat bread we had brought with us. While we drove, we chewed stone-hard dates until I would have given my right arm for some roast mutton.

After each stop, as we were getting under way, he would say, 'Insh' Allah', and then fall silent again. From then on all he would do was to move only his finger to show me where we had to take a turning.

But he was a most unusually reliable man who had lived in the mountains of Kurdistan almost without a break since his youth, and knew his way about. He had a free open look, and was proud, tough and strong. I liked him.

I decided to ask Djafar to hang on to him; a man of his sort was always useful. The two of them also would be well suited, since armed fighting was a favoured sport for both of them. Both were convinced that Germany was the friend of the Arabs.

This view stemmed from the time before World War I when Kaiser Wilhelm II had spoken words of friendship in Damascus, perhaps in hopes that the Ottoman Empire would side with the Central Powers in the event of war. Among the desert peoples, where sensational news reports were not yet an everyday occurrence and stories of days gone by were still retailed in the circle of one's friends, all that could not have been forgotten. There was always at least one man present who had fought through World War I on the Turkish side, and often there were several. For a Bedouin war is the most important thing in a man's life. They were therefore unconditionally loyal to any man who had direct contacts with Germany, who was prepared to live with them in their own way, and moreover went to the mosque with them.

We spent the night in the mountains. Towards evening we had reached Zamar, a little place where the Tigris flows out of a small lake. Here we were to leave the car with reliable friends of the Kurd's. Our plan was to cross the Tigris at first light.

Before we crossed the river, I put aside my European clothing. On the far side we clambered up a narrow sandy path to a palm grove, where a fellah was waiting for us with some donkeys. I would have preferred the local fast mountain horses, but the Kurd thought we would do better with the donkeys because of the steep paths.

Djafar had made the arrangements for the donkeys. On them we could quite easily cover the last 40 km to Alqosh. He himself was to be waiting for me on the high plateau. I don't know how the devil he got word that I had arrived. With neither telephone nor other rapid means of communication in the desert, new travels across it at the speed of lightning.

Slowly we trotted over the plain at the foot of the Kurdistan mountains, whose weird forms we could make out on the horizon through the mist that was shrouding them. By mid-morning, however, we were in the foothills. Towards noon we crossed a little bridge over a ravine. My donkey did not seem to fancy it. The roar of the brook at the bottom upset him. He stopped half-way across.

When a donkey refuses to go, neither beating nor cursing is of any use. There he stands, motionless like a lump of concrete. The best way to get him moving again is to take a bundle of dried grass, set it on fire and hold it under his tail. You must not forget, however, to keep a firm hold of the bridle, otherwise you will be sprawled on the ground and the donkey will show you a clean pair of heels.

He bucked a few times, but then, realizing that he had to give in, reconciled himself to his fate and on the other shore trotted along the steadily increasing gradient. On that side of the ravine there was a rock-face rising almost perpendicularly to the sky. Around one bend we suddenly came on a wild-looking character with an ancient blunderbuss under his arm.

Having intoned all the blessings known to the Arabic language and poured over my head all the benefactions of Allah, he informed me that Djafar was waiting for me at the top of the path. He gestured towards the opposite slope, where I saw another armed man leaning against a rock.

'And that man over there, who is he?' I asked suspiciously.

'He will be telling Sheikh Djafar that we have found you.'

I saw the fellow nimbly clamber up the sheer rock-face and disappear behind an immense boulder.

We went on up the ravine and met Djafar and some of his people in a pleasantly cool forest clearing up on the plateau. One of them was roasting a lamb on a spit and we waited, squatting in a circle, to be served with roast meat smelling deliciously of herbs.

Meanwhile I told Djafar all the latest news, and what I proposed to do about the other German agent. He had met him and described him to me, but I could not establish any resemblance to anyone I knew.

Djafar had recently been to Baghdad, and, while we were eating, he told me what he had seen and found there. First, the anti-British mood was beginning to collapse. We agreed that this was hardly surprising, since the Arab demand for the creation of an independent Palestine had been conceded in part. But Djafar interjected that the British had always promised a great deal, and he would believe them only when the Arabs of Palestine actually achieved their independence.

I explained that I was not concerned with politics and wanted only to verify what Hélou had told me about four officers who had organized a rebellion in Baghdad. Djafar said that Mahmoud Salman had set up a cell. 'That's all it comes to at the moment, but if he's doing organizing, it becomes a credible proposition.'

Now we were getting near the heart of the matter. This was something worth reporting to Aladin. The army was pro-German, pro-Italian and against the British, who of course wanted to prevent the cell from building up its strength any further. That was why the four officers known as the 'Golden Square' had been conspiring to start a rebellion. I had heard this from Hélou already. Now I had confirmation. Then Djafar enquired whether I knew that Husseini had been in Baghdad since the previous autumn. I said I knew this and that the Mufti was now trying to stir up trouble in Baghdad. But what distressed Djafar was that he had learned that the Mufti also knew that I was in the mountains with him.

'He always knows everything', I replied, in English for his ears alone. 'The trouble is, he's got such a damned good intelligence network. If you don't watch it, he'll give you a lot of trouble too.'

Djafar's people were taking no notice at all of our conversation. They threw themselves greedily on the pieces of lamb being passed round by the servant, tore apart the flat bread loaves and were chewing away for all they were worth.

I thought to myself things would be livening up from now on. Aladin distrusted diplomats and spoke of them disparagingly—they talked a lot, he said, and most of the time nothing came of it. In particular he considered those who dealt with Middle East affairs for all intents and purposes were nothing but amateurs, easily misled by Oriental cunning. He therefore wanted to know exactly what lay behind Haddad's mission and what the Mufti was doing. He had listened to Haddad's proposition in Ankara with misgivings, and was sure that he would be making all sorts of promises in Berlin about the Arabs' fighting prowess.

Aladin had no faith at all in the Arabs' fighting potential. As for money, nothing doing. Aladin would see to it that the Mufti would not have a penny. If the Reich Foreign Office was giving him some, that was no business of the Abwehr. I assumed that Haddad had most likely talked about money when he had met Aladin in Ankara, judging by the way Aladin was going on about the subject. So my instructions had been clear, and I was following them as best I could.

Djafar continued to explain about a growing movement in the Egyptian army, about the Mufti's plans to organize a block embracing all the Arab countries, with Egypt as well. I countered by saying that as far as Egypt was concerned, he would get precisely nowhere. The tradition of secret cabals did not exist there—that is, except for Hassan el Banna, but he was really a different kettle of fish altogether. I was his only German contact, or indeed European—he had no other connection, except possibly Italy, but with his anti-European feelings it was unlikely. I had never spread it about that I was on good terms with him, or on any terms at all. Perhaps the Grand Mufti would have done better to delay his edicts. In those days there was not even a glimmer of any Egyptian movement. Of course, later one could say the very opposite.

Time was passing. I wanted details of the strength of the British forces in Iraq from Djafar. He replied that Indian troops, including many Ghurkas, were arriving all the time on their way towards Palestine and Egypt. There was no sign of a weakening British position, even though some people in Baghdad thought differently. Djafar was referring to the difference between those excitable city Arabs and men like himself who lived apart.

Naturally the Mufti had blown the whole business up out of all proportion, just as he saw himself as the only true representative and leader of all the Arabs when he was nothing of the sort. He had told Haddad to speak of Arab forces in Iraq that did not exist, and as for the British, the inscription on the labels of one of their whisky bottles—'Still going strong'—remained as true as ever.

'Once the other German agent is over the border, you can go and see the situation in Baghdad for yourself', Djafar said. 'I am more inclined towards Rashid Ali el-Ghailani, not because he does not hate the English but because he looks at things more soberly.'

'And because he doesn't have Husseini's ambitions?'

As the head of a clan, Djafar was not interested in the Mufti, and wanted to talk again in a few months' time. By then one would have known whether the Italians had got anywhere with the offensive they had just launched in Cyrenaica. If the British withdrew their troops from Iraq because they needed them there, then Djafar would be ready to discuss the possibility of a revolt.

He said this with such conviction and so quietly that I knew right away what to report to Aladin. There was also the fact that Arabs instinctively ally themselves with the stronger side. In the present situation there could be no decision because everything was still fluid.

Suddenly Ramsis stepped into the clearing from the grove of trees behind us, and sat down between Sheikh Djafar and myself, having first greeted the others sitting in the circle with due Oriental ceremony. He was accompanied by a couple of his own men, who sat down on one side with the Sheikh's entourage, who were finishing off the rest of the lamb.

When Ramsis asked about the other German agent, who had been spying on me, I explained that there could be a number of reasons for this. Ramsis said that the other agent, together with his Assyrian companion, was only 500 metres from where we were sitting, and was being looked after by some of Ramsis's men.

When Ramsis said he wanted to know all the reasons behind this nasty manoeuvre, I explained that one could be that the people in charge in Berlin might doubt whether I was up to my job. There was also the fact that there were secret agents who work for two masters at the same time. There were agents who claimed to have very influential contacts while actually they had none. Perhaps things were not moving fast enough for the liking of the top brass in Berlin.

There were several possibilities, the most likely one being that the agent in question was working for a rival set-up we had at home. He was in a fix, because he did not know where to go from where he was, and that was why he had asked Ramsis for help. The man must have been trying to contact me, although he must have known that whatever he had to say would be of little interest to me.

Naturally I knew that the German was trying to 'turn me round', but that was no business of the Prince's.

'All very peculiar', murmured Ramsis in a far-away voice. Meanwhile it seemed to be my lot to be saddled with this fellow, whom I did not even know. A meeting could not be avoided. To have done so would merely have raised new unanswerable questions and sown further misgivings. But I got some amusement out of Ramsis's state of high indignation. The whole business was nothing like as serious as he made out.

The catch was that I now had to sort it all out; otherwise Ramsis would give me no peace. The time for playing games was past; so I had to send for the mysterious 'colleague'. Ramsis agreed to go and fetch him.

He got up, made a sign to one of his men and then disappeared into the woods with some others. They came back with the German, who was under average height. He followed Ramsis across the small open clearing, on each side of him one of Ramsis's men, who escorted him as they would a prisoner.

He seemed very indignant, this loose-limbed dark man with his beaked nose and bright blue, slightly watery eyes. I did not know him. As we looked one another over, Djafar just stared at the man. Ramsis looked glum. He understood a little German because he had once spent some time in Berlin, but it seemed he could make neither head nor tail of our conversation.

I told Shorty to sit down and get on with his story. I wanted the full details, and he knew damned well what would happen to him if I was dissatisfied with what he told me. Furthermore I reminded him that were he anything but German and in this part of the world he would be dead. He hesitated, though it was obvious that he was bursting with rage.

Ramsis stood up. He was in his element. With one leap he was behind the man and ready to draw his curved dagger. Djafar then restrained Ramsis by suggesting that it could be more useful to hear what he had to say. Ramsis sat down.

Our friend reached into his jacket pocket and produced a well-thumbed British passport. This bastard was depressing me. What kind of idiot did he take me for! I was neither impressed nor interested in his passport, no matter how good a forgery it was. I told him without mincing words that I knew he was working for Amt VI, and that he had better tell me which division and what his job was.

When he said that he had been assigned to the Kurdish guerrillas, I knew that he had to be with VI-C 13, Amt VI's Arab department; and I also told him that his chief, Heinz Jost, seemed to be unaware that the Kurds cared nothing for him and what he wanted to know. Then I pointed to Sheikh Djafar and said: 'Here is a man who could tell you what you need to know.'

'Anyway the Kurds in Persia seem to hold different views. I have a proposition to put to you.' He took his job quite seriously and gave his remarks an almost official tone.

I interrupted and said bluntly: 'You would like to use me, wouldn't you—to use my connections, to eavesdrop on what I find out? Or are you trying to recruit me as a source? That, my dear chap, would only lead to uncontrolled duplication, which would in turn lead to a confrontation. Since I like to know exactly where I am and avoid any possible misunderstanding, let's figure out how you are to get back over that border as quickly as possible.'

He looked thoughtful, but he did not seem to like my suggestion. Obviously he was not a man to be shaken off very easily. I was interested to see how far he was prepared to go, so I asked him what sort of proposal he had been instructed to put to me.

'We are extremely well informed', he answered. 'We can skip the preliminaries. I will come straight to my proposition. How about "all change" for you? Come over to us. You won't regret it.'

'How much?' I wanted to see how long he could keep this up.

'Three times what you are getting now.'

The amount was irrelevant—I was very well provided with money—but I disliked that bit about their being extremely well informed, though they could not have heard much. My contacts knew only what I chose to tell them, and not one word more; and Amt VI was not endowed with superhuman powers.

He asked again whether I was interested in collaborating, but I hardly heard him while racking my brains, trying to figure out who on the Tirpitzufer was the bastard tipping them off.

'Do you really think that all you need to bring a man round is money?'

'Don't forget, we have long arms. When all this is over, we shall have a lot of good jobs for the boys.'

He should not have said that. 'For one thing, you know what you can do with your jobs; and for another, who knows if your lot will be running the show.'

In Istanbul he'd been told that I was going to be in Iraq and what my cover name was, as well as where he was likely to find me. He must have been disappointed, because my contacts had been leading him round in circles until my arrival. He said that the people in Istanbul had hoped things would go a bit quicker than they had.

When I mentioned my contract with the Abwehr, he said it would not be an insurmountable obstacle, and that various details could be settled in Berlin. I had a pretty good idea why Amt VI wanted me as an agent, but my curiosity was aroused and I was having fun. Moreover I wanted to find out as much as I could because I knew that Aladin would not be amused when I came to tell him about this conversation. Given the right information, however, he would be able to take the appropriate action. He would not rest until he had found out who it was in Berlin who was leaking information.

The chap then remarked that his HQ knew that some sort of explosion was about to occur in Iraq, and that they wanted to build up a wide network in the Near East. For that they needed people who knew their way about—hence their interest in talking to me.

I told myself they wanted to use me to build up the network they had not even got round to establishing. It just was not on. If I played along with them, and got everything running smoothly, they would then cast me aside like an old sock. What a rotten lot! With a war on, which they all wanted to win, all they could do was trip one another up! Christ!

Suddenly I felt that I wanted to be done with this man; he was getting on my nerves. I had a contract and I was keeping to it. The only thing that counted now was how many contacts he had and how many friends of his there were up in the mountains. I challenged him by saying he was stuck, and his bosses in the Prinz Albrecht Strasse were pestering him to get something set up—that was why he had tried to buy me off. He could not be so stupid as to imagine that it would have worked. If he continued to follow me, I would have to shut him up for good. He had to understand that in this trade it was simply not done to poach, especially if you were supposed to be on the same side. He simply did not know his way around at all! Each time I took on a new cover name, all he would get to know was the one I had just cast off. That was all.

Enjoying my expertise thoroughly, I began to lecture him: 'Back home they crammed your head full with all sorts of stuff, telling you during your training that an oppressed people—in this particular case the Kurds—must be encouraged to resist. One goes to them, one stands by them, one trains them and organizes them. Sabotage is not enough; they must be taught to rebel. The undercover agent must devote all his strength in encouraging passive resistance, because that leads to overt violence and then to armed rebellion.

'This is what they taught you while you were being trained. Then, before they sent you out, they told you that you would only succeed if you got to that chap from the Abwehr and turned him round so that he would work with you, because he had been dealing with these people for a long time.

'Don't you find it odd that, if your people understand all this so well, they haven't taken their own advice in the territories taken over by the Abwehr? That they don't try to avert the open rebellion which is bound to come, and all too soon?

'No, you prefer to come here, chattering all sorts of rubbish because this golden rule doesn't apply here. It just won't do—waltzing up here, convinced that everyone here has only been waiting for you. Nobody has, and nobody wants to have anything to do with you. Take my advice: make yourself scarce before I make you.'

'You are behaving just like those dandies from the Secret Intelligence Service', he answered. 'To them, we are just upstarts. They too are very grand, and their snobbery knows no bounds. Even the cleverest Jewish refugees who had to keep clear of us can't work for them except to run sordid little errands. For them, everyone who isn't a member of their club—even their own colleagues in the Combined Intelligence Services—is an enemy.'

He seemed convinced that he had said something very clever, and sipped with a self-satisfied air at the coffee Djafar had ordered his servant to pour.

'Did they teach you that at your course too? If they did, they forgot to give you one little detail. There is racism to be seen elsewhere besides our side—especially in India. But they don't advertise it—they don't beat the big drum. It's a sound principle.

'They should also have told you that the SIS selects its people according to the following rules: consummate discretion, knowledge of languages, expertise, keenness, devotion to duty, detailed knowledge of the area and worldwide experience. Not blind discipline. No one in this world is less disciplined than your Oriental, which is why, if you tried, you would come up against a brick wall.

'Incidentally, the train I want you to catch leaves in an hour. It's not a fast train; actually it's a donkey. It will take you across the border. After that, if you know what's good for you, you will forget you ever met me. You can tell your people whatever you like.'

I turned to Ramsis who was beginning to wriggle about restlessly on his behind. He had probably been unable to follow everything that had been said. Ramsis had taken no notice when one of Djafar's men had come out of the wood while we were talking and had handed him a piece of paper, which after a cursory glance he had passed to me. It said that we must leave sooner than we had intended and get down into the valley. The note, which had come from one of Djafar's contact men, whom he had sent across the frontier, contained the name of the German and those of his three colleagues. Djafar's men had gone across the frontier a few days earlier to find out all that they could about this foreigner.

'You will see to it that Herr Mertens—which is what this gentleman is called—crosses the border tonight at Kol a-Shin.'

The stranger looked at me inquisitively on hearing his name and that of a place in Persia. Ramsis questioned my orders: 'Will you let him go just like that? Don't you think he is too dangerous? I mean for you—that's what I mean. When you get back home, they'll make trouble for you. If we get rid of him here in another land, nobody will suspect a thing.'

I objected to such a violent measure, and said that the German should be taken as far as Osnevyeh. Ramsis's man had better make a start pretty soon, because they would only get through the ravine unseen at night. From there on he would not have to go far to Rezaieh, where his colleagues would be waiting for him. But should he show any resistance—well then, Ramsis would know what to do. The German could on no account stay in this country.

Herr Mertens then asked how long it had taken to find out his name and whereabouts.

'Oh, it didn't take very long, really. As long as it took to go and come back and a few hours with the Sheikh's people—that was all.

You must have realized it. You've been here for weeks; you couldn't have imagined we were both blind and deaf. After all, the SIS too have been sending people in and you could well have been one of them. The Sheikh had you under continual observation; and this man here never let you out of his sight, although you may have been unaware of it.'

I pointed to Ramsis, who had understood and was now preening himself. Looking at him, I thought, It's small tokens of respect that keep a friendship going. He was as proud as a peacock to be praised in the stranger's hearing. Djafar, on the other hand, was concentrating intensely on the hubble-bubble one of his servants had got going for him. He knew that we were rid of the man and that we would then go down into the valley. In Ranya we would take one of those battered and overcrowded buses and travel unobtrusively as far as Kirkuk, whence we would go by rail to Baghdad.

The 'Abode of Peace', or Baghdad, has narrow alleys, ugly houses and any amount of dust. An entire perfumery industry would have its job cut out to mask the smells that waft through its bazaar. The garden suburb along the river, with its extensive palm groves, its riverside promenade and its shady trees is no substitute for the glories of bygone days.

We sat in the northern part of the city in the Al-Azamiya on the left bank of the river in Djafar's attractive villa, which nestled under tall date palms. A servant, stepping like a stork, carried his tray over the legs of the guests scattered round the room. It was all very Arab. The assembled company gave the impression of having just been awakened from a long nightmare of slavery. But I knew them, those cunning bastards, and I knew that they were all well off. Compared with them, the British were church mice.

For them, I was the man with the dynamite. I was the one who would blow those blasted British sky-high with as big a bang as possible. Then the great independence jamboree could begin.

If only they had known!

Admittedly the British were not exactly innocent tourists. They had come, and they had neglected to go away—and the landowners of Iraq disliked their presence.

In the beginning the Almighty had been somewhat mean with his distribution of the waters of the land. Instead of water, He gave them mostly desert. On the other hand, like a true Arab practical joker, He had hidden plenty of oil under all that sand and rock. He should have left well enough alone. It was because of the oil that the tourists had come and would not go away. Everything else was just a lame excuse to conceal that one real reason for wanting control of Iraq.

In 1901 a certain William Knox d'Arcy, a New Zealander, had secured a sixty-year concession to look for oil in Persia, giving the Persian government certain guaranteed profits; and after seven years of futile operations he had discovered the oilfield of Masjid Sulaiman.

The British government of course immediately realized the value of this discovery, made by a citizen of its Empire. They set up a company for the exploitation of the Masjid oilfield and of any others they might find. Their optimism proved justified. They found lots. As a reward for his services, d'Arcy became Director of the company—which was all he got. He was Director, not the owner. The British government, on the other hand, provided itself with a supply base on one of the most vital lines of communication of its Empire. In no time at all the British converted the Royal Navy from coal to oil.

After the British had snatched d'Arcy away from the Persian government, an Armenian colleague arrived in Iraq and got busy. No one knows how or when, but somehow an Iraq Petroleum Company came into being—and suddenly there were the British 'tourists'!

The British dubbed the Armenian, Kalouste Gulbenkian, 'Mr Five Per Cent', because they gave him 5 per cent of the profits—and immediately took the company under their 'protective' wing. The Iraqis got precisely nothing.

Now that you are 'reliably informed' about the background, we can address ourselves again to the situation prevailing at the moment of that crowded gathering in Djafar's villa. One man was missing still, as was indeed quite normal; men who matter are expected to be at least five minutes late for any meeting. Then he arrived, making the fullest use of his lateness, down to the last second, and walked loftily into the drawing-room. It was none other than Hadji Mohammed Amin el-Husseini, Grand Mufti by the grace of himself, and world champion of intrigue.

Naturally he took the place of honour, reserved exclusively for him. It was a throne-like chair of the kind peculiar to the Orient—vulgar and tasteless, with plenty of gold and tinsel, and its back upholstered in a most unpleasant green. He settled majestically in the armchair, and greeted the assembled company with much unction, as might the

Pope at one of his private audiences. He certainly did not suffer from an inferiority complex; he was every inch a Grand Mufti. The folds of his magnificent robe were arranged about him with enough grace to delight the eye of a Titian.

The conspirators in the room were nine. That excluded me. I was not of their number, but I alone knew it. The revolutionaries were convinced of the contrary, and that was where they were wrong. They also thought I had the dynamite and lots of money, and there again they were mightily mistaken.

The conspirators were quite certain that the hated British knew nothing, and there again they were also very much mistaken. The British knew quite a bit! The men in that room had no idea what they were letting themselves in for. Almost all of them believed in Kismet, and were convinced that with the help of Allah they could surmount any obstacle, provided they had faith in the precept that 'the Lord looks after his own'.

Besides, did they not have a direct line to Allah, via the Mufti?

The work of even the best secret agent is wasted unless his reports are acted upon properly when they arrive at their destination. I had no worries on that score as far as Aladin was concerned. But my reports would not stay with him. They would go further up the line—and then they could either arrive too late, or the man who had to evaluate them could make the wrong judgement or even let them gather dust on his desk because of some political consideration. Or the Great Panjandrum might possibly read my report, only to remark: 'Send this idiot to the front if he ever shows his face here.' Any report of mine on this secret meeting of revolutionaries would be bound to receive the last-named treatment. I decided to keep quiet.

There was a great deal of talking. The Mufti held all the threads in his hand. The Italians, he said, were on his side, and he was now expecting the Germans to do the right thing too. He had therefore already sent a confidential agent to negotiate in Berlin. In any case, without him, no reconstruction of the present régime, such as was now taking place in Iraq, would have been possible. He was moreover in constant contact with the Palestinian, Syrian and other nationalists. All this was his handiwork!

I could just see him—the new Saladin on his white charger, brandishing the sword of Allah, and waging holy war! He was setting up committees thirteen to the dozen. Had it not been the providence of

Allah that had sent him to Iraq? Only thus could this country obtain its forthcoming freedom.

He had it in writing that the Italians would stand by the Arabs and would not allow the British to occupy Syria or the Lebanon. Of course, they were in Iraq anyway, although to some extent lying low. The Battle of France was over, and consequently there were large quantities of weapons in Syria that could be used for an uprising. And now, as to money . . .

Aha! I thought. Now we're coming to it!

The insurgents themselves could raise very little, so his emissary was making the appropriate representations in Berlin. He looked at me sideways while he said it, smiling scornfully. I've pulled a fast one on you, haven't I? I don't need you, I can go straight to your lords and masters—he seemed to signify.

We sat till nightfall. For me the afternoon was not worth even a two-line report. I was beginning to feel bored.

Mahmoud Salman, a Colonel in the Iraqi Air Force, who was the real mainspring of the junta known as the 'Golden Square', seemed to feel much the same over in his corner of the room. He had never been very enthusiastic about Husseini. He had been much more inclined to put his trust in Rashid Ali el-Ghailani, who was Premier at the time, and also belonged to the circle of revolutionaries. He gave me a sign to leave.

'All that is easier said than done', he said as we were walking through the front garden of the villa and out into the street. 'Mohammed came back from Sandhurst recently. He will be staying for some time; but if the situation doesn't change, he will be going back to England to attend another course at Aldershot. I told him you were here; let's have dinner at my place this evening. He'd like to see you.'

'We'll talk about anything but this, Mahmoud. I must have realistic reports and "perhaps" and "should" are no use to me. You are a soldier; you know that it would only damage your plans if I were unable to report correctly that such-and-such is the situation, down to the smallest detail. Diplomats make politics, we don't. Should anything come of this coup, it must be won first. After that my department will have nothing more to do with the new situation that will have arisen. Our job is purely and simply to carry it out.'

We got into his Daimler and drove along the river to the bridge, where he let me off, saying by way of farewell: 'To you, politics is nothing; to me, it's everything. I'll be seeing you, Hussein.' With that he disappeared through the darkness.

I went down the Eastern Embankment to the Hotel Zia. The bar-keeper, Jesus, served me a double whisky before I went up to change for the evening.

Next morning I took one of those Nairn buses, custom-built for the rough tracks of the desert, which used to run to Damascus at a steady 60 km per hour. As we sped along, I had a perfect opportunity to assess the extent of the military movements being made by the British. There were convoys of military vehicles interspersed with light tanks in sand-coloured camouflage, their gun barrels pointing into the empty desert, their rattling tracks leaving an immense dust trail. Brand new tanks on special carriers, as well as other pieces of armour, were being transported to the North African front. They must have come all the way from Basra, where they had been unloaded from the ships. Apparently, the immediate destination for these supplies was Palestine, for final assembly before being put into action.

The identifying tactical symbols had not yet been erased from the various vehicles, and could be quite easily made out. I recognized a New Zealand division, some bearded Sikhs in Bedford trucks with Bren guns mounted on their driving cabs, several brigades of the Fourth Indian Division and some Australian units as well. The faces of the men manning their machine-guns were so encrusted with sand that their features were blurred.

The previous night, after the get-together I had attended, I had prepared a signal and sent it by courier to Ramsis for him to transmit at the prearranged time. Mohammed Salman, the Air Force Colonel's brother, was a Captain in the Iraq Armoured Force, and like many Arab officers since 1939 had been to various courses in Britain. We had known each other since spending a year together as boys at the English Mission College, and had kept in touch ever since. Before this latest trip of his to England we had met in Beirut and had arranged that should he come across anything of intelligence interest, he would send it to me at an accommodation address in Beirut. We had agreed on a code for this purpose. The whole thing had only been arranged between us in outline; it was nothing like a regular arrangement.

That evening Mohammed had told me, and said he was quite sure about it, that a secretary from some ministry or other (with whom naturally, he was sleeping) had heard that the British had cracked the letter code of the Italian Embassy in Baghdad. As a result they were able to monitor all Italian messages.

Technically speaking, I had done with the matter once I had sent off my signal; but perhaps they would lay aside my report as unreliable as they so often did. In any case, the Mufti, who claimed to have a direct contact in the Embassy, would be warned. Mohammed was to tell him about it in the morning.

Since the prospects of a *putsch* were still very much in the future (as I had been able to establish during my stay in Baghdad), I decided that it would be best if I went on to Cairo, the centre of British activity in the Middle East, which in any case was my brief. In Damascus I found Hélou, as arranged, at the bar of the Orient Palace Hotel. We discussed what had been happening during my absence, and I gave him a report which he was to forward via Adana and Mahamat Gülay.

Then Hélou told me that just three days previously he had arranged for a German major to be taken through the Palestine frontier by his people in response to a request from Aladin. When I showed surprise at his knowing that the man was a major, Hélou said that the German had learnt his Arabic, which he spoke with a Palestinian accent, in the Templar Colony in Sarona. Unfortunately his Arabic was apparently a bit clipped, a bit too military; Hélou had been afraid he might be spotted and had warned him.

When I enquired as to the man's unit and name, Hélou said he had received word through Mahamat to expect a man who would introduce himself as Paul and would give the number 1903, to which the reply was 'September', whereupon he would say 'the twelfth'. Aladin had also sent word that the German officer was to be taken across the Syrian-Palestine frontier immediately, otherwise the whole thing was off.

'Strictly speaking, you shouldn't be telling me all this, should you?' I said.

'Certainly not, but in the first place we have interests in common; and secondly it's important to you, isn't it?'

'Naturally; although I have nothing to do with him, it is always good to know that there are others running about in the area. I take it he belongs to Department II. That identification patter would be his date of birth, which he is unlikely to forget.'

'You should be prepared for one thing', Hélou said. 'The British have very strict controls now on the trains and at the frontier stations. You would be best advised to slip across the frontier at some lonely spot somewhere.'

'And how am I supposed to cross the Canal? Am I supposed to swim across and walk straight into the arms of some guard? No, Nadim, I need proper entry and exit stamps. The major's case is different because he has no genuine papers. He should have a safe address over there—at least I hope so for his sake.'

'Anyway, be careful; it's become a lot more dangerous.'

My thoughts were with this major who had crossed the frontier a few days ago. I could not help feeling a great deal of respect for him. While it is easy to say that life and death are all a matter of luck anyway, the fact remains that it does take tremendous guts to move about unnoticed among enemies.

How had he got to Beirut anyway, this Major Paul? And besides, why had he introduced himself as a major if he worked for one of the undercover organizations? That made no sense. In secret service work there are no ranks, only caution. The idea is to be as unobtrusive as possible, to be only one in a crowd.

Until shortly before my departure for Haifa, I sat with Hélou in a restaurant in Damascus. Then I went to the railway station.

The train crept into the small and insignificant station at Der'at near the frontier at walking pace. I watched from the window as a small group of uniformed men in almost brand new clothes split into groups of two. Each pair of them then jumped on the running board of one coach. The train was split up at Der'at. One third of the coaches went to Amman, but we would be going to Haifa.

The men from British Field Security were about to examine all passports and passengers with a fine-tooth comb. Not many minutes later I could confirm from my own experience that Nadim had not been exaggerating. They behaved very correctly, but they were quite firm.

If that major Hélou was telling me about were here now, I thought, he would have his work cut out trying to slip through the net. They took their time with the questions. They took pains to find out everything quite exactly. One of them, who stood in the background between the corridor and the compartment, must have been a passport specialist. He also had a list against which he checked the name of the passengers. When it was all over, on the other hand, everybody got his papers back; the security men apologized for any inconvenience and went on to the next compartment.

It was a pleasant journey. Apart from the passport control, nothing special happened. I felt well and relaxed.

All had gone smoothly in Qantara. The train ran along the canal, and I could see from my compartment window that the ship traffic was considerably lighter than it had been. Freighters loaded with raw materials and a few armed launches were plying in both directions.

I changed trains at Ismailia and again at Mit Ghamr, on the far side of the eastern arm of the delta, so as to be able to continue my trip via Zifta. I did not want to push my luck too far, either with the spot checks on the trains or with my own nerves. This way was slower, but correspondingly quieter.

It was late afternoon when my train arrived at Alexandria. Barrage balloons floated in the sky over the harbour, looking like pot-bellied cigars.

No sooner had I crossed the square in front of the railway station and turned into the Shariah Nebi Daniel, than the sirens began to howl over the city. From the harbour came the barking of the ack-ack; trace trails criss-crossed the sky; tiny white puffs blossomed out everywhere above my head. The harbour behind the Mahmoudia Canal must have been full of warships; that was where all the action seemed to be.

A Tommy carrying a sub-machine gun, his steel helmet at an angle over his right ear, came running over the street and yelled at me because I was the only person walking on the pavement. I stepped into the nearest doorway.

Half an hour later it was all over. You could still hear an explosion or two far off, but already the street had filled with people again, just as if nothing had happened. One might have thought it was all a dream except for the great change that had come over the town with the appearance of so many uniforms everywhere.

The inhabitants of Alexandria have always had a sharp nose for business. Now bars had mushroomed on every corner. In front of them stood hideously got-up females, waiting to relieve the soldiers of their spare cash.

The next evening I took a horse-drawn cab to Jovan's place in the

Kom el-Dik quarter, not far from the Grande Corniche. Just as the driver pulled up at the house, Jovan came out of the front door. We exchanged a brief greeting, and went into his flat. While mixing us both a drink, Jovan remarked that a lot had changed since the last time we had met, and that the Italian planes flew over frequently, though only briefly, as they had done the day before.

'You'd think that anyone who smacked in any way of Fascism would have been bundled behind barbed wire. But there are quite a few running around', he said thoughtfully, after a long pull at his drink. 'You can write Roberta off; she's gone off with an American. She isn't here any more; she is in Algeria or somewhere like that. Antonio Pulli knows where she is—he gets letters from her.'

I was taken by surprise, and it immediately occurred to me that this could have consequences. How much did she know? It could amount to very little, really, but she had clues—and that could mean trouble.

'How could she play such a dirty trick? I thought she was in love with you.'

'Dirty trick would be putting it too strongly. You must try to see it her way. As a poor kid from Reggio, naturally, she was always after money. On top of which she was worried that they would make it difficult for her here because she was Italian. She didn't tell me, but she did tell Antonio. All she told me was not to worry that she would talk about us. She would keep quiet.'

Shit, I thought! Shit! And yet again. Because she was so gorgeous, I had planned to get her to look after the British officers for me. They would have made a beeline for her.

'Anything else new?'

'I have just passed a few things on to Hélou. I've been keeping pretty busy, you know.'

'I know, Jovan; he told me that you have been sending a steady stream of reports, from your local correspondent. By the way, they found a name for you. They call you Oats, as if you needed the extra strength. Very apt, I think. I can't tell you how valuable the stuff is, because I haven't been back to Turkey. Besides it's not important at the moment, after what you've just told me. That's knocked me for six.'

I stood up and made for the window. Darkness had fallen, and down below the everlasting show of the town ran its course—people who only came out in the evening, the noise, and all the rest of it. For me, it was like watching a film.

The telephone rang.

'He is here', I heard Jovan say. 'Yes, see you presently, Ciao!'

He replaced the receiver and said: 'Pulli is coming over immediately.'

'OK', I said, rousing myself from my thoughts. I would have to move quickly now. Get out of town, or even out of the country. Better be safe than sorry. It was not Jovan I was bothered about. Heavens, no! It was Roberta. If she had gone off for money, then she was capable of doing other things for money too.

'Are you sure—you know what I mean, absolutely sure—that there is no danger from her?'

'I am quite certain. I know her sort of woman. They don't rat on friends, not even for money, although that's the thing that interests them most. What makes her tick is that she came into this world without a *sou* and she wants at all costs to be finished with that. She wants to cut free because it's a millstone around her neck. From us she can have pearls and things like that, but that's not enough. She wants to forget that she was born penniless, so she has changed her environment, because here she will always remain Roberta. And she doesn't want to be Roberta from Reggio anymore. I can understand that.'

If that was all, I thought, well and good. I could understand that too.

Jovan went to answer the knock at the door. Pulli came in as if he had not a care in the world.

'Why such a long face, my boy? Is it because Jovan has told you about the girl? Surely you didn't count on having her all to yourself? I refuse to believe it! I never thought we would be able to use her forever.

'But one thing you can be sure of: she is not a bitch. And she won't inform against us. She has gone off with an American. I know who he is. He's one of those who have been surfacing here lately. Lotfi has drafted a report about it, which I have seen.'

Well, he ought to know. He belonged to the command staff of the Egyptian Secret Service.

Antonio then told us that a whole operation was being organized by the US Military Secret Service and gave us some details, adding that it was of course obvious that the Americans would appear on the scene eventually.

After some while the three of us decided that we wanted a meal. We went downstairs, got into Pulli's car, and drove off to a restaurant in Stanley Bay.

Our jobs were changing. Up until now the business of collecting information had been something of a game. It had amused Jovan and Pulli, but now they were having second thoughts and were wondering how it all might end for them. The scales were beginning to dip in favour of the Allies. My companions were far from anticipating an Axis victory.

'What do you think? Will we have to run for it?' Antonio asked.

'I have no crystal ball, my boy. How should I know?'

'I think it'll be a case of many hounds and the one hare. I am Italian, but now I am an Egyptian. All this is none of my business. You must appreciate why I can no longer provide Jovan with information—it's become too risky. But should he be in any danger, I shall of course do all I can to help.'

I had expected this, and I could even understand him. Why should he risk his neck? What was in it for him? Nothing. Why should he sacrifice his position, morally repulsive though it was? He would have been a fool to do so. He had never pretended that he was acting from idealistic motives. It had been fun; it was fun no more. It was as simple as that.

At the very moment when reports on British movements were quite urgently required, they would be forthcoming more slowly; the trickle might even seep away like a river in a desert and simply disappear. I would have to find new people—idealists. That would be like looking for a needle in a haystack, because people of that sort were fond of talking without taking too many risks—except, that is, for the few suicidal maniacs who liked to play with bombs to draw attention to themselves.

'You can always count on me', said Jovan. 'But I quite understand Antonio's position.'

Jovan was one of those people one always underestimates. There was not a trace of idealism in his make-up, but he had guts enough for two men.

I said: 'Let's forget what's happened, Antonio. Let's remain good friends, but let's not do any more business.'

There was nothing more left to say on the subject. The trip had been almost a complete disaster because of the loss of Pulli as a contact. He was obnoxious but he had been useful.

It was 8 February 1941. Pulli was in a position to get hold of information before anyone else. It was not until the following morning that I read in the paper that the Italians had run away from the Desert Forces, not stopping till they had got to El-Agheila. Not until then did I fully appreciate Pulli's position. One does not stay with those who are retreating; one either stays put or goes over to those who are winning, if only for the time being. It was time to leave Alexandria.

Three months later the Orient Palace Hotel in Damascus was living up to its reputation even in time of war: I had my breakfast served on the balcony and it came with the latest edition of the daily paper. I wanted to enjoy at my ease one of those wonderful mornings in this city of many mosques at the foot of the Gebel Kasyun, one of the spurs of the Anti-Lebanon mountains.

Then I opened my newspaper to read that a rebellion organized by Axis agents had broken out in Iraq. It could develop into a holy war against the British throughout the Arab world. The windows of the British Consulate in Damascus had been smashed.

That was the end of my peace and quiet on the balcony. My breakfast remained untouched. It was not far to the British Consulate, and I was soon on my way there to see the damage for myself. I wondered how many agents were needed to start a rebellion in a country like Iraq. Perhaps one but more likely three, in every strategic spot—Habaniya, Baghdad, Kirkuk, Basra and Mosul. That would make fifteen and that would be too many. They would be tripping over each other's feet all the time.

The newspaper must have got it all wrong. There was no need to hurry, I would be missing nothing. I could simply book a seat on one of these Nairn buses to Baghdad which would leave the next morning, have my beard cleaned up according to the Arab fashion, put on a djellaba and all the other gear and travel as any other son of the desert.

The newspaper had also reported that the operation was fully integrated with a strategic plan Hitler was about to carry out. Since nothing had come of the invasion of Britain, and since the Blitz had been called off without producing any result, the German armies were now about to make for Mosul and Suez in a pincer movement.

Coming from the north, they had completely conquered the Balkans and Greece over a week ago; they had reached the sea coast opposite the Arab countries; and since 10 April Rommel's tanks had been at Sollum on the Egyptian border.

The bus between Damascus and Baghdad ran as usual. The interior stank as usual of garlic, onions and caraway seeds. There was no sign of any holy war. Some 150 km inside Iraq, at ar-Rutba, the driver stopped to let us stretch our legs. Wrapped in a cloud of sand, a column of vehicles came out of the Badiet esh-Sham. Without stopping they drove straight past us, and turned into the track. They seemed to have come from the direction of the Jordan. They were soldiers of the Arab Legion. British officers sat next to the drivers. These were no Djihad warriors. Somebody round here was fighting on the wrong side. Since it could hardly be the British officers, it must have been the Jordanians sitting behind them on the lorry benches.

Another Arab cock-up, I thought, as the Kurd sitting next to me said: 'They are going to Baghdad. Something is up; I read it in the paper. The English will give those Iraqis a sound thrashing.'

In Ramadi a British officer stopped the bus and ordered it to go on to Baghdad by a roundabout route. After our eventual arrival there, as we left the bus in Rashid Boulevard, I agreed with the Kurd that something was certainly happening.

The first two days of my stay in Baghdad—4–5 May—were days of great confusion. The British had reinforced the encampment and air-base at Habaniya with Indian troops.

Rashid Ali el-Ghailani, the chief instigator of the uprising of 3 May and Premier since then, had ordered the Iraqi troops to move to the heights to the south-west of Habaniya; but the Iraqi soldiers were a poor match for the RAF bombers. Hostilities had begun while, behind closed doors, the Mufti was playing a prominent role in political wheeling and dealing.

In an attempt to find out what was going to happen I arranged a meeting with Jaber Omar, the only man whose opinion mattered to me. Apparently, if the promised German help came quickly—as the Mufti had insisted it would—the *putsch* might be successful. I had to formulate some information to relay to Ramsis, who was sitting in the mountains and maintaining radio communication for me.

The only possible message was, It's a complete mess, no telling what's going on. Yet someone must have been extending promises of military support to the Iraqi officers. The question was—Who? And on whose behalf? And why was there nothing to show for it?

The British had clear-cut orders, and they had a plan. They were relying on no one but themselves and so far the advantage lay with them. As this was a matter of survival for them, they would hit hard. They had to control Basra, as a port of landing for American supplies and planes, and as the transhipment point for troops and raw materials from India and elsewhere in the Empire. After all, the Afrika-Korps was in Cyrenaica, and Rommel was not to be taken lightly.

British leaflets rained down on Baghdad, warning that the city would be bombed if the Iraqi Government did not immediately evacuate the highground overlooking Habaniya and stop shelling the place. Never! replied the Iraqis—and evacuated.

On 8 May I had lunch with Mahmoud Salman, his brother Mohammed and Jaber Omar at the Hotel Zia. Mahmoud, founder member and moving spirit of the 'Golden Square', had for some time been devoting himself exclusively to the preparation of the *coup*, and was full of good news.

'Help is on the way—aircraft and arms. The war has begun! We are standing firm!' he said, in high spirits. The Mufti had had a letter from Ankara containing these promises.

The Mufti in Baghdad, von Papen in Ankara . . . I thought. Even a political novice like me would not take all this at face value. Neither was a very attractive figure. Somehow they were very like one another. The Mufti was forever involved in politics of conspiracy, and von Papen was an intriguer of many years' standing. At one time he had even boasted that he would keep Hitler at arm's length and let him starve—or something to that effect. I found it all very puzzling.

I reminded Mahmoud that the *coup* could only succeed if the Axis powers supplied arms and planes, and, considering the enemy, they could only succeed after a long battle, because the enemy was no longer playing politics.

On the night of 11 May a courier came from Ramsis and told me that three Messerschmitts had landed at Aleppo on the 9th, and that a Junker had landed in Damascus with technicians whose job it was to arrange fuel supplies for the additional planes soon to follow. He also said that a Herr Renoir had likewise flown into Aleppo. Once again Ramsis had done his job very well. He knew that this Herr Renoir was actually Herr Rahn, and that he was the man responsible for the transport of arms from Syria to the Iraqis. But despite the receipt of arms and some help from the German Luftwaffe, the ability of the Iraqi army to combat the British forces had been greatly overestimated.

Even the Mufti was becoming nervous as the *coup* seemed to be foundering. By the third week of May, in the midst of the fighting between the British and Ghailani's troops, he asked to see me urgently. It turned out that he wanted to secure a safe retreat for himself in case the whole affair collapsed.

'Where could one find Ramsis if one had to?' he asked.

That is the least of his worries, I thought, but explained that I was the only person who knew where he was. This was not true. Jaber knew in which neck of the mountains Ramsis was sitting, so that he could go to the hideout should he be in danger. Ramsis's people would then get him across the frontier.

Ramsis was a bare 200 km to the north-east, right on the Persian frontier. And that was precisely where I was heading.

It was early in the morning when I arrived in the mountains. The dawn was slowly breaking, and I could see everything without straining my eyes. The mountain track, lined with walnut and oak trees, was fairly steep and often very narrow—almost too narrow for even one vehicle—but I was making good headway.

As I went further up the mountain, it became steeper and the precipice correspondingly deeper. Then, quite unexpectedly, there was the hideout. One of the Kurds who kept in touch with me was standing in front of a hut into which they told me Ramsis had moved a few days earlier. Until then he had been lying low in tents in the forest, because he and his agents wanted to be safe and above all undisturbed. But when they found that the village of Quraitu was never approached by Iraqi Frontier Guards or soldiers, they moved into more substantial quarters.

'A lot of planes have come over', Ramsis said as I went into the hut with him. He called in the Kurd, who had just returned from Mosul and Kirkuk, where Ramsis had sent him. Apparently German airplanes had landed in Mosul and Italians in Kirkuk.

'And Husseini is thinking of running away!' I told Ramsis.

'Sidqi won't be back today. I sent him to Haditta two days ago. The Arab Legion has overrun Fawzi Kawkatshi's position. He and his men must now be on their way to Tikrit or Baiji.'

When I complimented him on his organization and said that he had more information than Ghailani had, Ramsis explained that his twelve agents were Kurds and Sunnites like himself. You could hang, draw and quarter them and they would never say a word. They were all men from his part of the country. In Baghdad some sort of intrigue must have been going on, especially since that 'somebody' had arrived from Berlin, but Ramsis indicated that the *coup* was bound to come to a bad end.

When I asked whether his radio contact was still functioning, he assured me that Aladin had been kept fully informed. Then he said he wanted to show me something, and with that he went into a dark corner of the room, lifted a flagstone and from the hole beneath it drew forth a bag. He went to the table and tipped out a heap of lovely shiny Napoleons. They rolled over the table.

The money had been brought from Mardin over on the other side; Aladin had sent it with a courier. As I could see, he had no difficulty obtaining information.

It was a thriving business.

That evening Sidqi and the driver turned up in an old car I had left behind in Zamar for him to use. He told us that the British vanguard had got through the Wadi Tharthar.

'That means they'll reach the Tigris tomorrow', Ramsis remarked. 'It's barely another 70 km.'

'They'll get there even sooner—there's not an Iraqi to be seen', said Sidqi, who had come from the Falluja Corner, between Habaniya and Baghdad. 'They flooded the valley in a few places to hold up the British but it wasn't a great deal of use. The only people you do see are the German airmen. They are bombing Habaniya—that's all.'

Ramsis gestured to them to stop. 'Go and get some sleep. I know everything now. There is nothing further happening. Tomorrow you'll both go to Mosul and Kirkuk. You'll have three days. In Gilabah you'll collect some onions from Abdullah, pay him and sell them at the market in Kirkuk or Mosul. It's the best cover we've got; Sidqi has a licence to sell in the market. Bring the money back here and keep your eyes and ears open. I want you to give me a full report here.'

He was a hard taskmaster.

Then he got up, went into the next room and began to encode his signal for transmission during the night. The following day was 29 May.

Everything that day happened with the speed of lightning. The two men had just left in the old crate to drive down the rutted country road in the direction of Gorashala, a village on the Diyala river, which flows down the valley out of Lake Bendi Khan. I was just going back to the house when Jaber appeared on horseback.

I called Ramsis, who had stayed in the house. He came out, and when he saw Jaber Omar, his jaw dropped.

'Are you alone, Omar?' I asked.

'It's all a bit complicated, Hussein.'

'That means there are others, and I know who!' interjected Ramsis. 'And it's out of the question, Omar!'

'Just a moment, Ramsis; let him finish. You know we have nothing against Jaber.'

Jaber thanked me and said that he was to meet Husseini and Rashid Ali el-Ghailani in an hour's time a kilometre from the frontier just before Quasr e-Shirin. Then he explained that he had promised them that Ramsis and I would be there as well to escort them over the frontier into Persia. Ramsis had good contacts on the other side; they would have little trouble getting to Teheran.

Ramsis was furious: 'And now we're supposed to help them get away. If you had asked them ten days ago to do the most trifling thing for you, they would have told you to go to hell! To hell, do you hear me, Jaber! Especially that beady-eyed Husseini. He wouldn't even talk to you. I wonder whether these two heroes would ever do anything for me if I should ever be in trouble? Insh'Allah!'

They would not have been able to, even if they had been willing. The British caught Ramsis four months later when he was quite alone. But they only interned him as a political prisoner, because they wanted to avoid stirring up more trouble in the area.

As for the two heroes of the *putsch*, they had long ago crossed the Persian frontier and made their way to the safety of the Japanese Legation in Teheran. Rashid Ali el-Ghailani was eventually smuggled out of Persia via Turkey and on to Berlin. But the Mufti had greater difficulty in escaping, and barely managed to get himself to Italy and then to Berlin by November 1941.

Chapter 11

More Pieces in the Jigsaw

I was completing the ritual of my Turkish bath by pouring boiling hot water over myself, trying to get the whole business over with Oriental equanimity. In the past five months, since the Mufti's ignominious flight, a lot had happened, not all of it strenuous. After a few happy months with Sonia in Copenhagen, and after a refresher course in Brandenburg, I was back on a mission. Slowly but surely I was assuming the colour of a boiled lobster. I remember thinking what a peculiar idea of Aladin's—to meet in the hammam.

'Lüften Buyrum, Beg', the giant attendant said for the second time.

Despite the politeness of his invitation, I knew just what was in store for me for the next few minutes. I lay down on the slab without demur and waited for him to assault me. He seemed to have no idea of anatomy. He began to belabour my body with a wooden paddle rather like a shovel, until I thought I could feel every bone I had cracking inside me.

'How now, old friend! Isn't it marvellous the way these lads give one a going-over?' Aladin had turned up behind me, clad like me in a bath towel. He appeared to be revelling in the torture.

The attendant now began to rub my hide with a loofah. The coarsest sandpaper is like velvet by comparison. I got a certain amount of satisfaction out of watching another attendant throw himself on Aladin and work him over with a pair of arms bulging all over with muscles.

'Serves you right, you sadist!'

Utterly limp, we climbed off the slabs and crept into the rest cubicles, where they served us some marvellous tea to make us forget the torments we had just undergone. As always after a Turkish bath, it was only then that the beneficial effects began to make themselves felt.

'I thought it might be best to meet here before I leave Ankara. That's why I asked the Abwehr office's radio operator to arrange a meeting.'

'The brightest idea you have ever had in your life, I must say. Here of all places! Is this supposed to be fun?'

'None of the staff speak German', Aladin replied, laughing. 'And the Turks who come here are so preoccupied with their ablutions that they have no mind for anything else. And as for you, since you are our prize exhibit, it's out of the question to ask you along to the office. Or do you expect me to ask you along to the Para, where there is not a single café customer who is not a spy.'

'What's up then?' I asked.

'First tell me, what was it like in Spain?'

'Who told you I have been there?'

'Never mind, old friend', said Aladin. 'Somebody whispered it to me out of the corner of his mouth in Berlin, where I have just been for two days.'

'I hope they didn't radio it to MI-5 so they could make an entry on my index card. "Visited Spain from such-and-such to such-and-such a date." Then, should I ever get caught, they could shove the card under my nose.'

'Before we discuss our own business, I just wanted to tell you that Alex has copped it.'

'Alex? But he was such a careful type. Do we know how and when?'

'In Lenkoran, on the Caspian Sea, on the new stretch of railway line where they are building a number of important strategic installations. It happened a fortnight ago.'

'Alex had class. It's a blow.'

'Yes, he had that certain something that makes a good undercover man.'

'You mean he had that irresistible urge to discover secrets and to have secret power in his hands', I said.

'That's not an original remark of mine. It's something Canaris said to me one day in the Abwehr building, trying to explain my job to me.'

'He was right—those are the psychological mainsprings that make a good secret agent. Alex had them, and they made him a valuable agent.'

Each of us lay on his couch, a narrow space between us with a wooden stool at the head end, on which stood the tea service. The narrow confines of the place made evasion impossible. It was an odd sort of situation. I had been thinking about these things quite a bit. Some good people had fallen by the wayside recently, and that kind of thing is upsetting.

'One can't help thinking, especially now that Alex has been caught . . . On the one hand, we are winning everywhere, but I can't see any end to it. And, above all, I can't help wondering—can this war ever be won?'

He gave a dry laugh, leant over towards me and said: 'You can speak your mind; there's no one listening. Probably we have set our sights too high, which is why we are beginning to feel disappointed.'

'No, I have never had great expectations. I have always regarded what I have been doing more as an adventure. But naturally, I have allowed myself to be influenced, perhaps without realizing it. It's hardly surprising.'

'Just because we are winning now doesn't mean that one necessarily believes this war will end in victory.'

He had never spoken like this to me, although we had discussed the war before. Although I had realized that he was no Nazi who groped his way through life in blinkers, I had nevertheless believed that he was doing his duty without worrying about it overmuch, like a sort of automaton.

It was difficult to learn what these people honestly thought. One was always between two stools, and nobody had the courage to speak out. Perhaps they had no views of their own. Sometimes, when there was nobody about, they let drop a few casual remarks from which one could gather that they were of course against it, but . . . That left you free to think what you liked. Since there were never any witnesses to the conversation, they would be all right whichever way it turned out. The idea was—come on out into the open! If you refuse to show your true colours, I can only assume you belong to the other lot.

'So what are we left with? Songs about heroes!' I asked.

'I haven't seen the British begging for a cease-fire with their hands up above their heads. All our victories add up to a lot of humbug.'

'You're a pessimist.'

'No, I look soberly at the facts as I see them and as far as possible try to act accordingly. And that's not the same thing.'

'How then do you expect to win a war except by winning battles?'

'Of course they have to be won; but one doesn't get killed in the process', said Aladin. 'The idea should be to get a decisive result. The Allies are slow—but when they wake up, look out! And the British are just beginning to stir.'

'Don't worry; when everything has gone down the drain, the high-ups always have some excuse ready. We'll get the blame; there might even be talk of treason. They'll say: "Somebody told the enemy all our secrets. But for him, we would have won!" I am afraid it will be rather like the tale of the dog and the hare: if the dog hadn't stopped for a crap, he would have caught the hare. All those great commanders, with enough gongs on their chests to fill an ironmonger's shop, are still running about giving themselves airs; it won't be long before they will have their trousers full—only they'll never admit it.'

'Hitler says that by the winter Soviet troops are to be driven back beyond Moscow; but the British and the Russians between them occupied Persia a month ago. The former still remains to be done—if it will ever be done at all. The latter is all over and done with.'

'That's the end of the dream of a German motorized expedition through the Caucasus to Iraq', I said. 'That means I ran around Iraq for nothing and I wasted my time in Afghanistan and Persia too. I don't mean from the point of view of adventure, but from the point of view of results. Not to mention my other missions, which have also been a waste of time.'

'I haven't told you, but I ran into Alex before his mission to the Baku oilfield. I can say all this now that he is no longer with us and we shall never see him again. Call it insubordination or worse. I have never been subordinate in my life. But we were good friends and I am glad we had another chance to meet.'

'He too will have died for nothing—and if I don't look out, it'll happen to me too.'

'Have you ever known a secret agent who wants to die—just like that?' asked Aladin. 'I haven't. What for? Maybe soldiers dream of dying a hero's death. But an agent knows perfectly well that there is no such thing.'

'What a rotten way for Alex to die!'

'Would you like to be interrogated by the Russians? I wouldn't. You can imagine, can't you, what they will do to him! Just remember the Order on Commissars promulgated by Hitler at the beginning of the Eastern campaign. It's an altogether different war now. They'll make Alex feel that order; and we can't really even blame the NKVD for putting him through the mangle.'

'I hope he tells them everything at once', I said. 'I hope he sings and doesn't have any silly pride. I hope he sings like a canary—that way, he'll die quickly and less painfully. Why should he give himself any airs and graces?'

'Do you really think a general would not talk?' Aladin asked bitterly. 'He'd talk all right, and he doesn't even have to. But Alex does, because thumbscrews are sheer delight compared with what a NKVD can lay on—which doesn't mean to say that our own SD's methods are any prettier.'

Now it was his turn to speak his mind. If he hadn't, I would have been wrong.

'What's our solution? Run along to Tommy and tell him all we know? Tell him we are the most terrific anti-Nazis; and wind up with a nice peaceful time for the rest of the war. But it won't do, my friend, will it? You wouldn't come.'

'I am no quitter', I said. 'But I do look at things objectively. We must see it through somehow, there's no doubt about that; and it's not what really matters. But I don't want to do it blindly. I want to know why.'

'Don't let any party bigwig hear you say that! We'd be carted off to the nearest concentration camp before you could say 'knife'. We're political innocents—you're right about that. We've never understood that part of the business at all, and I am very much afraid we are in for a horrible awakening. To think that there are some people who are dreaming of calling the whole thing off in good time now, although it was they who gave Hitler and his paladins a ride to the top on their own backs! Now they want to get rid of him, but they lack the guts to do it. I think it maybe best for us just to carry on.'

He was not like the others. It was nice to know that. I had always liked him.

'That's enough of that now; there is no point in such talk', he said, and I realized that we were far too small, as small fry went, to be allowed any say.

Of course there were people who opposed the régime but did not dare to try anything. Perhaps they played the part of an opposition—a very insignificant opposition. But that was none of my business. I did not know them, nor did I feel like throwing my life away in some show of bravado. I had no desire to be the little hero whose head was chopped off. No thank you!

Aladin broke into my thoughts: 'Do you remember the report you sent through towards the end of 1940 about that decoy unit in Cairo?'

'What about it?'

'They checked it, and assessed it as most valuable material.'

'Now you are talking to me about doing one's duty. Loyalty, and that rot. That was eighteen months ago; how long did they need to check one report?'

'I'll tell you what the checking consisted of. When a column of innocent-looking lorries opened the most devastating fire and they slowly got over the shock and the heavy losses, some chairborne jackass in Berlin dusted off my report and said, That chap—what's his name again, who's running about out there in the Middle East and chucking our money out of the window? He must have had a spot of luck. Didn't he send back some report or other about some decoy units sometime or other? Give him a pat on the shoulder! It doesn't cost anything.'

'That's where you are wrong, my friend', I said, 'because we ourselves have now opened a shop just like that!'

I could still remember well the afternoon when I had been driving down the Shariah Soliman Pasha in Cairo with Fuad Osman, my contact man in the Canal Zone, in a Chevrolet I had just bought at the Eleftheriou Garage in el-Faghalla. He was telling me that in a small courtyard of the house behind the Groppi Tearooms he had seen some very odd-looking vehicles being got ready. It was a throwaway remark he had made while we were eyeing the pretty girls walking on the pavement. He kept whistling after them, but they did not turn their heads; a wolf whistle was nothing new in the streets of Cairo.

Suddenly it occurred to me that an old acquaintance of mine from my schooldays lived exactly opposite the place. I turned towards the Shariah Maarouf to fetch my binoculars. One never could tell; perhaps Fuad had stumbled on something.

I thought I should be able to look down into the courtyard from the roof of the house. The servants' rooms were up on the flat roof and the windows overlooked the courtyard. I had to get up there, so I drove home as fast as I could.

Before we got to the Shariah Maarouf, I drove over the Kasr el-Nil bridge, past the Guezira Sporting Club and up to No 4 Shariah Salah el-Din, where I had a hideout. It was in an attractive villa with a large garden in front, full of palm trees and flowering shrubs, so that the house could hardly be seen from the street.

For security reasons I had rented a studio in the Shariah Sherif Pasha, where, in full sight of all the other tenants of the house, I was cohabiting with the belly-dancer Carioca, at that time the toast of the Badia Massabni Oriental Theatre. It made little stir. A rich young Egyptian living with a dancer was bound to be away a lot. How many other sons of rich fathers were doing the same! I was therefore free to travel wherever I wanted. If anyone enquired after me, the story was that I had gone to one of my estates but I would be back soon.

For my radio transmission times and anything else to do with my undercover work, I had the villa. The husband of the elderly Armenian widow who owned it had been an attorney at the *Tribunal Mixte* in Cairo, and had furnished the villa with every imaginable comfort. He had been a very prosperous attorney. After his death she had had to move to Alexandria to live with her sister. She could not bear to live alone.

In January 1940 I had paid the rent for a year in advance and instructed the Banque Misr in Cairo, where I had an account, to pay the next year's rent when it was due. They also had instructions to pay the wages of my servant Mahmoud, who lived in the house and saw to everything necessary there. I could pursue my activities undisturbed and could even travel abroad.

To make my cover complete, I went to visit my old friend René Rehbinder, who lived at the Midan Falaki, two minutes from the Bab el-Louk suburban railway, where he had a flat right at the top of a five-storey building. It was unbearably hot up there in summer, so I invited him to come and live in the villa. Count Rehbinder was the only one apart from my two contact men, who knew what I was really doing.

He had for years been a popular and unusual figure in Cairo society, with his entertaining stories about his time as a guards officer in Tsarist Russia. Now penniless again, René had a marvellous gift for spinning a yarn. We would listen to him utterly captivated, for hours. His stories took on a slightly different colouring with each retelling, which did not bother us in the least. They were famous all over town. He was one of those rare people who are never bored, which made him so delightful to have around.

There were a few elderly Pashas who, like himself, were turf-mad, and who were to be seen milling about on every racecourse in Egypt. They had set him up with a small pension. It was not very much, but it enabled him to live and—what was more important to him—to remain idle. As far as the Count was concerned, work had not been discovered. They only time he did work was when the object of the exercise was good food. For a good meal René would walk miles.

René was to live in my villa all the year round, occupying the bottom floor. For me his presence provided an ideal cover. The arrangement suited both of us excellently.

Mahmoud was raking the garden when I arrived at the villa. 'Fen el-Chawagh'a Rehbinder?' I asked him.

'He is sitting in the back garden with a gin and lime', the boy replied.

It was René's favourite place of an afternoon as the sun was setting in the Western Desert, when a light breeze would spring up from the Nile.

I wanted to take René to town with me. The idea was that he should buy some films, and I would take some pictures if what I found in the courtyard was worthwhile. I could then study these at my leisure at home. Even if I could not take them with me, because I did not yet know how I would be leaving the country, they would be useful.

It is always dangerous to maintain observation from the same place for too long. That applies to a flat roof as much as to any other place.

We parked the car in an alleyway next to the house where my acquaintance lived. René had left us earlier to get the films. Fuad remained on the steps while I talked to Hamdi. He agreed immediately, called his servant and asked for the keys; and the two of us climbed up to the flat roof.

The view into the courtyard was perfect.

The place looked like the backstage of a theatre or a film studio workshop. The innocent observer might have thought they were working on a war film. Four men picked up a Mark VI tank and without any trouble carried it across the courtyard, loading it on to a waiting lorry. It was made of rubber. Even from as close as this, from just across the street, hardly 50 m away, it was indistinguishable from the real thing. They had quite a number of tanks piled up in a corner. They seemed to be mass-producing them—right in the middle of a big city! Propped up against the walls of the courtyard were parachutists realistic down to the smallest detail, standing about as though having a five-minute break for a smoke. If it had not been for their height, which was barely three feet, one would have taken them for real people.

Camouflage and decoys seemed to be very highly thought of by the British. Fuad had earlier brought me material from the Canal Zone that bore this out. There they had simply covered over a part of Lake Timsah with sacking stretched over stakes. They had painted the upper side with desert camouflage. It was superb. It was so well done, Fuad had said, that it was bound to mislead any pilot and no one would be able to spot it.

They had covered the lake over from a point immediately after you leave Ismailia behind the rue Mohammed Ali, just past the mouth of the stretch leading to Cairo that runs alongside the lake, right up to the Canal fairway at Gebelmaryam. They had even covered the Memorial, which is 30 m tall, making it vanish completely. They had in fact extended the length of the Sweet Water Canal! It was a stroke of genius.

Further to the south, between Toussum and Serapoum, nearer Suez, they had covered over a 15 m wide sweet-water channel for a distance of 10 km. Seen from the air, all landmarks had been obliterated. Bombers making an approach were bound to be hopelessly disoriented.

Fuad had also said that there were dummy submarines on the Great Bitter Lake. I did not believe him, but later I had to admit that his observation had been correct.

What I saw in the courtyard was of course only a very small part of a very big project. It fitted into the immense jigsaw of a great offensive, which was to start not long afterwards. On 23 October 1942, three hours after sunset, when the desert lay under bright moonlight, that offensive was heralded by a solid artillery barrage on a front 1 km wide, a mere 80 km east of Alexandria.

Chapter 12

Hitler

Within two months I was summoned back to Berlin.

After my steamy confidential conversation with Aladin early in September 1941, events and personalities in my sector moved rapidly. A mere two weeks later the British captured Teheran and stepped up the hunt for the two prime pro-Axis Arab leaders—Rashid Ali el-Ghailani and, of course, Hadji Mohammed Amin el-Husseini, the Grand Mufti himself. They did not know that Ghailani had left Iran late in July and was under Turkish protection. The Mufti had not been so lucky. Everyone was looking for him, friend and foe alike, but the wily man once again went into hiding, and for once kept his mouth shut. The British did manage to capture his cousin and Haddad, his private secretary, who were extradited to Iraq and executed.

The Mufti took refuge in the Japanese Legation in Teheran, and severed contact with everyone, including my own people. He remained invisible and mute for several weeks and then, just as he had eluded British surveillance in Jerusalem, he gave everyone the slip by disguising himself and quietly walking into Turkey. Within days the Turkish government disembarrassed themselves of his unwanted presence and the Mufti found himself in Italy. Ten days after his arrival there he had a meeting with Mussolini, on 27 October. About ten days later he was in Berlin.

The Mufti was installed in a splendid villa deep in the Zehlendorf Park. The first time I went to see him there and approached the unarmed SS guards at the gates, they commented: 'Not another of those buggers!'

I quietly showed them my green Abwehr identification card, and they promptly stood straight, threw their shoulders back and clicked their heels. Making no excuse for their rude remark, they smartly conducted me to the door of the house.

He received me. He had certainly lost none of his presence, despite the squalid way he had managed to reach Germany. Dressed in his graceful jubbah, he could even have impressed von Ribbentrop. He talked to me about his visit to Rome and his meeting with the Fascist Leader, who he assured me, was eating out of his hand. There was nothing to impede the progress towards the creation of a United Arab movement with the help of Rome and Berlin. He was going to have a meeting with Hitler himself, and for that occassion I was to be his interpreter—an honour, I thought, of dubious value. The prospect of coming face to face with Hitler, if such should happen, since official invitations to the Chancellor did not necessarily mean an introduction to the Führer, frankly upset and at the same time attracted me. Even if I distrusted Caesar, I had to admit that not everyone had the opportunity to shake his hand.

The Mufti sighed with relief and said: 'I am glad you have come. I was afraid they might assign me a German interpreter.'

I soon took my leave and waited for the summons. The days were spent visiting friends, and the Mufti once more, and knocking about in the Abwehr offices. Then came startling news, that Ghailani himself was in Berlin. Officially it was known that he had escaped from Turkey on his own, and made his way across the Black Sea and on to Germany by way of occupied Bulgaria. In fact he had been disguised in bandages, and had boarded a German plane from Ankara as one of eight press officers. The whole scheme had been put into operation by von Papen himself. So now both Ghailani and Husseini were here!

Two days later the telephone in my apartment rang. I was to proceed at once to the villa in the park. The meeting with Hitler was to take place that afternoon.

The huge Mercédès drove us through the heart of the city to the famous Chancellory. The monumental stairs outside were guarded by two SS men standing on small plinths like two statues. The enormous building, like a pompous Roman temple—impressive and chilly, clean lined and heartless—was filled with huge corridors bathed in a romantic semi-darkness, with gigantic dimmed torches. The great hall itself, as huge as a railway terminus though less crowded, was still thronged with busy functionaries—stiff SS men, some in the black uniform of the state troopers and some in the field-grey of the military.

I hardly felt at ease in all this Germano-Roman imperial decor, surrounded by six-foot giants coming and going and emphasizing my shortness. We waited, arms folded behind our backs, looking here and there, and listening for the approaching steps to announce that we were to be led into *the presence* itself. After about a quarter of an hour a uniform came to inform us that the Führer would receive us in a few minutes. He then gave us instructions on how to greet Hitler once we were in the room: we were to say 'Heil, mein Führer', and extend our arms horizontally, not vertically as done in Italy. Assured that we would not embarrass the leader, the officer left. A few minutes later we were approached again, this time by von Ribbentrop, who told Husseini that several memoranda had been passed to Hitler during the last few days and that the Führer was completely *au fait* with the facts and plans for a pro-Axis United Arabia. Then we were led to the enormous doors, and searched perfunctorily by two guards before the vast portals were opened dramatically and the three of us went in.

The room was so immense that the back walls were all but lost in shadow. The huge windows were covered by heavy curtains, which kept the monumental cavern in demi-shadow. Hitler was seated behind his desk. After a moment he looked up, rose and came to greet the Mufti with his hand out. I was a bit startled to see how short he was, and how simply dressed in civilian clothes, his shoes so highly polished they reflected whatever light there was in that chamber. Yet his eyes were piercing, and one could appreciate the hypnotic effect he had on so many people. He took the Mufti's hand and said: 'I hope your stay here is a pleasant one and that you do not feel homesick.' He then turned and shook my hand, and asked: 'Well, sir, you speak Arabic. Is it a handsome language?'

I could see the depths of ruthlessness and cruelty in those eyes. 'Yes, mein Führer, it is a lovely language.'

'And where did you learn it?'

'I was born in Alexandria, mein Führer.'

The pleasantries and formalities finished, we were shown to some armchairs. Once seated, the Mufti spread his garments and began his tirade. Their enemies, he said, were mutual enemies: the Jews, Britain and Bolshevism. He would raise a legion that would exterminate the Jews, route Britain and her allies and destroy forever the Bolsheviks. He would raise the standard for the unification of the Arab States and establish a pan-Arabic-Moslem entity which, with the Axis, would dominate the Mediterranean area and extend throughout Russia to the gates of China and the passes into India. Together he, Germany and Italy would declare to the world that the domination of the Moslem world by the Jewish-dominated Allies was at an end.

He went on in this vein for at least fifteen minutes. At times I was hard pressed to translate these fiery platitudes with some degree of conviction.

Then it was Hitler's turn. Once more the Jewish-led Allies were the scourge of the world. It was they, and they alone, who held the power, and by their devious methods exploited the peoples of the world. However, he told the Mufti: 'A promise to raise an Arab legion will be valueless on its own. The only assurance of real value is one that rests firmly on victorious armies. And only when the war is won will the hour of liberation and the hopes of Arabs he fulfilled.'

He then explained that a declaration of Arab aims could only re-inforce the enemies of the Axis and the Arabs. If the French thought they would lose their mandate in Syria, the Gaullists would have colonists flocking to their side. This would only strengthen their efforts and make the war in Western Europe more difficult when Germany had to concentrate on the battles in the East. Only when the forces of the Reich had subdued their enemies in the South Caucasus—which he assured the Mufti would be in a month's time—only then was a declaration possible. Together, then, they would wage a war to the end on the Jews of the world, destroy the Jewish element in the Arab countries and remove any hope of a Jewish nation in Palestine.

Even with the pauses for translation, which I made sound as fervid in Arabic as the tirade had sounded in German, Hitler's tone of voice was as certain as the one he used when addressing an assembly of thousands of Germans. He assured the Mufti that, once the inevitable victories had been rightfully gained, he, Husseini, would have a decisive voice in all Arab affairs, and that he would be the Grand Mufti, the leader of all Arabs everywhere.

There was a pause. Then the Mufti, anxious to seal the matter, suggested the drawing up of a secret declaration and a secret treaty. I translated this message, and noticed a slight change on the Führer's face. He was not pleased with this. He barely listened to my last words, before he declared in an ice-cold voice that a secret agreement, treaty or declaration known to several people could not long remain secret; in any event, he had given the Mufti precisely that confidential declaration just now. I could not, in relating this to the Mufti, convey the Führer's frigid tone, which denoted that the matter was settled; but in a more amiable manner I concluded the translation with words that sounded hopeful and worthy of trust. As an Oriental prince, the Mufti considered the explanation with superb dignity.

Hitler then rose. It was the signal for us to rise. He took the Mufti by the hand once more, and in taking leave of us said to me: 'Tell the Grand Mufti of Jerusalem that he must treat Germany as his own home. I have instructed the Foreign Office to watch over him; he will have nothing to worry about, he is to receive every attention.'

The Führer accompanied us to the doors, which were quickly opened, and we left. The interview was over. As the doors shut, leaving Hitler in his office with von Ribbentrop, I began to wonder, as we walked down the corridors once more, how much of what had been said would ever happen. How much did either of them trust the other? There had been promises and handshaking. Was there anything else?

Chapter 13

Operation Salaam

It was early May 1942. Alexandria was a sealed port, inaccessible to ships and aircraft. My job was to get into Cairo unobserved and establish regular radio contact with Rommel. It was too dangerous and impractical to be parachuted into the desert to make my way into Cairo. That was why our column of vehicles was racing along the Gulf of Sirte Road. We were behind enemy lines. It was a good thing I did not know that it would be my last journey for some years, and that some unpleasant surprises lay in store for me.

There was nothing happening at the front, which was in the middle of a three months' lull that everyone was enjoying. Both sides were exhausted, but re-equipping for a new passage of arms. Rommel had his eyes on Egypt and the near East, which was why I was now driving down the Via Balbia. The Tommies still held the Gazala/Tobruk/Bir-Hacheim line, but Rommel was preparing feverishly for an offensive that would take him to el-Alamein. The battle for Egypt was about to begin.

Malta, that unsinkable aircraft carrier of the British Empire and thorn in Rommel's side, which Hitler had inexplicably left undisturbed, had virtually crippled supply operations across the Mediterranean. Kesselring was getting nowhere with the bombers he sent over the island. You cannot sink a rock—not even Hitler could. The thing to do was to take it from the air, as we had taken Crete. But Hitler would not be told. The greatest warlord of all time, he had prepared a grave for the Wehrmacht in eastern Europe and was now fully occupied with that enterprise.

Count László Almásy sat next to me as we drove, smoking a cigarette. He told me with a grin that the tarmac road down which we were driving was originally supposed to have been 50 cm wider, but while it was being built, Italo Balbo, after whom it was named, had found that his coffers were empty and needed urgent replenishment. The road-building project was best suited for this purpose, so he had proceeded in a somewhat unorthodox manner. He assembled the contractors taking part in the project and ordered them to build the road 50 cm narrower. They would pocket the net saving, one-third going to them and two-thirds, of course, to the Marshal. After all, what's 50 cm? But over a stretch of 1,000 km it would be worth a couple of bags full of lire to them. It was a good thing the Duce never found out! The Marshal made sure the little joke was kept a secret from him.

In token of his gratitude, Balbo built the great Arco dei Filene, which towers over the Sirte for miles around, as an 'everlasting' memorial. He had the Duce commemorated in bas-relief like a Caesar, with an inscription for all to read:

BENITVS MVSSOLINI
SVMMVS REI PVBLICAE IDEMQUE
FASCISTARVM DVX

Balbo's accounts were in order once again and his lord and master had been made immortal—at least for the time being.

'It couldn't happen in Germany, you know, László.'

'That's as it may be', he growled. 'I wouldn't like to be there when they audit the accounts of the Atlantic Wall.'

The assurance of this man Almásy was truly enviable. He had not changed since that day in 1935 we had broken down with engine trouble near the great Mohariq Barkan Dune. We had been searching for a lost oasis and were resigned to awaiting the end, but he quite calmly repeated: 'The last moment has not yet come. Someone will turn up and get us out of this.' And right enough, someone did just about at curtain time. It was Robert Clayton, who took us back to the Nile Valley.

The episode had left Lázsló quite unperturbed. No sooner were we back than he propped himself against a bar at the Mena House and asked the barman, Gaston, for a whisky with plenty of soda, just as if nothing had happened.

Ever since Rommel had begun his third African campaign in January, I had been wondering about Clayton and the others—like ourselves, desert trackers. Where were they now? I was not too sure that I wanted to know, just in case they were doing the same job as we were but for the other side. Now, on this mission for Rommel, I had to voice my fears.

'It's not just Clayton who's knocking about here', I remember László saying. 'Bagnold, Prendergast—you name them—they're all cruising around in the desert. They've always had a good nose for it. And they know that if anyone is rooting around here on the German side, it's bound to be us. It must have been quite obvious to them that we have in fact been doing it for some time.'

'So you feel quite sure that they are all with the Long Range Desert Group?'

'When I was in Mamelin doing my course, they were talking about someone called Mitford, who is supposed to be one of their commanders. But no one ever heard of the name in Cairo.'

'I saw Mitford in 1938 in Palestine', I told László. 'He was working with a survey team from the Royal Geographical Society, travelling around Sinai with Bagnold. Now they've fitted their vehicles with 30 mm Bofors and anti-tank guns. They're still surveying the desert, and playing war at the same time. Nothing has changed. Personally, I think it's rather fascinating.'

'We found out during our interrogations that our people attribute the greatest importance to the Long Range Desert Group over on the other side. Little wonder! The Tommies know their desert; they can use these units to patrol and to make pinprick attacks that can be extremely damaging. They can introduce agents behind the lines, just as I am now doing with you; they can gather intelligence as easily as emptying a letter box—all in our rear. And when they have finished, they can vanish unseen among the dunes of the Great Sand Sea.

'It would be a waste of breath to tell all this to our lords and masters. It's not in the Prussian military textbooks, therefore it's not true. They'd just shoo you away when you started telling them. And were you stubborn enough to insist, they'd kick you out.' Almásy looked once more at the last few hundred metres of Mediterranean coast before we turned off to the south.

We were heading for the last Italian outpost—the Gialo Oasis, where we would stay for a few days to prepare ourselves for the journey itself. We would check our supplies and vehicles and stock up with water before pushing on into the desert.

There were practically no maps to be had for a trip south of the Tropic of Cancer, so one had to take maps consisting mostly of blank areas. The Italians, who had been in the country for years, had marked out a track to the southern Libyan oasis of Kufrah. They had planted 3 m steel posts into the ground at 500 m intervals and had christened the result Balificata. Meanwhile, however, half the posts had rusted away or the Beduoins had found a use for them and had pinched them. The track, which had originally run along the edge of the Calanscio Sand Sea, was now some 20 km to the east of it, but no one had bothered to mark this on the map. For simplicity's sake, the printers had just put 'Dunes' on the map. If there were some there, the printer was in luck; if there were more, it did not matter, for no one would ever check it anyway.

Those maps cost us many unpleasant hours.

We found that the Balificata was closed. The Free French were sitting in the Kufrah Oasis. Colonel Leclerc had marched north from the Chad via the Matan Bisharah up to Kufrah, where he had dealt swiftly with the Italian garrison and was now turning his thoughts to giving Rommel a thoroughly unpleasant time.

The super-strategists of the Abwehr, including their chief, Angelo, the initiator of Project Dora, had in the good old German fashion commissioned an evaluation by university professors of the chances of a possible counter-offensive from the Chad area. Highly qualified road builders from the Organization Todt had stated that no road could be built from Fort Lamy to the Mediterranean. It would have been an impossible achievement, to cover a good 2,000 km as the crow flies across the Sahara to the sea.

But Leclerc did not bother his head about roads. He moved fast, covering 1,600 km without roads or watering places—only sand dunes and merciless heat.

All Angelo's and his friends' trouble had been for nothing. Their 'research' and the conclusion of Project Dora—that it would only be possible for a column using the most modern equipment to traverse the Chad-Cyrenaica route—was all nonsense. There were some pretty red faces among the experts hired by the Abwehr—Orientalists and road engineers alike—when they learned that the Italian garrison in Kufrah had been surprised by Colonel Leclerc and his men. He had established himself in Kufrah without having to worry about experts.

Before us lay Gialo oasis. When one hears the word oasis, one imagines date palms and trees bearing oranges, lemons, peaches and other delicious fruits. An oasis is a port one reaches at long last after an interminable voyage full of privations. Every caravan makes for an oasis. Without oases it would be unthinkable to attempt to cross the desert. The oasis, with its cool covered streets, its rectangular white-washed houses gleaming in the glare of the sun, and date palm trees everywhere, is the coveted goal.

The shady streets are frequented most exclusively by men. One could get the impression that there were no women about at all, but for the occasional glimpse of some beauty, veiled up to the eyes, stealing a curious glance at some passing desert sheikh. It is she, the woman of the oasis, who is the staunch guardian of all tradition. Behind her veil she is the very embodiment of Oriental eroticism. All one can see of her are her almond eyes, hands and ankles, but that little titillates the male imagination all the more. She has the charm of mystery, which arouses all a man's senses. But she is also the guardian angel of the house.

I had seen all this many times before. But each time I rode or drove into an oasis out of the desert after a long absence I was fascinated by it all over again.

There are none of this to be seen in Gialo, however. There are no purling brooks there, no wonderfully scented fruit and no mysterious black female eyes. In fact, there is no romance to be found there at all.

On the north, coming from the sea, you have to traverse tough dessicated scrub for mile after mile. To the west a sort of devil's garden reaches up to the very first huts of the oasis. It is a vast and impenetrable area of thickly strewn boulders as far as the eye can see. To the south stretches the unending Sarir Calanscio. It is a tableland 400 km long by 200 wide; a flat land where you can lash your steering wheel, set the throttle to 100 km p.h. (60 mph), and confidently go to sleep in your car. There is not a stone, not a single depression, not even a hillock to disturb your sleep. You drive by the compass there. To the east is the equally vast wall of the Great Sand Sea.

As for the Gialo Oasis, the springs are brackish and the inhabitants surly. A thousand palm trees and filthy mud huts stand in a hollow in the middle of the desert. The wind howls ceaselessly—there is never an end to it. Over the centuries the sand has been slowly covering the oasis. The people protect their miserable little gardens with palm fronds, but the wind just blows straight through them, as it does through everything, everywhere. The nearest source of drinking water is 20 km away in the east, where a stream breaks the surface. It is good cool water, which has to be laboriously fetched; and by the time it arrives in the oasis it is almost hot. The women are muffled in black and gaze dejectedly through their veils. The men go about bent and taciturn. You hear no one laugh in that oasis, and the streets are not roofed over. The fruit tastes insipid and the dates are all as hard as stones.

The Wahat Jalu, the area in which the oasis lies, had changed hands twice already. Patrols S1, S2 and T2 of Long Range Desert Group 'A' had taken the oasis on 27 November 1941, after General Reid had occupied the Wahat Jalu with his Punjabi regiment. Everyone wanted the oasis as a base for reconnaissance patrols. Rommel had retreated northwestward to a line running from Marsa el-Brega to the Maradah Oasis, around which he had constructed defences.

The Long Range Desert Group were operating sabotage missions against the fuel and ammunition depots of the Afrika-Korps and were planting agents behind the front. Gialo was the ideal point from which daring men undertaking risky sorties could operate.

On 21 January Rommel had pushed out from his base positions, again thrusting forward, and by 26 January the Desert Rats had evacuated the Wahat Jalu. Once again they disappeared behind the Great Sand Sea.

As our column drove into the oasis, the soldiers of the small Italian garrison were sitting in the shade listlessly chatting about their girl friends back home; we exchanged greetings in a desultory way. Our limbs were leaden and our brains numb. We needed a long break.

The sun was rising over the dunes in the east. It was 11 May 1942.

It was 5 o'clock and the night was visibly clearing over the endless sand plain to the west. It was cold—bitterly cold. The bonnets of our vehicles were drawn abreast and pointing south. The needles of their Askania gyro-compasses had been checked against each other. Their steering had been tightened. We were waiting for the command to go. Fingers stiff with cold were warmed for the last time round hot tin tea mugs, from which we took short sips. Seconds later we were streaking over the surface of the Sarir, baked hard over millions of years.

Soon the cold gave way to searing heat. Before us stretched days of nothing but sand, heat and desert—and that damned sun, which roasted us from morning till night. It burned so hot that our brains withered, our tongues swelled and we saw nothing but black before our eyes. We were automata, not human beings.

We drove hour after hour, day after day. Perhaps somewhere beyond our windscreens, in a valley between two dunes, eternity was lying in wait for us. All night long an eerie ghost-like music wailed through the stillness—the singing of myriads of grains of sand contracting in the cold of the night, rubbing against one another and slithering down the slopes of the dunes.

We had set out on a fantastic journey, one that had not even been attempted by the famous Long Range Desert Group, the greatest experts on the Libyan desert. Whenever possible, they used existing tracks and ancient caravan routes. For safety reasons and so that we should not be seen by them, we were driving across the Great Sand Sea. Our ambition was to reach the Nile Valley 400 km south of Cairo. Slap across the desert—and what a desert! Not even a brackish water-hole would we come across, lost in the immeasurable vastness of sand.

We proposed crossing an area of 60,000 sq km without water-holes, trees, shade or grass, where death opens before you and closes behind you like the undergrowth in the depths of a wood, as the Bedouin says when he speaks of the Great Sand Sea. Here and there on the sandy plain lie the desiccated corpses of assorted migratory birds. Exhausted on their long flight over the Sahara, they simply fell out of the sky. In normal times such a journey in May, when the heat is quite deadly, would have been madness; but then the war, for which we were making the trip, was madness anyway.

In the late afternoon of the first day, after a monotonous drive down this infinitely wide 'motorway' on which not even the smallest stone is to be found, we made camp at the foot of an immense sand dune 450 km south of the Gialo oasis, our point of departure. It was a wonderful place to camp. We spent the night on sand as soft as silk. We ate our dinner together and chatted for a quarter of an hour or so. We were pleased with the first stage of our journey. Then we crept under our blankets and were out like a light until next morning.

The stretch we had put behind us had been the easiest. The following day we kept getting bogged down in the sand, our vehicles balanced over the edges of dunes 80 m or more high. We bumped and banged our way dangerously along the craters in the depths of the dunes. Our foreheads streamed with the sweat of fear as we hurtled over ridges, expecting any second to land under the vehicles, or end up with a broken neck in a valley between the dunes.

But tomorrow was another day—and we would see!

'Good', László said one morning, climbing up to join me on the ridge of a dune, his inevitable cigarette in the right-hand corner of his mouth. I had climbed up ahead of him.

'Point the nose of your car dead east down that dune over there in front of you. Then turn immediately to the south when you get down into the valley. I myself and the others will travel down this valley here behind us. After 10 km you'll turn due east again, up to that great sand dune over there you can see on the horizon. It must be at least 100 m high—you can't miss it. I shall look for a way through further to the south. We shall meet at the Big One.'

'A good idea', I agreed. 'Perhaps this way we'll find a quicker route through the Sand Sea. We ought to be somewhere at the latitude of the Farafra Oasis, which should be some 550 km to the east. From there into the Nile Valley is just a short step, in a manner of speaking.'

'Quite, if you can call 300 km just a short step. In that case, you're quite right. But it's fair enough, we both know that stretch pretty well; what does bother me is the stretch between here and Farafra.'

We walked on the crest along the rim of the crater from which this type of dune takes its name. It is called a 'barkan' from the Arabic word for the half moon. This spot gave the best view. In front of us lay a sleeping sea of sand, the dunes like huge breakers. Eternity could not have been more still.

'I have a nasty feeling we'll never get out of this', Almásy said, looking grim. We drove for two hours, each following his own route, and met at the high dune. László was the first to jump out of his vehicle.

'It would be foolish to go on like this. It's hopeless to try and break through. We'll only crack up the cars and get stuck—and die of thirst', he said. 'We'll have to find another way.'

We drove once again between two ranges of dunes, 100 km further south. Once more we clambered on to a ridge. The men, just about all in, sat slumped apathetically in their vehicles. The two of us stood gasping for air at the top, and looked over the surrounding sea of sand.

'Just look at it!' László said. 'It's huge! There's no end to it. Let's go further south. Let's try climbing four more of these shifting dunes. Maybe we are not far from the end of the southern spurs of the desert. These goddam maps have nothing but blank areas on them. We'll have to guess, and that's as dangerous as hell. If there's no change after that, let's go south, even if it means risking coming across an LRDG party.'

Without looking round, he ran down the slope, got behind the steering wheel of his vehicle, pointed its nose at right-angles up the wall of the dune and flew up it, his foot pressed hard on the accelerator. László had guts, because behind that wall there was again the endless business of the wheels sinking into the sand, which meant that the equipment in each truck had to be unloaded before we could dig ourselves out. Shade? There's no such thing in the Sahara. What do you want shade for? Just let your brains dry out. Who needs a brain just for shovelling sand? Put sand mats behind the rear wheels. Second gear. Give her just a little throttle. Careful now, gently! Like walking on eggs, creep out of the sand drift. Reload the vehicle. Drive on!

The engine screams, the wheels spin, the truck won't shift. The whole grizzly grind starts all over again, the temperature is 50°C (122° F). A blinding sun, a killing thirst, stinging eyes that stare out of deep sockets on to an unreal landscape. Then sand mats under the wheels again. Out of the sand drift again. Reload the car again. My God, the amount of shit people carry around with them throughout life!

Another 100 m, and into yet another sand-drift trap. Distance covered during the day, 40 km. Thousands more to go.

It seemed that Operation Salaam had been conceived under an evil star. It comprised altogether eight men. On the third day of the first stage, the doctor we had taken with us was struck down with desert fever—a case of 'set the fox to keep the geese!' The Sergeant-Major's heart—the German army always has to have a sergeant-major's finger in every pie—said it had had enough. One of the drivers, who was from the Brandenburg Special Duties Regiment—every man as hard as nails—developed the galloping shits. There was nothing for it—it was back to Gialo.

It was the only solution. There was no time to lose. A few days later one captured Ford V-8 was left behind in Gialo so that the casualties could get back to the Mediterranean coast. That left us with four vehicles, and Operation Salaam started out again, this time with only five men.

This time we were to attack the Great Sand Sea by driving clean across it, but we were once again to find the going very slow—only 40 km a day. On the fifth day, with nerves already badly frayed, we suddenly came on steel hard land with thousands of shallow sand ridges at close intervals, no more than a few centimetres high. It was like driving on corrugated iron, and the road bed hammered ceaselessly against the suspension of the vehicles.

The dunes became smaller and smaller until they disappeared altogether. Ahead must be the Garet es-Saghar—the Devil's Garden—a huge stretch of granite boulders, ranging in size from a fist to the height of a house, all thrown about the landscape by the hand of Satan. Millions of years ago a volcano must have strewn them on the surface of the land, covering an area as large as that of a city of a million people.

The famous British explorer Bagnold had surveyed the southern edges of the Sahara in 1937 while searching for a new route from the Nile Valley to the Oasis of Kufrah. That was how the Garet had come to be known about—but not known. He had not ventured even a mile into it—and how wise he was!

But we had to get through, we had no choice. We agonized our way through this garden of madness laboriously, twisting and turning at walking pace, continually shifting rocks out of our path. Shortly before sunset, it was all over at last. The Devil's Garden lay behind us.

No one wanted anything to eat. We had even almost forgotten our thirst. Hardly had the monotonous roar of the engines fallen silent than we lay down, just as we got out of the vehicles, right between them, utterly worn out. We pulled the blankets over our heads and slept as if we had died till daybreak.

At very first light of our first day on the far side of the Devil's Garden a slight but hot breeze sprang up. That is unusual and can mean only one thing. There was not time to pause for thought. We had to draw up the trucks into a hollow square very quickly, because a searing hot Gibli was about to hit us.

Already a thick yellow veil had spread across the southern horizon. It consisted of sand and gravel, coming at us at a speed of 100 km per hour.

A flock of tiny birds, driven ahead of the storm, dropped into our stockade of vehicles, looking for shelter. They were birds of passage. Panting they settled in the searing hot air under the trucks. They made no attempt to move away when we lay down next to them. They did not touch a drop of the water we set down before them. They seemed to have lost all will to live in the merciless heat and the storm. Finding it pointless to live any longer, they were surrendering to death.

But we could still stand, burnt a dark brown as we were, and sinewy, with nothing but muscle and bone under our leathery skins—not a ounce of fat left on our bodies. Utterly dehydrated, we sheltered behind our vehicles against that goddam storm, cursing it. That storm played hell with our projected schedule.

'It's a good thing we remembered to put wire mesh over the windscreens. After this Gibli we would have had the choice of going on without windscreens or returning to Gialo', said László. His face muffled in a scarf up to his sunglasses, he cursed as a hundred thousand grains of sand stung every inch of exposed skin, like so many needles.

Both Arabia and Africa have their own hot winds. Egypt has its Khamsin, Arabia the Sherkiya, Algeria the Samun. But the three of them together would have their work cut out to equal the power of the Gibli. It chaps your lips and tears skin off your face. The windows and metal of our vehicles looked as if they had been sand-blasted under high pressure.

Suddenly it was over. It had raged for four hours, and now it was gone. We watched the last dust cloud moving over the dunes to the north. This burning hot wind of hell had gone as suddenly as it had come. Yet hours afterwards the stones and sand still gave off heat.

We climbed back into our cars and raced over the Sarir, our feet clamped hard down on the floorboards. At last we had good going again, and could make up for lost time. We drove until nightfall, and there before us, only a kilometre away, stood a black wall, majestic in its unbounded wildness.

It was the Gilf Kebir Plateau, soaring 800 m out of the plain, and almost as large as Switzerland. It was 200 km long by 100 km wide, and shaped not unlike the African continent on which it stands. Together with the Jebel Uweinat, which lies further to the south, it is the most impressive tableland in the eastern Sahara.

Ten years earlier Almásy had sought and found the Oasis of the Little Birds, the 'Zarsura', in the Gilf Kebir. Together with the Englishman Clayton, who was knocking around not far from us as our enemy, they had travelled down the Wadi Hamra and had found a hidden valley in the south, amid the high crags of the Gilf, which could only be the 'Zarsura'. It is known to the Bedouins of the Sahara, who tell each other all sorts of stories round their campfires. One of them is the tale of the 'Zarsura'.

It was supposed to have been as green as the Garden of Eden and full of antelopes and gazelles. It was said to have been inhabited by thousands of small birds and to have had—water! Above all water, any amount of it, flowing down a wadi.

On this plateau, which was inhabited a great many years ago, Almásy and Clayton had also found rock drawings in caves. They named the dry river bed in which the caves were found Wadi Sura or Valley of the Pictures. The wonderful rock drawings are of swimming men and grazing antelopes, giraffe and buffalo; and of hunters chasing lions and women building fires.

'Tomorrow morning I'll dig up a canister of water I buried here in 1937', Almásy boasted, as we were setting up camp under the precipitous wall of the Gilf.

'*Chante, beau merle, chante*', say the French, when someone is showing off. So he proposed to find the canister of water he had buried years ago, where there were no landmarks or even a track, did he!

'I'll pour the canister over your fat head, my little friend; that'll teach you!'

That evening Sandy, our expert radio operator, who was to go down to the Nile Valley with me (if and when we arrived at our destination), sent a signal to Intelligence HQ, Mamelin. 'Sandy' was the name I gave to Sandstetter, a German from East Africa who had assumed the name of Peter Monkaster and carried an American passport as a businessman. His radio message to headquarters would inform the Afrika-Korps of our whereabouts. After crossing the Gilf, we had about another 800 km to cover to the point where we were to be dropped off above Asyut.

The following morning I was the recipient of a canister of Nile water over my head. We admired the rock drawings and Almásy, who had a nose for the trail like a bloodhound, that afternoon found for the second time the el-Aquaba Pass north of the Wadi Feraq, which he had first crossed with the British desert traveller Penderel in 1931. It was Clayton who had given the Pass its name.

One of the Bedford trucks, which we had nicknamed 'Flitzer', got irretrievably stuck in a fissure of rock on the Gilf. We were bound to lose one somewhere along the way. For all I know, it's there to this day.

At its widest, the pass is no more than 10 m across, but one can drive through those places in one's sleep. However, there are only a few places as wide as that. Most of the time on the way up to the Plateau the right wheel of the car was using only half the width of the tread. The other half was turning on air over a sheer drop of several hundred metres.

When we had got to the top and climbed out of our trucks, Wieland, the Brandenburger from South Africa, said: 'I was shitting bricks during that little drive.' He was not the only one! From then on, however, it was all child's play, if we did not run into a native of the Sudan Defence Force or into the Long Range Desert Group.

Once over the Tropic of Cancer we could turn north, and at Abu Ballas, where twin mountains rise to the sky like the breasts of a woman, we turned northeast and drove through the 60 km gap of sand between the green Dakhla Oasis and the great Oasis of Wahet el-Kharga. It was hard sand, a Sarir on which the cars would travel as if hell-bent to get to the land of the living again.

The Great Oasis—Wahat el-Kharga! There we stood, parched, unwashed, unshaven and thirsty, at the rim of the murderous desert we had traversed. At last we could look down on a real oasis, and on its thousand date palms, its green gardens and scattered mud huts. It lay in complete silence. Only a few lazy clouds of smoke drifted over it.

'The lucky bastards', said László at my elbow. 'There they sit, eating ful medami, onions, slices of radish, with fresh-baked bread!'

'Shut up, or I'll run down there immediately, knock on the first door and ask them if I might have some, please.'

'What's that you're talking about?' asked Sandy, our radio operator. 'Ful medami—that must be marvellous from the way you both drool over it.'

'Forget it', said Almásy. 'You'd never eat it. It's only lousy beans, steamed with herbs and prepared with lemons, olive oil and cayenne pepper. It's the favourite food of those people, particularly of the poor; but the rich are just as keen on it.'

'Just think, we might even have a bath', said Wieland in a flat tone of voice. 'A bath—remember? Oh, to splash about in water as long as you like!'

We were to have none of those things—no ful medami, no onions, no radishes, no baths. But with kilometres of desert behind us, we could be excused for dreaming a little.

The stars were still bright in the clear sky overhead, but over in the east, where the Nile Valley lay, a pink flush was beginning to spill over the horizon. It was time we moved into the oasis, to face the acid test. If the British had occupied Kharga, and if one of their patrols turned up where we were camped, our struggle across the desert would have been for naught and we would be marched off to a prisoner-of-war camp.

Five puny men could hardly fight a small war of their own in a remote oasis. So, carefully, like thieves, we drove down the slope and continued on past the mud walls surrounding the oasis and into the centre of Kharga. A skinny dog was nosing about on the road. Not a soul was to be seen. Somewhere a donkey let out a long-drawn heart-breaking bray. Some hens were clucking behind a wall.

We had hidden our Afrika-Korps caps under the seats of our vehicles. The uniforms were khaki, much the same as the British. We should not attract too much attention. Before we had started, we had smeared the German military emblems on our cars with sand and mud. But, just in case, they were still there underneath. If we were caught, it would be quite easy to make them visible again.

We went round the corner, and there stood a R'affer with a rifle over his shoulder. All over Egypt this hybrid—half gendarme, half nightwatchman—patrolled the villages at night, well trained to shoot first and ask questions later. Better safe than sorry was their motto.

Behind the R'affer we could see two Egyptian soldiers in puttees. Their bayonets hung down to their knees, and their rifles were slung over their shoulders like bags of flour. They were not dangerous, but the nightwatchman-cum-gendarme was.

'Stanna!' We pulled up.

Pushing his regulation fez to the back of his head, he looked through the open window. By saying 'Sabah el-Kher, j'ah Beshchau-wish!' I promoted him to sergeant-major with as much unction as I could summon, and that seemed to please him mightily.

Then he asked: 'Whither so early, Chawag'ah?'

I immediately explained that I was the Egyptian Divisional Interpreter attached to the British general. The other men in the car were officers in the British Army, and we were on our way to Asyut to find quarters there. Then, to avoid any further delay, I warned him to get out of our way in double quick time, and that it could be that the general, who was not far behind us, could come along and tear a big strip off him; in that case the Mudir of Asyut, as the man in charge of the Kharga oasis, would post him to the Sudan for the next twenty years.

'M'ah Salama, y'ah Effendi.' He had promoted me to the rank of Lord, or Master, and wished me peace. He turned about and went off with the two soldiers, who throughout had been leaning against the wall.

I suppose he wanted to avoid meeting that infidel, the general. He probably went off to the village café, to smoke a hubble-bubble and keep well out of sight.

Kharga is no small oasis. It is almost 100 km long. We found ourselves on the road that runs through Muhariq, an inhabited place, if consisting only of a few mud huts. We stepped on the gas, past the airfield, which lay to the right of the road, and reached the first few hovels of the village. Everyone still seemed to be asleep, except for one fellah who crossed the road to get to his camel, which was lying down. Without further mishap we reached the Jabsa Pass, which runs steeply up to the plateau. Asyut is not far from there.

'If you only knew what a weight has just fallen off my mind!' said László.

He was the first among us to speak. The rest of us were still too dazed by our luck with the R'affer. We had all been quite resigned to being caught.

'There must be someone particularly thick on the British General Staff, someone who's never been in an oasis', Almásy said. 'I hope Clayton never gets word of it—that there isn't a single Englishman posted here. I am quite sure he is convinced I am knocking around somewhere.'

'Well, the main thing is we've done it', Sandy said. From now on he reverted to the name Peter Monkaster, born somewhere in the American West. That was what it said on his passport anyway.

The passport had been genuine enough in its time, and 'Monkaster' himself had that cocky manner Americans showed in those days, when they thought they were just about the wisest guys on earth. He played his part well, and I was sure that he would not be noticed in Cairo. In those days America seemed very far away—just a place in the New World where rich uncles lived.

'We're not in the clear yet', I said. It had all been too easy; it had all gone too well. But why not? If we were going to be picked up, it would have been in Kharga. Nothing much could happen now.

The two of us would go down to Asyut, the others would drive back to Cyrenaica the way we had come, and that would be that. We had solved a great problem—that of living together in the boundless wilderness like members of a ship's crew who must learn to get on with each other for months on end at sea. That was not an easy thing to do. There had been a few frictions, but we had learned to trust each other, so that everything had gone pretty smoothly. We had completed our journey and overcome hardships that we once might have considered unendurable. Having achieved so much, we felt nothing could go wrong for us now.

From then on Sandy and I would be on our own. Despite the fact we had been together day and night for weeks, we knew very little about each other. Long ago in Berlin I had struck up a conversation with him quite casually, and without him suspecting anything. We chatted awhile as soldiers do. He had struck me as a good chap, and I had had the impression that we would get on. He had lived among Englishmen for a long while, knew them, was familiar with their idiosyncrasies and spoke their language excellently. One could not have wished for a better companion for a mission—only it meant that I would no longer be on my own. That was what really bothered me.

We had arrived at the highest point of the pass. There it was, that old blue sky of the Nile Valley, somewhere between dark blue and turquoise. The only painter who ever managed to capture this blue was Nattier, and he never saw Egypt. There was not a cloud in the sky. The shimmering ribbon flowed down the middle of a Garden of Eden between two deserts—through green fields and white mosques with their slender minarets. Tall palm trees moved almost imperceptibly in the breeze.

We had arrived at our half-way house. Operation Salaam had been completed and now Operation Condor—our mission in the Nile Valley—would begin.

Chapter 14

Condor

One of our vehicles was parked a little way off the road, concealed from sight behind a large rock. Almásy, who was at the steering wheel of another of the trucks, drove on with the others a few hundred metres further, to the point where the road dipped down into the valley. He let his car roll to a standstill, put on the handbrake, lit a cigarette and said: 'That's it, chaps. Let's keep it short.'

We took the suitcase with our civilian clothes and changed. Sandy assumed his new identity of Peter Monkaster and I took on my old one, in which I had always felt at ease. I carefully checked all papers and other small details, such as my Egyptian driving licence, address book and club membership card—all those little things a man carries about with him in his pockets that prove he really is who he says he is.

I too wanted to get on. Moments like these produce an onrush of sentiment that would have been out of place on this occasion. Everything had worked fine; the first stage had gone strictly according to plan.

My superiors had great hopes in this operation. Because of the object of the exercise, it had been prepared with great care. After the success of the offensive he had just launched, Rommel intended to make his next steps dependent, among other things, on our reports from Cairo.

Almásy turned his truck around, the second truck followed him, and they were on their way back. There we were, two agents who had to get to Cairo, despite the omnipresence of the British Army.

There was a bend in the road. On either side of the straight stretch that lay ahead there was a British army camp. We could see barracks and soldiers marching about. The road ran straight into the camp. I can still remember Sandy saying: 'Are we looking at the end of our mission?'

I tried to reassure him by explaining that not a person in the British camp would suspect that we could be enemy agents, because only two complete lunatics would have attempted the route we were taking to Cairo. Outwardly calm, we strode along the road.

A British major standing in the middle of the road as we came within hailing distance said that we looked like a couple of door-to-door salesmen who pestered people in the country back home. He asked us where in the devil's name we had come from!

I explained that our car was some way back behind the hill and that we had broken down. As we had managed to get this far, we should be grateful for a lift to the railway station, since we had to be in Cairo by the next day. I can still hear him asking in amazement. 'To the station? I can't do that without knowing who you are. We are not running a taxi service, you know.'

I immediately introduced Sandy, my American friend, who had wanted to see the desert before he returned to the States. Then, showing my passport as Hussein Gaafar, I let it drop that he had probably heard of my family in Cairo. The major seemed suitably pleased to meet us and suggested that we all go and have something to drink. After that, he would arrange for some transport to Asyut.

It was a simple as that! We had some marvellously cool whisky and soda, served by a batman. There was some lively talk about the desert, which had after all been a topic of everyday conversation with us for the past three weeks and on which we were therefore pretty expert.

Some of the officers said that we must have been clean out of our minds, and that one should never go into the desert without a second car to accompany one. I agreed that they were of course quite right, and that we had been very silly to drive into the Sahara unaccompanied. Then there was an invitation for lunch, which was just about to be served. It tasted marvellous—no substitute malt coffee for the British officers' mess; they capped their hospitality with a cup of real coffee before driving us to the station.

'If you pricked me now, you know, I really think there would be no blood', Sandy said as the driver disappeared out of sight and we went up to the ticket office.

'What makes you think you are the only one?'

Then I did something that would have cost my radio operator his life if he had had a weak heart. This being long before the time of Diners' Club and similar credit cards, we carried our cash (expense money and allowances) with us in a suitcase. There was so much money in the case (both in sterling and Egyptian pounds) that nobody but a bank robber could have dreamt of walking about with such loot. As to our other suitcase, it contained a very superior radio transmitter, purpose-built for long-distance communications work—a neat little 40-Watt transmitter/receiver. It was a top-secret kind of set—1942 Spring Model, you might say. In other words, there was dynamite in both cases.

Having reserved two seats on the first-class Pullman on the late afternoon Luxor-Cairo Express, I wanted to stretch my legs in the square outside the station and to get the feel of my new surroundings. I could send the cases 'Personal Luggage in Advance', but when it came to collecting them in Cairo, the Field Security inspectors would be certain to turn them inside out. Since that had to be avoided, I had a problem to solve.

I had been lucky once already that day, so why should I not have one more stroke of good fortune. As I strolled around the square, I noticed four pitch-black Nubians sitting propped up against the wall of the railway station building. Suddenly, an idea came to me. All of them had almost certainly worked as house-boys in Cairo. As I approached them, they sprang to their feet and planted themselves before me. As with one voice, they said: 'Ahlan wa Sahlan, y'ah Bey!'

All four bore the same tribal markings on their faces—two strokes on each cheek. The strokes had been drawn very close together, with great precision, identifying them as tribesmen from Dongola.

Dongola is a place in Nubia between the third and fourth Nile cataracts, where the desert creeps up to the very doors of the mud huts. The inhabitants of the place would have died of hunger long ago if it had not been for the rich people in Cairo for whom they worked as servants. They needed no references—Nubians from Dongola are honest. Not even the missionaries, for all their painstaking efforts, had succeeded in turning them into dishonest Africans.

I pointed to the youngest, because I knew that their tribal custom was that the youngest should be given the first opportunity. He must have been about seventeen and was called Mahmoud. I explained to him that I was looking for a servant who would come to Cairo and keep house for me there; and he almost immediately agreed to accompany me. But not before we engaged in the delightful Oriental process of haggling about money. We carefully went through the prices of the various foods then prevailing, which he invariably claimed he could buy at derisory prices. Like all Orientals, he worked for nothing.

Should I make him a present of £E5 a month, all his family back in Dongola would pray for my health. However, should my generosity run to £E6—why then, Illustrious Bey, since Allah has made you a gift of all the wisdom of this world, the prophet would this very day order you a divan from the heavenly carpenter, on which you should experience heavenly joys with three virgins, delivered fresh, each day.

I promised him £E6. The prospect of being blessed with three fresh—and naturally surpassingly lovely—virgins every day after my departure from this wicked world, and of enjoying the delights of paradise with them, made me forget my instinctive meanness.

Meanwhile Sandy, who was keeping an eye on those suitcases full of dynamite, looked as if he had never seen me before. When I went up to him with my brand-new servant, who promptly picked up the suitcases and disappeared with them, Sandy gasped and looked frightened enough to faint.

After being given enough money for a third-class ticket to Cairo and travelling expenses, Mahmoud reappeared without the cases and asked where he should wait for us in Cairo. I suggested at the bottom of the steps outside the Midan el-Mahatta exit of the Cairo Main Station.

Mahmoud bowed in agreement and returned to his friends, one of whom was already using one of our suitcases as a headrest. Very quietly I mumbled to Sandy that no British Officer would bother to check on a Berberie. He asked angrily how I proposed to explain the loss of those two suitcases when I got back to Berlin. I told him that we would not starve, and that whether we got back to Berlin or not depended on who won the war.

Indeed, when we walked out of the station in Cairo, there sat Mahmoud, waiting patiently on the bottom step, a suitcase on either side gripped firmly under each arm, wide-awake and watching everyone who came down the steps with searching eyes. I exchanged a triumphant glance with my radio operator, who just then had pointed to the Nubian with his forefinger to show me that he really was sitting on the step and waiting for us. It was hard to comprehend how Mahmoud could sit there with those suitcases, waiting for two people who would not dare to summon the police if he should disappear with them.

The first stage of Operation Condor had gone without a hitch.

It was a muggy humid early June day. The taxi took us through Tewfikya, to the Shariah Maspero, then drove quickly along the banks of the blackish-green Nile to the Kasr el-Nil Bridge and on to el-Guezira. If it had not been for the presence of so many British soldiers, you would never have thought that a few hundred kilometres to the west a dreadful war was raging in Libya.

It was the pleasantest time of day to be in Cairo. The population sat chattering outside the cafés and restaurants, drinking zibib or beer and eating vast quantities of meze, smoking their nargilehs, sipping coffee, and laughing. The city was brightly lit. Groups of people were loitering on the banks of the river, and those aboard the graceful feluccas on the water were enjoying the river breeze.

At Guezira we could at last spend a night in civilized surroundings after our murderous journey through the desert. At one and the same time I felt both thrilled and worried, because there was a great deal more to accomplish if Condor was to be a success. But uppermost in my mind was sitting down to a first-class Arab meal at Ali Hassan el-Hati's restaurant after first spending an unconscionable amount of time having a shower.

As we left the taxi outside the villa I had rented from the Armenian widow during my last mission, I could smell the heavy scent of jasmin from the hedge outside. The elder Mahmoud—for some unknown reason Nubian house-boys are mostly called Mahmoud—came to meet us down the gravel path between beds of roses in full bloom. He looked in some amazement at the newly arrived Nubian, who belonged to a tribe other than his own. Then he explained that René Rehbinder had left Cairo a week earlier in a hurry for the pleasanter climate of Alexandria, following his generous patrons, the Pashas, whose horses were now running on the Alexandria racecourses.

As Mahmoud was talking, I thought how that free and easy style of life in the lively seaport was really quite scandalous! All those clubs, nightclubs, receptions and beach parties—all that boozy social life—would be over in a flash if the war began knocking on the city gates. The smiles would soon be wiped off faces. Destruction and fear would reign supreme. To hell with this damned war!

While I was having that much wanted shower, Sandy sent the signal to say we had arrived in Cairo. Later, much later, I learned that on that very day, at 8 Midan Sheikh Yussuf, not far from my villa, a very different signal was being monitored. The British Secret Intelligence Service decoded the message:

> GERMAN MILITARY ATTACHE LISBON BOUGHT FIVE COPIES DU MAURIER'S NOVEL REBECCA IN MARCH 1942.

Alarm bells were sounded at the Special Investigation Branch of the Military Police. Major A. W. Sanson of Field Security had ordered the word to be passed—do not give up the chase until Condor had been brought to the kill.

In his book *Wüstenfüchsen* (*Desert Foxes*) Paul Carell gives the German version: '. . . when early in June Almásy reported back on his mission to Rommel outside Bir-Hacheim, he saluted and said: "Herr Generaloberst, Operation Salaam has been successfully completed. Operation Condor can begin." Almásy was then told what had happened. It was Rommel himself who told him, and Almásy's distress was quite evident. At the start of the May offensive Rommel took away our radio operators in Mamelin (Aberle and Weber), and incorporated them with his own radio staff. After all, Rommel said, he needed every man he could get, and the two men might just as well wait for their signals from Cairo in his signals unit, where they could do other duties as well.'

But what the two men had done was something quite different. They had taken with them a copy of *Rebecca* (containing the code for Operation Condor); and when they were caught by a New Zealand patrol that mounted an attack on Rommel's headquarters and interrogated, Daphne du Maurier's novel was found among their possessions.

This is how Sansom tells the story in his book *I Spied Spies*:

> 'Have you read this book?' Bob asked me, showing me a book. It was the best selling novel *Rebecca* by Daphne du Maurier.
>
> 'Yes, when it first came out. Why?'
>
> 'We found it among the possessions of a couple of German POW's. It was the only book they had.'
>
> I said nothing. The most unlikely books are found among people's possessions and Bob knew that as well as I did. I waited for what else he had to say.
>
> 'Neither of them knows a word of English. They were captured at a mobile field radio-monitoring station in the desert. A New Zealand patrol caught them literally with their pants down. It was just before dawn. The

German signals men were brought to the Interrogation Centre at Maadi, and that's where I came into the picture.

'I was looking through their personal effects when I found this book,' Bob told me, indicating *Rebecca* again. 'As you can see, someone had rubbed out the price.' He pointed to a roughness of the paper on the corner of the fly-leaf.

The book was in mint condition and the net price was printed on the dust-jacket, so the fact that a price had been pencilled inside meant almost certainly that it had been sold abroad. Bob had found out where from a forensic photographer, who had deciphered the impression of '50 escudos' on the fly-leaf. That meant Portugal.

I sent a cable to London and asked them to investigate. The answer gave me the first, as yet insignificant, lead on Eppler. At least now I knew for certain that this must have been the code book of an agent and that the man concerned was certainly in this country. It wasn't much—but it was a start.

Resuming Carell's narrative in *Wüstenfüchsen*, Count László Almásy wonders:

> Was there no alternative? Was it necessary to risk such a carefully thought-out operation, on which headquarters in Berlin had lavished so much care, just to add two men to the frontline strength? Almásy tried to make the interview a little less constrained by talking about 'Salaam'. He said: 'Herr Generaloberst, I could have taken a whole regiment with me to the Nile.' Rommel patted him on the shoulder and said with a laugh: 'Count Almásy I hope to get there with my army by a shorter route.'

Rommel never did get there. The odds were too heavily stacked against him. But the carefree life of Alexandria continued undisturbed. To Rommel, Sandy and I were just two agents working away in Cairo, and we were expendable.

On this marvellous June day—marvellous because I was in Cairo again—I had taken my time over an excellent meal and was sitting in the best of spirits at the Kit-Kat, across the river from el-Zamalek, and asked Mac the barman for a whisky. I wanted to see Hekmat Fahmi, the beautiful belly-dancer, whom I had known for some considerable time—and not only in my official capacity. I wanted her to work for me. The nightclub was the ideal spot, being a favourite resort of officers from the British HQ Middle East and of officers on short leave from the front, many of whom could snatch a few pleasant hours in the company of lovely women.

The sweet scent of a thousand roses in bloom mingled with the

French perfumes of brown- and white-skinned women. The figures round the tables were barely discernible in the subdued light that filtered through the flowering shrubs in which the lamps were concealed. Stinking rich Egyptians, Greeks and Armenians, who could not have cared less about that awful war, were making up to assorted lovelies hung with precious jewels. Everyone who was anyone in Cairo was having fun. The people there were 'in'; they fancied themselves as 'belonging'.

He was immaculate in flannels and blazer. A dark red tarboosh sat on his head. His features were firm and virile—the face of a man—and would have been even without the moustache. Though not tall, he was powerfully built and handsome. He settled himself on the free bar stool next to me, and pulled slowly on his cigarette, inhaling the smoke deeply. Without being asked, Mac put a White Horse and soda before him.

'Cheers!' he said, raising his glass.

'Cheers!' I said.

'It's a warm night; makes a man thirsty. Will you join me in another?' he said in flawless Arabic.

'I don't mind if I do', I said.

'Sansom', he said. The name meant nothing to me.

I could see, as I introduced myself, that mine meant equally little to him.

'Glad to know you', he said and raised his glass.

We drank a few more together that evening until I left with Hekmat, the belly-dancer. He could hold his liquor. In the end I left owing him a round.

I discussed everything with Hekmat during the remainder of the night, in her fabulously furnished houseboat, while we lay in her wide sensuous bed under its silken mosquito net. We perfected our plans down to the last detail.

My wristwatch said 6 o'clock. The sun was just rising over the Mogattam Hills. Its rays, having struck the citadel and the dome of the Mohammed Ali Mosque, slowly lit up the town, which still lay in the penumbra of the valley. I was on the way to my second rendezvous.

A few people who had just arrived on the train were crossing the Midan el-Mahatta, in front of the main railway station. I drove round the station and into the Shariah Choubrah which runs north as straight as an arrow for 3 km. About half-way, at the intersection of the Shariah Ibn el-Kourany, stands St. Mark's school and its chapel.

Being no churchgoer, I did not know how to behave on entering the House of God. The only thing I knew was my password, 'Alma Mater'. I was supposed to talk to a priest who would be celebrating early morning Mass. Should I be unlucky, I would have to keep coming to the church until I had found the right man.

Headquarters had sent a transmitter to Cairo via a diplomat in Budapest. The transmitter, I had been told, was set up in the church. The priest was in the habit of supplying Rommel's headquarters with meteorological reports at irregular intervals. But his transmitter had been silent for some time now.

I hated this kind of set-up; it could so easily turn out to be a trap. I disliked contacts that had been arranged by other people, preferring to build up my own; that way I could work with my mind at rest, because before making a contact I always painstakingly checked the person concerned.

I parked Hekmat's Cadillac, which I had borrowed that morning, in a side street about 100 m short of the crossroads, and walked the rest of the way to the church, an inconspicuous building. Candles were burning on the altar. In front of them, his back to the handful of old ladies scattered among the many empty pews, stood a priest. His eyes were raised to heaven, his hands clasped. His face was turned away; I could not see it. What's the difference? I said to myself; you don't know him anyway.

I tiptoed up to the door of the vestry, as I had been told. He was bound to come that way once Mass was over. Now I could see his face. It was not that of a young man, but it was the face of a good man; and my misgivings were allayed. He could never have gone through the world without attracting attention; his lean face with the shock of white hair crowning it, the dark brown eyes with their humorous twinkle—they were bound to make him stand out in a crowd. He wore his *soutane* as a Prussian officer wears his uniform. Judging by his furrowed face, he must have spent many years of his life in countries with tropical climates; nor did his unusual appearance suggest the run-of-the-mill parish priest.

When the service was over, he approached me with slow and measured steps. As he passed me on his way to the door, I whispered: 'Alma Mater'.

'God bless you, my son', he said.

He opened the door of the vestry with deliberation and walked into the semi-darkness of the room. As straight as a flagstaff, I thought, as I followed him in. But we had not yet completed our introductions. I still had to say a sentence to him to which he must give me the appropriate answer. Not until then could we speak without restraint.

'Facere significationem', I said as the door closed behind us.

'Cor ad cor loquitur', he replied.

He's my man, I thought.

'Why, mon Père, have you not been sending any signals for some time?'

'Since the failure of the General's flight it has become somewhat unsafe. You must appreciate that I cannot take any risks', he said.

I could well understand it. The amateurishly prepared escape attempt over a year ago of General Azziz el-Masri Pasha had been bound to fail, because it had been so stupidly organised. The British had naturally discovered it, and all those who had directly and indirectly taken part were still very frightened men. I too was anxious to keep my head down and avoid possible unpleasant surprises. I had to escape becoming another hero in shining armour – no easy matter, considering the keen scent of Field Security's bloodhounds. It could happen easily enough. But I was not interested in 'going over Jordan'. I was not interested in finding out what there was, or was not, to be found there. I had a pretty shrewd idea that there would be an absolute void.

I tried to convey all this to the Reverend Father, not in the crude terms in which I was thinking but in a somewhat milder form. As we parted, he said in his pleasantly modulated voice: 'Do you believe in God?'

'No, Father, only in chance', I answered as I left the room. I considered that our discussion was at an end. I knew that I would never return, not only because things were so dicey, but also because I could not really approve of installing a transmitter under the altar of a church and, moreover, operating it from there. That was asking for more brass neck than I had.

I got back into the car and drove through the town to the Bahr el-Ama section of the river. Hekmat's houseboat was moored there, between el-Guezira and the western bank.

Hekmat was something special. She fitted well into undercover work. Instead of bothering her head about life after death and all that stuff, she catered to the pleasures of the flesh on this earth. Not that she went with just anyone who came along. No, she was very particular.

She owed her fantastic body, which had such an irresistible effect on almost every man, to her belly-dancing. Whenever she appeared on stage, not one of them could tear his eyes away from her erotically twitching, lascivious abdomen. While they were watching, no doubt they all dreamed of a romp in bed with her. Certainly she was a terrible strumpet, and, once she made up her mind, could conquer any man, even the most obstinate.

Sometimes even I would be bitten with jealousy, though we knew each other so well and our liaison was by no means recent. If I ever spoke of it, she would reply coolly: 'Are you really so unsure of me, taking such risks as I do for you, that you think I could be keen on that fellow?' She gave me proof of her faithfulness later, during some very unpleasant hours she spent in the hands of the Secret Intelligence Service.

I parked the great car not far from the houseboat, or dahabiha, a little way up the Shariah el-Mountassar, so that it could not be seen from the Shariah el-Nil, where the houseboat lay. It was a safety rule we had. Perhaps it was not a very original idea, but it reassured us. Then I walked towards the river through el-Agouza, a newly developed area with attractive new villas. The East and Europe take the upper hand in Cairo by turns. I like it that way: it is the Egypt of my childhood, more beautiful by far than any fairytale. There are the Egyptian women, with those golden bobbins on their noses, from which black veils fall over their faces; and the gait of the fellaheen—their long slender necks sitting on broad shoulders, their flat powerful backs and their heads crowned by turbans. They go about their business, dressed in long black or tobacco-brown shifts reaching to the ground, poor but proud. No European, no matter how elegant, can ever match the way they walk.

At the corner, where a white lookout-tower stood like an exclamation mark next to the wooden-barred harem windows, I crossed the street towards the Bahr el-Ama arm of the Nile. I walked up the gangplank leading to the houseboat.

'Where have you been so long, Hussein? Come here immediately', said Hekmat, comfortably seated in a deckchair, sheltered from the sun beneath a bright awning.

She was extremely beautiful, and justifiably the most adored of belly-dancers. She had a head of lustrous black hair, and sensational green eyes inherited from a Circassian grandmother. Her nose was the delicate aristocratic nose found in ancient Egyptian paintings of women. As she sat there, she had that same dreamy face to be seen on the bas-reliefs of God knows how many dynasties in upper Egypt. Her features were so finely drawn they were almost stylized, but wonderfully lively. Her skin had a tawny colour that was the perfect foil for her deep green eyes.

'What's the hurry?'

She had found a houseboat for me, only a few hundred metres down river from her own, immediately before the Zamalek Bridge. She wanted me to come quickly to meet the woman who had agreed to rent it to us.

As we walked along the Nile bank, she explained that another houseboat just above the one we were to use was at present occupied by a major in the Secret Intelligence Service. Nothing could happen to us with a neighbour like that! Surely no agent in the world would have the cheek to move in right next to him! Because she was 'keeping her eye' on us, we should have nothing to fear in being so near the enemy.

Hekmat knew all about the major; he was, after all, in his sixties and she was young and enticing. Then she asked whether I had ever seen a beautiful Egyptian cat playing with a mouse. Her voice was velvety and her movements those of a cat about to show her claws.

It was a very attractive dahabiha, with a great sundeck complete with a bar made of mahogany and a whole wall covered in bottles of every known and unknown variety of alcohol. In the staterooms below the bulkheads were covered in attractive materials and the furniture had been chosen with great taste. It was pleasantly cool; one felt snug and safe there. Very pleasant quarters indeed.

A padded passageway led to a short steep flight of stairs up to the deck. I noticed that there were two ways out and was well pleased, because one might need them in a hurry.

Later, when I showed our new quarters to Sandy, he found a marvellous hiding place for his transmitter. One of the rooms had what was almost a purpose-built radio cubicle, right under the bar. The bar had a great radiogram let into it. There was a small trapdoor right behind it, which led into our radio cubicle. The door in the padded passageway was also fitted with padding, so that you would never suspect there was a room there at all.

Our aerials above the sun awning would not attract any attention either, because the bar on deck, with its great radiogram, was invisible from the street. Only if one was standing or sitting at the bar itself, might one be forgiven for thinking that the aerial was perhaps a trifle too long for such a very high-powered radio. But nobody would give it another thought in a town where there must have been many other large VHF radios. That was confirmed by the major's batman when he said in all innocence to Sandy, who had just finished erecting our aerial: 'That should be good for a range of 1,000 km, for transmitting as well as receiving.'

Since the beginning of Egypt's history all her invasions have come from the east. Never has any army penetrated the country from the Libyan desert. But this time it looked as if the Nile Valley might be conquered from the West.

General Pierre Koenig was near the end of his tether at Bir-Hacheim with his Free French Brigade and his Jewish Volunteer Battalion. Although General Ritchie advised him to break out of the deathly grip of encirclement in which he found himself, he sent Koenig no relief.

On 10 June Rommel took Bir-Hacheim. Ten days later it was Tobruk's turn, and then he swept on to Bardia and Bir el Gobi. The Western Desert Forces were on the retreat, and Rommel planned to use Tobruk as the ideal jumping-off point for an attempt to reach the Nile. Before long he would be a mere 100 km from Alexandria.

Cairo was in turmoil.

As the German tanks rolled over the frontier, knocking down the barriers, Egypt's many banks were having to honour their customers' deposits. Foreign currency on the black market dropped 50 per cent, and the true value of British money could only be had from their paymaster corps. That money had to be honestly declared, and in Egypt honesty is not easily come by.

Among a few thousand Jews, Greeks and the flotsam of various nationalities—that is, among those who had enough money—the cry went up: 'Let's get out! The Germans are coming!' Everyone else stayed in town, put their trust in Allah and awaited whatever fate held in store for them.

Only one character behaved as if nothing whatever was happening—Tommy!

In time General Alexander replaced Auchinleck, and Montgomery took command of the Eighth Army. He proceeded to establish defensive positions between the coast and the Qattara Depression.

Rommel now had a vastly extended line of communication, and 45 per cent of his reinforcements, sent across the Mediterranean, were being sunk in their transports. The decision to delay the invasion of Malta was beginning to have its repercussions. On the other hand, the streets of Cairo were loud both by day and by night with the rattling of the tracks of tanks rolling up to the front. The Tenth Army was on its way from Syria and Palestine, and the first American units were setting eyes on the Land of the Pharaohs.

One wonderful night, when the moon was full, I was sitting with Hekmat on the deck of the houseboat when an Indian unit, dusty and dog-tired, stopped for a brief rest. They were immediately across the street and easily identifiable. The unit could be seen from a long way off, so bright was the moonlight. The field kitchen was operating on the pavement and the exhausted men were queuing up in front of it for a bite to eat.

I can still imagine the conversation taking place between two of the soldiers, who were looking towards us as they waited for their food.

'Those two over there don't care a damn about this war. They are sitting there and lapping up their whisky and letting things take their own course—it's all the same to them, whatever happens. And then they'll be going and you know where!'

'But those two are not English surely. They are Egyptians, or something. In any case, they will be having nothing to do with the war.'

'And you? I suppose you are an Englishman! I suppose you are having something to do with all this! You are just as liable to be stopping a bullet—and for what? For damn all! And I am just as crazy as you are.'

'And what are you going to do about it? Nothing—nothing at all.'

They jogged across to the far side of the road with their full mess tins to join their comrades sitting there. They did not know what else to do but to troop off with the rest of the herd after they had been fed.

My own situation was not unlike that of the two Indian soldiers. None of us could alter the course of events.

From Hekmat's sources I had received some essential information about the Allies' growing military superiority: at that very hour 100,000 mines were being taken up to the Alamein Front, and a new defence line between the sea and the Qattara Depression was being organised. Hundreds of brand new American tanks were ploughing through the sand on their way to the front. I knew that the Allies' material superiority was growing steadily—that the enemy was swimming in fuel and up to his ears in tanks and artillery—and that all this would shortly be thrown against Rommel's army. Our work had all been a complete waste of effort.

Hekmat had wasted her time and risked her life in vain worming secrets out of British officers. In vain had I been nosing about at the Turf Club, the meeting place of Allied staff officers. In vain had I crept round the perimeter of the Eighth Army supply depot at Abassia to take down details of what was being loaded and unloaded there. Someone back home, having established that the two radio operators had been captured at Rommel's headquarters, had cut off our line of communications and had stopped acknowledging our radio signals.

Then we received this message:

STOP! MISSION ABORTED. BEWARE OF BRITISH DECOY INFORMATION. DON'T REPLY. WE'LL LIE LOW.

This despite the fact that it was as obvious as the nose on your face that British Field Security could not possibly have tracked us down yet. They knew our code manual, but everything else was bound to be just guesswork. Any competent intelligence officer on our side would have come to the same conclusion. He would therefore have accepted our reports, since he could cross-check them—at least some of them. Moreover, our people had screening units that would have been able to establish whether we were genuine or not. They must have been employed as part of Rommel's battle plan, which had meanwhile been decided on, because our people did not hesitate to use some forged maps left behind by the enemy in a minefield.

Sandy kept on transmitting, although he realized that nothing was being received at headquarters. The Herr Oberst had decided that 'those two characters in Cairo had to be walled in'.

The houses in the street leading to the el-Malek el-Saleh Bridge are huddled tightly together. The area is full of open-fronted shops where swarms of black flies cover the merchandise. Carbide lamps hang from the ceilings, swaying in a light breeze, and casting their glare, and eerily swaying shadows, into the street. Poor Arabs, both young and old, stand or squat by the house walls, Oriental music grinds from a coffee-stall, and veiled old women hurry down stinking alleyways leading into old Cairo.

I parked the car well short of my destination, behind the Kasr el-Eini Hospital, several streets north to avoid drawing attention to myself, amid the crumbling walls of the old quarter—and also to give myself time to think carefully about the meeting with Masri Pasha. Once we were face to face, I would have no more time for reflection, apart from which the utmost care was indicated, in any case. Three times before General Azziz el-Masri Pasha had tried to escape, and three times the attempt had failed. On these occasions his people had organized his escape like complete fools. First the idea had been that the General should be taken abroad by a U-boat in Lake Burullus, east of Alexandria, where one of the arms of the Nile flows into the sea. What they had forgotten was that the lake is so shallow in some places that one can easily wade across it. Since not even the Germans had any U-boats on wheels, this escape attempt fell through.

On the second occasion they had sent word through the priest that the rendezvous would be a small airfield near Kataba on the fringe of the desert, without realizing that there were immense British war-material dumps there that would of course be swarming with troops. After that, they chose the Gebel Rozza, a height in the Western Desert not far from Cairo, near which there was hard-packed sarir on which you could land an aircraft. I had been elsewhere but Almásy was available; and as an experienced military pilot in the Austro-Hungarian forces in World War I, who had made pioneering flights over the Libyan Desert, he did not need to be asked twice. He took a machine and flew it in. But the General did not turn up, because his car had broken down on the way to the rendezvous. It had chosen that crucial day of all days to give up the ghost, almost within sight of the prearranged meeting place.

This time, however, the General did not want to leave anything to chance. He wanted to use an Egyptian military aircraft to give the British the slip and simply fly to the Afrika-Korps. This time nothing would go wrong, and Rommel would welcome him with open arms.

Later his 'foolproof' scheme to join the Afrika-Korps added a fourth to his escape disasters. The pilot, the organizer of the three previous attempts, ran his machine into a post. It seemed evident that Allah had once more raised his hand. He did not wish General Masri to leave the country. What poor Allah had to do with the clumsiness of the pilot I failed to figure out. But we were after all in Egypt, where many things can happen that are hard to understand.

But the British had not been asleep! They gave Kismet a bit of a helping hand; the General was put under surveillance. I suppose they were afraid that he would have all the aircraft of the Egyptian Air Force flown into telegraph posts; and they were not in a position to supply new ones since they needed all the machines they had, what with German pilots in the skies over North Africa.

The house I was making for stood on Manyal el-Rodah across the bridge, in the middle of a large overgrown garden. A high white-washed wall kept out the glances of the curious. On the right, immediately past the dilapidated gateway, stood an old gnarled olive tree, on the lowest branch of which hung a freshly cut palm frond as a signal that the coast was clear.

It was Anwar el-Sadat who had arranged for this to be done. If there was no palm frond hanging there, the meeting was off, meaning that General Masri had been unable to come to it unobserved by the men who were watching him.

To someone who had lived all his life in the Levant these precautions seemed exaggerated, since the men assigned to keep an eye on the General were Egyptian officers, who had given their word of honour to Colonel Lotfi, then head of the Egyptian intelligence service, that Masri Pasha would not engage in any conspiratorial activities. But since almost every Egyptian wanted to see the British in hell, Lotfi was ready to turn a blind eye when the General occasionally took longer than the prescribed time over his daily walk.

Anwar was waiting for me in the dark hallway of the house. I could just make him out by the dim light of a half-open door at the end of the passage. The General was sitting partly obscured behind a standard lamp next to his chair. He was so small that his feet hardly touched the carpet. He was smoking a cigarette in a jewelled holder.

The lady of the house, the widow of a one-time senior Egyptian civil servant, was of Austrian origin. She had been assimilated so well by her surroundings that she would have passed unobserved as an Egyptian.

As I sat down next to the General, I naturally did not know that all three of these people were known to Field Security, who had been following them for some time. After some general small talk, we chatted about a drive to Cairo through the Sahara; and the General seemed immediately to understand why I had chosen this long and laborious detour. Anwar did not seem to grasp it quite so clearly—which may have had something to do with his suspicious character. Masri Pasha then began to tell me in great detail about his various attempts to flee and about everything he could have been doing for us over on Rommel's side had one of them been successful.

While he was telling me all this, I reflected on what a high opinion generals always had of their own importance. If he were to escape, what use would he have been? None. He would have been taken to Berlin, where he would have spent the time in the company of the Mufti Husseini and others of that type. Because of his name, they would probably have sat him in front of a microphone and turned him into an Arabic propaganda commentator. It would have been a pity for a man like that to spend his time talking into a microphone. What is more, he would not have enticed a single fellah on to a barricade if he had done so. Years later Anwar el-Sadat was to talk of the 'streak of ill fortune' that dogged Egyptian patriots when discussing these attempts to spirit the old man away to the opposite side.

The myth that Anwar el-Sadat first cooperated with the Germans in 1941 and 1942 has persisted to this day, and still surfaces from time to time in periodicals and newspapers. They say he worked for the Abwehr and was involved in anti-British sabotage. In other words, that he was a contact man.

Well, he was, but there was no question of any sabotage. During the course of the war the Abwehr's Department II (sabotage and subversion) did not make a single sabotage attempt in Egypt. Sadat never had any direct dealings either with the Abwehr or with any other German service unit. He was not known by name either to the Intelligence Branch of the Afrika-Korps, or to the Abwehr itself.

In 1942 Sadat was in direct contact with me, but no German service unit was notified about this. Nobody was listening to my radio transmissions, since I was supposed to be at risk; and in any case I would not have referred to Sadat, as he was my contact.

He was and still is a Nationalist—an Egyptian Nationalist—and a member of the army. Anwar el-Sadat belonged to the young cadres who, on the basis of the Anglo-Egyptian Treaty of 1936, had been given the opportunity, thanks to Premier Mustafa Nahas Pasha, to complete their studies at the Military Academy, which until then had been exclusively reserved for the sons of the propertied class.

These young officers—Nasser, Sadat and the others—were influenced almost entirely by nationalistic ideas. They were members of Hassan el-Banna's Moslem Brotherhood and of the Wafd Party; and some of them were also Greenshirts, a pseudo-National Socialist party that later developed into a Socialist party. They had two things in common—a hatred of the British, and an awareness of the need to do something for the rebirth of Egypt, above all to make sure that she was never again subordinated to another nation.

Naturally, I knew that Anwar could tell me if there was any group in existence that merited the description of a resistance group. I wanted to know whether there were officers who had organized anything that might be of interest to us. It was, after all, part of my work to find out what was happening on the enemy side. I could easily establish that much in the course of an evening. But primarily I had come to ask Anwar, who at that time was a lieutenant in a signals unit and understood about radio communications and equipment, to examine my transmitter, or, if necessary, to supply me with another set. Because Sandy was not making contact, he thought our set must be faulty.

My meeting with Masri Pasha and Anwar proved a waste of time: it was actually an exercise in patience—my patience. I knew I had to be polite in order to get some advice about the radio on our houseboat; and only by appearing interested and concerned could I be sure that in return Anwar would give me his expert opinion. And so, later that night, at 11.30 he checked over the radio and assured me that it was in working order.

Sandy was not prepared to give up yet. He transmitted punctually on the minute, although he no longer believed that he was being received or that he would get an acknowledgement.

Anwar had left our houseboat angrily. He did not approve of the cover we had chosen, although it was none of his business. He took it for granted that an agent ought to live like a hermit. Anyway, I had other worries and did not care how things looked to him. I was fed up because it had all been such a waste of time. I felt like a blind man having to grope around without knowing where he is. I felt as browned off as a man on whom an enormous invisible fist descends every second, beating him into the ground. It was all very depressing.

The night was hot and I sat on the deck of my houseboat. A searing hot wind was blowing across the Nile valley from the Western Desert, making one sweat continually. Sandy was crouching in his radio cubicle under the bar. It was his scheduled transmitting time. He was sending a signal as long as your arm. In the still of the evening I could hear the soft tapping of his key. The morse signals died away without any response, for the simple reason that there was no one at the receiving end to take them down.

All of a sudden a strange calm came over me. I got up like a sleepwalker and poured myself a drink at the bar. It was an outsize Scotch, four fingers of it, without any soda. I was just sitting down on one of the bar stools when Sami the money-changer came up the gangway.

'It's like a bad dream', he said, as he sat down next to me on the other stool. I poured him a gin. It was the only poison he touched.

'What's like a bad dream?' I asked.

'Your pounds are counterfeit, Hussein. Because I have known you for years, because I know exactly who you are, I just can't believe it. Nevertheless, they are counterfeit. But people like you and me don't handle counterfeit money—not even if we are up to our ears in trouble.'

I had been afraid of something like this; but I could hardly explain to him how it might have come about. 'Nonsense! What are you talking about?'

'I have just had a call from Eli. You know, he's the one who always takes them off me. Today he received ten notes to change bearing the same serial numbers as yours from an official British source—that's how he noticed. The ten British ones are of course genuine. He hasn't told his bank anything; he simply can't. Now he's sitting right in it. Needless to say I can't offer him any more notes!'

So there it was, the second blow. First the business with the radio, and now counterfeit money. *Jamais deux sans trois*, I thought. When would the third blow fall?

'There are other banks.'

Instead of answering me, he just said 'Cheers', and drank up his gin.

He had exchanged almost all my English pounds in regular

instalments. At the moment there was no danger that we would find ourselves in financial straits. For me, this matter was of no great consequence. But there was Sandy to consider. It occurred to me that I could use my family's money in order to pay my contacts. No, that definitely wasn't on! The two of us could still get to Turkey with what we had left—only in that case we had better make up our minds pretty quickly.

'We must get rid of what pounds you have left as quickly as possible', I heard Sami say. 'But it will be expensive.'

'What do you mean expensive, man? They are forged, aren't they? Just scraps of paper!'

He pretended he had not heard me say 'scraps of paper'.

'Because it is dangerous, very dangerous. On the black market I have to declare my hand, because I can't risk the neck of the man who buys them. He must know that they are duds—it's the only way he will be able to get rid of them. But in that case he will want a hefty profit.'

It would suit me to ditch them double-quick if it could be done. They were hot—red hot.

At that moment they were still stowed away below deck, well hidden. I went to fetch them. As I did this I thought, Sami, the Jew, would come out of all this as the most honest of us all.

An hour later, we were with a really dirty crook. He took them for a quarter of their face value, but at least I was rid of them.

Next day, when I told the story to Sandy, he summarized our predicament precisely: 'No radio contact, up to our arses in hot notes—if you ask me, some bastard is trying to set us up! One more reason to get stoned, sing the *Deutschlandlied* in Swahili and send off one last great big one. Perhaps then they'll come and get us. It can't be long now, anyway.'

With that he disappeared in his cubicle, not before helping himself to two bottles of whisky. I left the houseboat, got into my car and drove into town. It was the time of the day when everyone in Cairo was loitering on the pavements—young and old, well-dressed men, elegant pretty women, acting as if there were no war on.

I had an appointment with my money-changing friend Sami. He really had helped me at a time when most people would have dropped me like a red-hot brick. We had been fellow students at the San Stefano College, where the maths master had foretold Sami's future as being one devoid of any business sense, he was supposed to be so bad at his sums. How and why he became a money-changer, and a fairly shady one at that, I never understood. His family had been established in Cairo a long time and were frightfully respectable. He must have done something to blot the family escutcheon for his father to have thrown him out. In any event, with his gift for quick sums, he had landed on his feet. Sami's great weakness was clothes, and he always looked as if he had just stepped out of a band box. Perhaps he felt that it gave him an air of respectability.

As we were walking towards the tailor shop, Sami let out a soft, low, flat, somewhat toneless whistle through his gapped teeth. People with such teeth are said to be lucky—and certainly Sami was, no matter what the future looked like. As he whistled, I knew he had seen Edith. Now, I have known many women—pretty ones, beautiful ones, and some who were not so beautiful. Some were blondes, some brunettes, redheads or any other colour; some were white and some were black—but of them all Edith was perhaps the most beautiful.

Her eyes were doe-shaped and slanted, her mouth blood-red without a touch of make-up. Her eyebrows were perfectly symmetrical arches. She had wonderful teeth, like those girls with frozen smiles in toothpaste advertisements. Her hands were delicate and expressive, her hips shapely and her breasts firm and pointed. Her long legs could drive a man wild; her skin was soft to the touch and firm all over her body. She was as beautiful and finely made, as fragile and slight, as only a young Jewess can be. Everything about her seemed perfect.

Edith was with a friend, an ugly girl, on the other side of the street. Edith was more than somewhat narcissistic, and always went around with ugly girl friends. I do not believe she knew any pretty women.

Sami asked me if I had known Edith long and I replied that it had been about two months since we had first met. He admitted to having known her much longer—not in that way, of course, merely to greet each other or chat at a party—but nothing beyond that.

'Why do you think I'd like to know her better?' I asked him. He did not know how really well Edith and I knew each other.

'Tell me, Hussein, are you in love with her?'

'What do you mean, am I in love with her?'

'She says you are.'

'Edith? I'm afraid I am going to have to disappoint her. She's on the wrong track, completely.'

'Then she is lying to her bosses.' Sami dropped this bombshell as we went into the tailor's shop.

The tailor danced attendance on Sami as he was fitted for his new suit. During the fitting session I sat in a chair and wondered how it was that he knew Edith well enough to be able to tell me that she was lying to her employers. What sort of employers? I had always assumed that she had no need to work.

Sami filled me in at Groppi's Swiss tearooms. Some of what he told me I already knew and some I did not: about the Hagganah, the conservative Jewish para-military underground movement; about the extemist Stern Group, two members of which were acquaintances of mine, which he could not know. It was strange that even then, when it would have been in the interest of all Jews to make a common cause with the British—for the duration of the war at least—the Hagganah were unwilling to fight alongside the British forces and the followers of Abraham Stern—fighters for the freedom of Israel—continued to work underground against the British. Sami himself disapproved of the Stern Gang, like most Egyptian Jews, but Edith, it seemed, was a member. It was her boss in the Stern Gang she had been lying to—the head of the movement in Egypt.

That was all I needed in this time of trouble, for Sami to reveal that he knew what I was actually up to in Cairo. But I had to be sure that he really knew, and the best way was to sound him out on other matters. If he did know, then I would have to do something about it immediately.

'Why on earth should she talk such drivel to her group leader?'

'There's only one possible reason', Sami said, without changing his tone; 'they need a good cover, because the British are keeping an eye on them. He must have put her up to it because it is known that your family are so Anglophile.'

'I suppose that makes sense.' But actually I thought something quite different: if only the three of them—Sami, Edith and her boss—knew what a rotten cover that was!

Then Sami talked about the Bnei Brith organization, which the American Jews had set up to help the poor Jewry of the world. It was something to which Sami himself belonged, and in which he believed, in spite of being a money-lender.

All the while he was going on about this I could sense that there was something on his mind. It was a rare occurrence, to feel that someone was seeking a way to tell me something indirectly, but I remember the sensation vividly: he knew something of the utmost importance that he wanted to impart to me. What he had talked about and what he had told me were in some ways useful, but none of it was significant.

'Now, Sami', I said, 'the Stern Gang can't be so interested in Edith's usefulness or connections that they can afford to dress her in the style she is accustomed to. Have you ever seen her in the same outfit twice? A wardrobe like hers costs a lot of money, Sami.'

'Oh, that doesn't come from the Stern Gang, Hussein. Her bosses have trained her too well. She gets the money from the Midan Sheikh Yussuf. From the British.'

So that was what I had sensed. Edith was not so perfect, after all. She was working for Field Security. For Sansom. She was an informer for them and kept an ear alert for her own boss at the same time. She was a double agent. It came down to the fact that I was a bad judge of people—as bad as that maths instructor who thought Sami was doomed as a businessman.

Suddenly a lot of things I had overlooked came back to me: once when she was visiting me on the houseboat I had gone below to fetch something, and half-way down—God knows why—I looked around. She was standing by the post (above the radio cubicle) that kept the sun awning up and next to which the aerial wire was hanging. She could not see the aerial luckily, because it was concealed above the awning. But she was examining the wire to see what it led to above the sun awning. When I had surprised her by turning round, she had pretended to be looking for a glass behind the bar, although Edith never drank alcohol in the morning. Moreover, she knew perfectly well that everything non-alcoholic was in the refrigerator round the back under the shelves and could not be got at from the front. I remembered the incident very clearly.

I had to settle the score with that girl, and immediately!

It was around 3 o'clock in the morning. I lay on my bed. Through the window came the intoxicating scent of jasmin from the garden hedge of a nearby villa. The room was pitch dark and the night quite still. Every now and then the quiet was broken by the croaking of bullfrogs. The chirping of the cicadas in the sycamore trees along the banks of the Nile came in sharp little bursts.

Every day a man lives takes him nearer to the graveyard. It brings him joy, adventures, amusement—and lots besides. Unless he goes through life unseeing, it can also bring with it experience, which, as it accumulates, sharpens his senses.

My senses had had enough years to sharpen. I felt the sensation for just a second—and then I shot out of bed as if fired from a gun.

They were here!

There was a barely perceptible splashing on the water, like fish jumping. But this was not the time of year when they jumped.

The intruders must have wrapped their oars in rags in order to approach the houseboat as quietly as possible. Some other men must have been creeping up on the boat from the road and slipping down the steep bank and into the river.

I had no time to get dressed.

I thought of slipping through a window into the water and swimming past the boats to Hekmat's boat. That would mean staying under water for at least a minute though, which might take some doing.

My only chance was surprise, which the British might not have anticipated. They wanted me alive—I was no use to them dead. If they had wanted to, they could have shot me before now, on any street corner in Cairo.

I crept into the main cabin on the side away from the river bank. I could hear whispering outside. There must have been a boat right under the window. A shadow filled the frame. The window was securely closed.

The shadow hovered motionless for a moment, only to fall out of sight.

Should I fetch my gun? No, it would be crazy. I would be outnumbered. It would not get me anywhere. They had surrounded the houseboat completely; if I shot, they would riddle the boat until it was like a sieve.

I could hear footsteps and whispers out on deck.

The only way to open the door was from the inside, and it was securely bolted with two heavy iron bars at the top and bottom. It would be impossible to force it from outside.

Where was Sandy? I had almost forgotten about him in the heat of the moment. I went down the passage to the concealed radio-transmitting cubicle and knocked.

'I am setting fire to things—hold them up—I'll be through in a moment. They won't find anything—I'll see them buggered first!' he called out, laughing.

'I've opened the hatch; they will have a hell of a job salvaging this tub. In a quarter of an hour she'll be at the bottom. You do the same!'

I went midships and lifted up the trapdoor we had sawn into the double hull to hide the bung let into her flat bottom. As I knocked the bung out, water began to gurgle in. I replaced the trapdoor lid, shot the bolts back into position and returned to my room, where the water was already coming up between the floorboards.

Up on deck I could hear the crashing of falling glasses and bottles as they climbed on board from the stern and looked for the stairs that led below. They could not come downstairs; the door was bolted fast.

Sandy pulled out the fuses. It was pitch dark.

I wondered how would he get out of the radio cubicle? They were right on top of him! I was still thinking when I heard a loud crash.

I felt my way to the door and opened it. In the dim light I saw Sandy crawling out of the wall. He had fought his way through the partition, clad in nothing but his pyjama trousers. He was holding a torch.

The water slowly rose in the passageway.

On a chair near the open door into my room lay a pair of black socks. I grabbed them and rolled them up into a ball.

'Get behind me and shine your torch. I'll open the forward door and hold these socks up to my mouth, seem to pull the pin from a grenade and throw it on deck. It's a long shot—but if they duck for cover, we can dive into the water and swim towards Hekmat's boat.

He turned on his torch and I went softly to the door.

The water was now up to our ankles, but the men on deck would not have noticed that the boat was sinking imperceptibly into the river.

Slowly, very cautiously, I lifted the steel bars out of their hasps and let them slip quietly into the water on the floor.

I heard them calling: 'Police, open up, we're coming in.'

Then one of the men came down the steps. He must have taken a run for the door and, as he came, I pulled back the catch—just in time for him to fly through the open doorway, past Sandy, and slip in the water on the floor.

Meanwhile the other men had trained their torches on the door. So I grabbed the socks, pretended to tear the pin out and threw them on the deck.

'Look out—hand grenade!' somebody called, and threw himself on the deck. My plan seemed to be working.

'Don't fire—duck!' called out the man in charge.

They all threw themselves flat—except one man. A small wiry cockney stood by the door and stuck the barrel of his sub-machine gun into my ribs, just as I was about to take off.

'Stick 'em up mate!' he said, and I raised my arms.

Sandy tried to make a dash for it across the deck but he was stopped as well.

I recognized the man in charge as he stepped out of the darkness wearing a uniform, a uniform in which I had not seen him before. It was Sansom.

'I owe you a drink, Sir!' I said. I made a joke but was frightened out of my mind. He replaced the Colt in the holster at his belt and gave me his hand.

'Good morning. Take it like a game. In every game there is a loser and a winner, you know.'

They were now playing the beams of their lights into the gangway of the houseboat and could see the water slowly rising.

'Major', I said, 'in ten minutes she will have settled on the bottom. There is no time to lose. Let's go.'

It was still dark and the air was pleasantly cool. In the east there was a thin pink line just above the Mogattam Hills. Soon it would be light; another cloudless blue sky would break over Cairo.

At the Central Detention and Interrogation Camp, 15 km south of the City of a Thousand Minarets, everyone was busy. Two cells had been prepared. The interrogating officers ate a hearty breakfast. They knew they would have no time to eat for the rest of that day.

Postscript

Between the summer of 1942 and the Autumn of 1946 my future and Sandy's were controlled by the Middle East division (SIME) of the giant Secret Intelligence Service. All our contacts directly involved in Condor had been allowed to go free before we were released.

Almost all the documents, part of the Intelligence Staff and both the radio operators who should have maintained radio contact with Condor were eventually rounded up by SIME during the British commando operation against Rommel's headquarters behind the Ghazala Line. The radio operators answered the relevant questions put to them (there was no need for them to) because, like all prisoners, they were afraid and because people of higher rank had also made statements. Every interrogating officer, without exception, had been alerted when Sandy and I arrived at the Central Security Detention and Interrogation Camp that morning—alerted to apply the rule that an intelligence service must wring out of every prisoner every last scrap of information.

No one interrogates with kid gloves on. Since time began, interrogation methods have been hard, prolonged and brutal. But they have never been as hideous as they are now because, although men have always fought wars, they have never before been as brutalized as they are today.

The British were perfectly within their rights to use the methods suited to their purpose. It was after all a war. Reproaches are out of place.

Apart from a mass of newspaper articles and features in illustrated magazines, eight people have mentioned Operation Condor in their books. Three of them—Leonard Mosley, A. W. Sansom and Sadat—were directly involved with me in Cairo. Mosley, as British war correspondent, had access to War Office records. All the other accounts of my mission for Rommel were written from hearsay and without reliable documentation.

If an agent is lucky enough to get away with his life, he should put his feet up. And that is precisely what I have done.

Condor was the only attempt the Abwehr made, apart from one still-born operation, which cost a life, to infiltrate an agent into Egypt from North Africa. It is for this reason and because there are so few exciting spy stories about the Abwehr—because so few ever happened—that Operation Condor has excited the imagination of writers.

Every agent needs one thing he cannot learn—luck! If he has other trump cards to play as well, so much the better. I did have some, with my family contacts in Egypt. It is thanks to them, and to them alone, that I am still alive today.

No one is better qualified than my one-time adversary to testify about those family contacts. As Sansom explained in his book:

> He was German and I was British: but when we first met we spoke Arabic. Each of us took the other for an Egyptian. Eppler as a matter of fact had been one most of his life. Although he was born, like me, in Egypt of European parents, his father had died when he was a child and his mother had married a rich Egyptian who had adopted him and, although another boy was born, brought him up as his eldest son. His name was changed to Hussein Gaafar; baptised a Roman Catholic, he became a devout Moslem and made a pilgrimage to Mecca. He forgot that he was German and had no interest in politics . . .
>
> Then at 25, he gave up the life of a rich young Egyptian to fight for a Fatherland he had never seen and a Führer who despised his stepfather's race. Why? For adventure, I suspect.
>
> A qualified pilot and a daredevil in his fast sports car, young Gaafar liked the smell of danger.
>
> 'So he became (John) Johannes Eppler again and made his way via (Greece) Turkey to Germany, where he was interviewed personally by Admiral Canaris. For he was an obvious candidate for the German Abwehr . . .
>
> Hussein Gaafar's stepfather was a highly-respected magistrate friendly towards the British. In other words, he was an important man for us. He hadn't seen his stepson for a long time and didn't know what had become of him. We found out only that he was also known by the name of John Eppler. Should we ever track him down, we would have to watch our step, because we didn't want to get into any political trouble in Egypt I was therefore forced to proceed very carefully in my hunt for him.

Leonard Mosley, as a British war correspondent, writes in his book

The Cat and the Mice:

. . . and that, so far as espionage is concerned, is the end of the story of John Eppler. Of all the German spies captured during World War II, he and Monkaster were the only two not to be executed. True, he was put through a court martial which sentenced him to death, but it was postponed.

With the discovery of the code, however, the end had been achieved. What use was an execution, in the circumstances? He was a fair enemy who had come unstuck because a general had blundered. Since Eppler's stepfather, Saleh Gaafar, had been a good friend of Britain in Egypt, it was decided to treat him as a political prisoner rather than as a spy.

He has us British to thank for that to this day.

News from our side that he would never face the firing squad was given to his stepfather on his death-bed twenty-four hours before he died.

John Eppler and his radio operator, Monkaster, were taken to a camp for political prisoners. After the end of the war, he was flown to Hamburg-Neuengamme and interned in a camp for war criminals. The Secret Intelligence Service had him released from there because no charges could be made against him. With that, he became a free man.

The others?

Hekmat Fahmy, released after a year in prison, went on dancing for a while and then retired to upper Egypt where she lives to this day.

Lt. Anwar el Sadat became Nasser's successor. After two years in captivity he joined a resistance group. That group had not properly come into existence until he joined it, Nasser having meanwhile been transferred to Cairo. During the time of the Nasser régime he was Propaganda Minister and later Speaker of Parliament. He is now the President of the Egyptian Republic.

After his year in prison, Sami did not change any more money. He went to Melbourne and is now a wool exporter in a big way.

Edith now lives in Israel and has become what all women want to be—a mother.

Some of the others are still alive; others have moved on.

Index